THE HUMAN DIMENSION OF QUALITY

The Human Dimension of Quality

Brian Thomas

McGraw-Hill Book Company

London · New York · St Louis · San Francisco · Auckland
Bogotá · Caracas · Lisbon · Madrid · Mexico · Milan
Montreal · New Delhi · Panama · Paris · San Juan
São Paulo · Singapore · Sydney · Toyko · Toronto

HD
62.15
.T5
1995

Published by
McGRAW-HILL Book Company Europe
Shoppenhangers Road, Maidenhead, Berkshire, SL6 2QL, England
Telephone 0628 23432
Fax 0628 770224

British Library Cataloguing in Publication Data
   Thomas, Brian
   Human Dimension of Quality
   I. Title
   658.562
   ISBN 0-07-709051-9

Library of Congress Cataloging-in-Publication Data
Thomas, Brian (Brian Alun)
   The human dimension of quality / Brian Thomas.
      p. cm.
   Includes bibliographical references and index.
   ISBN 0-07-709051-9
   1. Total quality management. I. Title.
   HD62.15.T5   1994
   658.5´62–dc20

                                   94-29588
                                            CIP

12545 BL 98765

Typeset by BookEns Limited, Royston, Herts.
and printed and bound in Great Britain by Biddles Ltd, Guildford, Surrey

For Emma, Emily, Rhiannon and Robyn

Contents

Foreword

To function efficiently, organizations must determine the exact ends they wish to achieve and adopt the most rational method of pursuing them. Few organizations take the trouble to think out their goals clearly. It might be supposed that the aim of a business is merely to make the maximum profits, but this in itself is vague. Should it maximize profits over a given financial year, over five years or over ten? And should it balance profit against the deterioration of the environment caused by its products? The aim of the health service should be to increase the health of the population at minimal cost. But how is cost to be offset against benefit? Should the old receive less care than the young since they will on average benefit over a shorter time period?

Until organizations are less hazy about their ends, there can be no possibility of taking the best means to achieve them. Moreover the ends of the individual members of an organization are often at variance with those of the organization. Executives may disrupt their relations with workers by taking massive pay rises themselves, while expecting their employees to be content with a miserable 2.5 per cent, while some workers may be lazy and others may sabotage the workings of the firm out of spite.

But greed and self-seeking behaviour are not the only problems. As I have shown in detail elsewhere[1], everyone behaves, without knowing it, irrationally for much of the time. They take without thought the decision that is the most obvious but not necessarily the best; having formed an opinion they are reluctant to change it even in the light of new and conclusive evidence; committees can be disastrous—most members seek the approval of others by taking the majority view and even exaggerating it; top executives are often confirmed in their mistaken opinions by the lip service they receive from others.

No organization can completely overcome the irrationality of its members, but it can be set up in such a way as to minimize irrationality and its damaging effects. Total Quality Management is a method for ensuring that an organization works in as rational and therefore in as efficient a way as is possible despite the irrationality and selfishness of its members. One of its central principles is the requirement that organizations maintain a clear focus on process management and the effective collection and use of relevant and accurate information: this is a necessary but not sufficient condition for operational success in any sector. Organizations have financial, material and human assets and in any age in which crucial material aspects such as information technology are available to all, it falls to people to provide the competitive edge that differentiates one organization from another.

A good deal has been written about the technical and procedural aspects of TQM yet little of any consequence has been written on the nature of *human performance* as it applies to the ideals of the TQM philosophy. To combat people's deficiencies, we must first have a clearer understanding of the reasons *why* they so often take the wrong decision.

The *Human Dimension of Quality* tackles this challenge. It examines, among other topics, the crucial organizational implications of our understanding of process variation and probability theory and questions the inherent effectiveness of a number of cherished managerial concepts such as performance-related pay. It explores in detail the psychological and social processes that constitute the most difficult problems faced by organizations in attempting to change their existing cultures.

The book is clearly written and its abstract precepts are illustrated with concrete and compelling case histories. I would hope and expect that it will be widely read by managers and other staff throughout the world. But reading it is not enough. It is difficult to change existing organizations and to introduce radically different patterns of thought—a difficulty that Brian Thomas faces squarely in his discussion of how to change the engrained psychological and social processes. Perseverance is required, but those prepared to make the necessary long-term commitment will be rewarded by seeing their efforts reflected in the greater success of their organization.

Stuart Sutherland

[1]Sutherland, S. *Irrationality: the Enemy Within* (Penguin Books: London; Rutgers University Press, Rutgers NJ)

Preface

This book aims to fill a gap in the literature on implementing Total Quality Management (TQM) within organizations. This literature, past and current, has focused overwhelmingly on the technical and procedural aspects involved in implementing TQM and has paid only superficial attention to the crucial human factors, social and psychological, which must be addressed if TQM is to become a reality. This imbalance must be effectively addressed.

In the final analysis quality really is about people. This, of course, is a basic catechism in the official quality liturgy that, along with other noble proclamations, asserts that 'our people are our greatest asset'. They are, but in the majority of organizations they are not always treated as if they are. The egalitarian rhetoric of TQM is commendable but the reality of everyday organizational life is commonly very different. Good intentions must be acted upon if we are to achieve the results we desire, far too often the rhetoric has stood alone.

The majority of quality initiatives have focused on systems and procedures, aiming to stabilize the consistency of output of processes (e.g. BS5750) and/or to achieve greater productivity by redesigning them (e.g. Process re-engineering). The systems-procedures approach to quality improvement has serious limitations in practice and the promised results, frequently proclaimed with missionary zeal, have largely failed to materialize. This is completely predictable. Sustainable and continuing improvements in organizational effectiveness will not be achieved by focusing on work processes alone (as some would have us believe). Process engineering and re-engineering are necessary but not sufficient elements in the transition to TQM organizations. Process improvements must be accompanied by equivalent improvements in the basic *human* aspects of organizations (hence the title of this book) if we are to have any real chance of achieving the immense benefits that TQM promises. The human interactions that constitute the everyday realities of working life must be fundamentally changed.

The central argument of this book is that TQM usually fails because the human dimension of quality is not given adequate consideration. However, I do *not* mean by this statement that the challenge is principally one of improving the effectiveness of training and development or 'human resource management'. The real problems are rooted in the assumptions, norms and practices of everyday organizational life and conventional human resource strategies barely address them, other than at a superficial level. They are problems that, in the absence of effective management, emerge spontaneously when human beings come together in pursuit of a stated goal. Their effects can be observed across the full spectrum of activities, from the demise of multi-nationals to the failures of the smallest teams. They are linked to power and status, are nurtured by the petty jealousies and internecine squabbles that strangle the most brilliant strategies; they propagate through dysfunctional systems of communication and create diffracted 'them and us' cultures; they are rooted in the vagaries and limitations of human cognition and social processes and they culminate in the irrational and destructive decisions that groups and individuals so often make. Organizations frequently bring out the very worst in human nature; destructive competition, irrationality, excessive stress and anxiety, downright cruelty. This, in many ways, constitutes the 'hidden dimension' of organizations and it has received only cursory examination in the literature.

Many (most?) TQM initiatives are 'techniques driven'. They are based on the assumption that implementing the systems, tools and procedures of quality management constitutes the principal challenge of TQM; get that right and everything else will somehow follow like clockwork. Indeed, clockwork is an appropriate metaphor for the approach: it is highly mechanistic. The problem, of course, is that people are not machines (no matter how much the quality control fanatics despise the fact that they are not) and it is extremely difficult, if not impossible, to simply slot them, like component parts, into an idealized production process.

People are people: cautious yet reckless, rational but also emotional, curious to try new things yet resistant to change; all the paradoxes that make human beings so unpredictable and management such a difficult art to perfect. However, love it or loathe it, people *are* the key and TQM will succeed or fail because of them.

It is a regrettable fact that a substantial proportion of people hate their bosses, their jobs and the organizations they work for. It is also regrettable that, apart from a small minority, they have *become* this way as a result of their experiences of working life. This needs to change, *really change*, and soon, because the environment in which organizations must survive is changing dramatically. As President Lech Wallesa has rightly commented, 'the world market for words is rapidly disappearing'.

The philosophy and techniques of TQM provide a unique opportunity to tackle these human challenges head on, but this will not be easy, it will be the most difficult part of the whole process. In the chapters that make up this book I will examine the nature and complexity of these challenges from a perspective that is firmly rooted in practical experience of the central difficulties involved in implementing TQM within organizations. In doing so, I will describe the major obstacles I have encountered, time and again, in a number of different contexts. These obstacles commonly emerge from a diverse (though interlinked) range of factors, some 'hard' (i.e. technical, statistical, etc.), and others 'soft' (i.e. to do with such things as human emotions and human thought processes). Because of the diversity of these problems the resulting book is, in many ways, a number of books in one. It addresses the important technical challenges (particularly in relation to understanding) and also examines, in detail, the major social and psychological difficulties that stand in the way of success. I hope that on completing the book the reader will discover the fact that the seemingly diverse range of subjects I cover are synthesized in the philosophy of TQM.

The book is organized in four parts and begins with an in-depth analysis of the two guiding principles of TQM; customer orientation and process management. Experience suggests that these principles must be understood at the deepest level (what W. Edwards Deming describes as 'profound knowledge') if TQM initiatives are to succeed in anything other than a superficial manner. In Part I, therefore, I flesh out the major implications of these guiding principles, particularly in relation to non-manufacturing areas and set them in the context of the issues described above.

In Part II I examine the principal psychological and social factors that are central to an understanding of the human challenges we face in implementing TQM. The philosophy underpinning the whole of TQM draws heavily on notions of rationality. A TQM organization is, above all, a *rational organization*: driven by data that is both objective and focused, managed through techniques which facilitate the logical integration of critical processes and engaged in the perpetual challenge of continuous improvement. Fine in theory, difficult in practice. Again, the central problem is people. People are often neither rational or logical, are frequently limited in their ability to solve problems and are prone to believe what they want to believe rather than accept the objective but contrary evidence that stands before them. Part II explores human irrationality in some detail, with particular reference to those aspects that impede the development of TQM.

In Part III I use the notion of organizations as being similar to living things in order to examine the principal requirements for strategic management in a TQM environment. A great deal of practical management insight can be gained from an analysis of the natural world and in this part of the book I focus on the process of evolution by natural selection in order to draw important parallels with organizational development and the principal factors influencing long-term survival.

Part IV is concerned with the practical changes that will be needed in order to convert the rhetoric of TQM to reality. In particular, I focus on the role of the individual and explore the notion of individual responsibility, competence and personal management 'style'. I also introduce a number of tools that can be used to analyse existing situations and provide a framework for positive action.

Although I have used the philosophy, concepts and principles of TQM as the central platform for this book, its relevance is not restricted to quality management issues alone. The challenges detailed here are not exclusive to organizations attempting to implement TQM, they are generic. It is therefore a general management book and it will be relevant and useful to managers, trainers, lecturers, students of management and organizational theory and consultants in a wide range of organizations and management disciplines.

Brian Thomas
Wales
May 1994

Acknowledgements

First I am particularly indebted to Professor Stuart Sutherland who gave detailed and extensive advice on both the content and structure of this book and kindly allowed me to quote freely from his own work in the area of human irrationality. His astute criticism, not always comfortable to receive, has made the book a much clearer account than it otherwise would have been.

I am very grateful to Julia Riddlesdell at McGraw-Hill for supporting the initial idea for this book and for her patience and gentle yet effective 'encouragement' when I slipped behind schedule.

Finally, the process of writing a book inevitably results in alternating periods of excitement, frustration, boredom and elation. My family have endured this with their customary aplomb. My children simply ignore my antics during the process and my wife, Charmian, who is the first 'customer' of all my writing, invariably provides enlightening comment and always encourages my endeavour to 'tell it as it is'. They make a difficult process possible and also worth doing.

Introduction

A great deal has been written and spoken on the subject of quality and TQM in recent years. Yet despite the plethora of gurus, 'How To Do It' implementaion programmes, case studies and exemplars, the majority of organizations that have attempted to implement TQM have not achieved a great deal. This failure to convert theory into practice has fuelled an understandable level of cynicism. The following story characterizes the nature of the problem.

A group of French, Japanese and British managers is taken hostage by terrorists and told they are to be shot in retaliation for their particular country's support of opposing factions.

The managers are informed that nothing personal is involved: they are simply the unfortunate individuals upon whom symbolic retribution is to be exacted. As a gesture of their sympathy the terrorists offer to grant each group a last request before their execution. The French managers ask to be given a final meal of grilled lobster, seasonal vegetables, truffles and copious quantities of vintage wines. The Japanese managers ask to be given a final opportunity to clearly outline the long-term strategic advantages of adopting a company-wide approach to the implementation of Total Quality Management. The British managers ask if they can be shot before the Japanese managers as they cannot face another lecture on quality! The story reflects a growing sense of boredom with the subject of quality and the notion of TQM. Certainly, this is understandable, but it is extremely bad news.

If we are to succeed in achieving the desired outcomes of TQM (I will focus on outcomes in order to prevent myself and the reader from falling into the seductive trap of considering TQM to be an end in itself—it isn't) then we must understand why so many organizations are finding difficulty in translating theory into a clear business advantage.

It seems to me that the fundamental principles and methodologies of TQM are unarguably correct; the blueprint is sound and the foundations are sound. Why then do we experience such difficulty in building upon these foundations and why do so many well-intentioned structures collapse after a relatively short period of time?

Peter Drucker has commented that TQM is a good idea but, like many good management ideas, it has the unfortunate tendency to degenerate into hard work. He is right. TQM *is* hard work. It is not hard physical work, it is hard emotional and mental work. The term 'emotional labour' is, I feel, appropriate in describing the effort required to introduce and maintain TQM within an organization.

The successful implication of TQM is hard work because it requires many people, and managers in particular, to change beliefs and attitudes that have proved relatively successful in the past, to think more effectively and most importantly to change what they *do* in the contexts of their working lives. In my own experience the effort needed to achieve success is also directly proportional to position within the hierarchy, the higher up an individual is, the more change is required.

The challenge of TQM is, first and last, a human challenge. It is not simply about techniques, systems and procedures, it is primarily about values, attitudes and, ultimately, business ethics. We must recognize these facts if we are to be truly successful. The changes that TQM requires are not superficial, they are profound.

Most organizations discover very early on that introducing TQM is very different from other attempts at staff and organizational development. TQM is a can of worms, and to understand why so many difficult problems arise it is necessary to understand the overt and covert nature of organizational life.

The vast majority of organizations (probably 99.9 per cent) are composed of 'official' (visible) and 'unofficial' (hidden) structures, rules, values, norms of behaviour, lines of communication and power networks. In many instances it is at the level of the 'hidden organization' that most of the real business is carried on. Access to, and knowledge of, the hidden organization is also inversely proportional to elevation in the hierarchy. The further up you are the less detail you will known about it.

At each level within the official organization management tends to be aware of (and often, for various reasons, turns a blind eye to) some element of 'what goes on' at the level below. In all probability this knowledge constitutes a maximum of 25 per cent of the unofficial views and practices that exist. Because the unofficial practices known at one management level are commonly not communicated to the management level above, this means that the management function will *in total* be aware of only 25 per cent of the unofficial practices that exist throughout the organization.

Also, the more management levels there are, the more will be hidden as we ascend the organizational ladder. In an organization comprising 11 layers of authority, top management will be aware of only 2.5 per cent of the total unofficial practices that exist.

It is clear therefore that senior management is commonly not party to a vast amount of *hidden information* within their organizations. This information includes the genuine feelings of staff at all levels; feelings about the morality of the organization, its practices, ethics, values and aspirations; feelings that management must influence if TQM is to become a reality. Senior management must therefore acknowledge that what they are shown and told within their organizations will, almost inevitably, be only part of the complete picture. To believe it is the whole picture is to be seduced by considerable amounts of appropriate pretence, somewhat equivalent to the Queen believing that the whole world smells of fresh paint.

The 'problem' with TQM is that it tends to rip the lid off the hidden organization and lay bare the underlying dissatisfactions that lead to resentment, various degrees of non-co-operation and covert practices. But it is precisely at this level, *inside the hidden organization,* that the real battle for TQM will be won or lost. The following (unofficial) quotes from staff and managers in organizations attempting to implement some form of quality improvement inititative underline the reality of the challenges we face.

> They tell us about JIT ('Just in Time' inventory management) and Kaizen (continuous improvement) and why we need it and, yes, I can see ways of cutting out steps in my job, to make assemblies faster. But if I do that, what will they do? They'll speed up the line, that's what they'll do, and I'll be working harder for the same pay.
>   (Assembly worker, large domestic electrical equipment manufacturer)

The above company had attempted to encourage the notion of the internal supplier–customer network. To facilitate the development of this idea management distributed a 'customer survey questionnaire' to first-line employees asking for detailed comments on the effectiveness of their support line-maintenance teams. Again private comments are revealing.

> The line-maintenance guys are useless, they hold us up for ages even with little repairs and then we've got big production backlogs to cope with. We try to fix most breakdowns ourselves and only call them in if we can't do a repair. Their job is a doddle. But I'm not going to put that on the form. I'm not going to help put somebody out of work at a time like this. No way.
>
> I'm not filling it in (the questionnaire), it's a load of rubbish. If they sent one about the management here I'd fill that in. They'd probably give me the sack but it might just be worth it.
>
> (Two first-line employees)

In another (non-manufacturing) organization attempting to introduce a continuous improvement programme a bright young line manager said:

> They need to get the basics right before they start trying to put the icing on the cake. They're asking us to make this extra effort to improve processes when there's so many basic gripes that they don't do anything about . . .
> I mean, just look at this office! [Tiny, windowless and in need of redecorating].
>
> (Medium-sized distribution company)

Another common problem stems from the fact that senior managers often underestimate the rate of change that can occur when staff become enthusiastic about the application of TQM principles in their own work environments. TQM is often 'sold' to non-managerial staff on the basis that it will increase their autonomy and allow them to use talents and abilities that have previously been stifled. Of course, this again is a basic tenet of TQ philosophy and it is fine in principle. Problems arise, however, when staff underestimate the amount of time it takes for *management* to appreciate the implications involved in converting the rhetoric into practice. Sometimes change moves too fast for them. Again some real-life comments are instructive.

For a while we had the lunatics running the asylum.
(Managing director, medium-sized leisure company)

This refers to the 'overenthusiastic' actions of a quality improvement team that had taken the rhetoric of employee empowerment seriously.

People are going straight over my head. I never had any of these problems with my staff before all this started, it's ridiculous.
(Warehouse manager, medium-sized distribution company)

This comment followed an improvement suggestion from a junior member of the warehouse staff that was taken straight to the managing director after his announcement of an 'open door' policy on improvement suggestions.

Most of the serious difficulties that arise when organizations embark upon the quality journey can be ascribed to common human weaknesses. Protecting one's own turf, petty jealousies, erroneous assumptions, crooked thinking and mental lethargy constitute a formidable barrier to success. The overwhelming majority of the existing literature, action programmes and implementation initiatives ignores, or dramatically underestimates, the critical nature of these factors.

It is pleasant and intellectually stimulating to preach the sermon of quality and extol the virtues of a future in which people and organizations progress in mutually enhancing harmony towards excellence and the delight of their customers. The pursuit of this 'quality future', as a philosophy, is virtually unarguable. People frequently complain that it will never happen in their particular organization but not one single person, in my experience, has ever questioned whether the goal itself is worth while. However, the preaching may be easy but the reality is hard. Such a future is not an impossibility but it will not be created easily or without *fundamental* changes occurring along the way.

The central difficulty, of course, is that TQM is really about changing people, not systems, and people are exceptionally adept at *not* changing established patterns of behaviour. They are also exceptionally good at identifying where others need to change but are usually somewhat less able with respect to themselves. In the overwhelming majority of instances, however, *everyone* in the organization will be required to change to some extent, and some will be required to change dramatically, if TQM is to succeed.

There is, unfortunately, no guaranteed answer to the challenge of implementing TQM: the 'How To Do It' plans do not work. Like those for slimming, smoking or time management, they work only for a while. They ultimately fail because they are merely *followed* rather than *lived*. They will only work when change is genuinely desired and when we accept that the benefits of that change will inevitably involve costs. Too often the 'How To Do It' plan suggests that it is possible to achieve the benefits without incurring any of the costs. It is never that easy.

Most organizations that embark on some sort of quality initiative recognize that they need to improve; the problem is that they frequently wish to improve while staying fundamentally the same. What they ideally require is that their problems are removed without changing the organization from which these very problems derive! This, obviously, is not possible.

This book is, in many ways, the antithesis of the 'How To Do It' variety: it is concerned mainly with the barriers to achieving TQM and it focuses on the nature of the enemies we face. This is both necessary and timely; much past and current literature on TQM oversimplifies or ignores the fundamental human challenges involved. Real TQM is not easy to achieve, little of value ever is, but it is achievable.

One final comment encapsulates the nature of the challenge:

> The more I understand it (TQM) the more I see that it's right. But there are going to be huge problems in making it work. An awful lot of people will have to change, and I mean really change. It's going to be very hard to do.
>
> (Manager, British Rail)

This book is an attempt at clarifying and responding to the human challenges involved in applying TQM principles in the real world of work. It is based on experience of leading training programmes on quality and quality implementation, conducting personal research and, most importantly, of working with managers and staff in organizations, large and small, that have embarked upon the journey towards a future that no one derides.

Part I

Quality revisited

'For an idea ever to be fashionable is ominous, since it must afterward be always old-fashioned.'

George Santayana

Quality is a radical, emotional intellectually stimulating idea and it has a tendency to create divisions. There are those who buy into the quality message with an intensity that borders on the obsessive and those who eschew it with equal vigour. In the middle are the non-committed; waiting to see what will happen in the long run. These divisions are present in current management literature and thought and certainly manifest themselves within organizations that undertake some form of quality improvement inititative.

My own experience indicates that the basic philosophy of Total Quality Management (TQM), if communicated effectively, creates little immediate hostility. Indeed it is very difficult to argue coherently against it. The problems arise when organizations attempt to translate the theory into operational reality. Then, frequently, all hell breaks loose.

There are a number of recurring problems associated with the implementation of TQM. Broadly speaking they can be grouped, in no particular order of importance, under the following headings:

- Underestimating the organization-wide implications of embarking upon a TQM initiative.
- Failing to make profound changes to working practices.
- Failing to link a TQM initiative to base-line business performance indicators.
- Underestimating the effects on interpersonal relationships.

- Attempting to change too rapidly.
- Failing to integrate individual quality development initiatives.
- Failing to manage human resource development effectively.
- Failing to change recognition mechanisms.
- Failing to generate effective data.
- Failing to allocate resources strategically.
- Misunderstanding fundamental quality management concepts.
- Overapplying quality management techniques.
- Jargonizing.

All these difficulties arise from people rather than systems or machines. It is people who misjudge, subvert, avoid difficult problems and give up when things get tough. Also, of course, only people are capable of generating passionate enthusiasm, leading, supporting, coaching and creating fundamental improvements. People are *the* key to successful TQM.

In this book I will tackle the major human challenges we face in making the necessary changes to our existing methods of organizing, producing and delivering goods and services, and there must be no doubt that such changes are indeed *necessary*. Without wishing to add to the outpourings of the doom-and-gloom merchants we are running perilously short of time in which to become competitive in home, European and world markets. It is also well to remember that the quality message is not confined merely to 'for-profit' enterprises, it applies equally to publicly funded provision such as education, health care and social services and also to voluntary activities.

We must change the way we operate if we are to reverse our current descent toward becoming primarily a third-rate, low-skill, cheap-labour economy. However, I wish to avoid the 'hell and damnation' variety of exhortation to adopt quality management practices; the time when such an approach was effective is long gone. We do not need exhortations; we need action. What is required is that our organizations are staffed with competent and motivated people who are given the authority to make the changes necessary for long-term survival. This will not be easy to achieve because the changes required are not superficial.

As I have commented elsewhere[1] I do not believe that organizations have a death wish in not applying TQM principles and I also do not believe that they are necessarily foolish in not doing so. People make decisions according to their knowledge, perceptions, current pressures and objectives. Quality management principles may or may not link in with these. A decision may be rational in the short or long term: it all depends on what our objectives are.

TQM techniques are founded on the assumption that investing for long-term survival is a desirable objective. No one really argues with this as a principle; it is the *level* of investment required that often causes concern. Many managers point out that (by definition) investment requires the allocation of existing resources to activities that do not yield immediate results. Indeed, the mere act of investment does not, of itself, *guarantee* success in the long term. TQM, in the final analysis, is a gamble; a rational gamble admittedly, but a gamble none the less. It is also a gamble that will have, for better or worse, long-term effects. Many managers express the real concern that, if improperly attempted, quality initiatives can be positively detrimental to the organization. It is a justified concern. Insincere and half-baked quality initiatives can do a great deal of harm.

1

The pressures for quality improvement

Quality improvement pressures have been generated almost exclusively by customers. There are, however, two market contexts in which it is likely that customer-driven pressures for quality improvement will be of little effect:

- in a sellers' market
- in a captive market.

In a sellers' market demand outstrips supply; this situation existed in the USA and much of Europe in the two decades following the end of the Second World War. Captive markets exist in much of the public sector and some of the private sector today. In a sellers' market the majority of customers will take whatever is on offer and the minority who complain, or choose not to buy, can be effectively disregarded. It is basically 'take it or leave it'. This situation exists in many employment markets at the present time.

In a captive market the dynamics operate somewhat differently. In a captive market there is usually no effective 'leave it' option. For example, unless you are of adequate financial means you will be obliged to take what the state provides in terms of education, protection from crime, and medical care. And, unless you have access to a well, a generator and methane deposits you will be obliged to accept the services of the water, electricity and gas companies.

I am not suggesting that what you receive in these captive markets is, *ipso facto*, substandard. But what is important to note is that the delivery and quality of service you do receive will be dictated largely by the providers themselves. Quality improvement initiatives are difficult enough to initiate and sustain when customers have the option of walking away. When they are effectively handcuffed to the walls the difficulties are increased by an order of magnitude.

In many captive markets, deprived of an effective customer-driven pressure for quality improvement, there will be a strong tendency for suppliers to focus on productivity increases in order to improve bottom-line financial results and to structure and organize in ways that minimize their own operational difficulties. The sellers' market-place is disappearing rapidly: it began to disintegrate around the beginning of the 1960s. During this period customer-focused innovators such as Ray Kroc (McDonald's) in the USA began to take customer needs seriously and to deliver service value that far exceeded their previous experiences and expectations. But the largest influence of all came from the opposite side of the Pacific ocean.

During the 1960s the Japanese launched a concerted attack on established western markets in electronics, steel manufacture, shipbuilding and motor vehicles. The results of that onslaught are well documented. In doing so they changed the rules of the game forever. In effect they moved us away from the world of Henry Ford in which we could have whatever colour car we wished as long as it was black, towards one in which we may soon be able to have any colour that is humanly possible to produce, and have it in double quick time. The Japanese, above all others, empowered the customer.

Of course this empowerment did not restrict itself to the field of electronics or motor vehicles; customers began to make value comparisons along a whole spectrum of provision. Being well catered for in one area they transferred their raised expectations to others. Suddenly the balance of power in the customer–supplier relationship shifted dramatically. Some innovative organizations such as J. C. Penney in the USA picked up the scent of this revolution and acted promptly. They quickly stood out among the plethora of mediocre competitors and further raised the general level of customer expectations, once again encouraging innovators to emerge. In this way a chain reaction was begun that has spread relentlessly in all directions. The old world is dead and gone and organizations are now effectively faced with only two real alternatives:

- To institute a systematic quality improvement programme as soon as possible.
- To do nothing about systematic quality improvement and hope

that no one else in your particular market does anything either (someone will).

There are no safe havens any more. Organizations that successfully implement systematic quality improvement initiatives establish standards of excellence that customers will inevitably transfer to other contexts; there is no going back. Also, organizations that succeed with quality initiatives in one particular market are often capable of transferring to another: the tools of quality are context independent. Thus the Japanese first established themselves in manufacturing areas such as steel, shipbuilding, electronics and motor vehicles (mopeds and motor cycles first) and then moved into property, leisure and financial services. Japanese interests now own the Rockefeller Center in New York, a good deal of the film and music industry and the six largest banks in the world are Japanese.

The Japanese success story is complicated, it cannot be attributed solely to the application of TQM principles within manufacturing organizations although this has played a vital part. Alongside the early application of quality control techniques under the guidance of Deming and Juran in the 1940s and 1950s, the inherent structure and culture of the Japanese nation provided the most fertile possible ground in which the immense benefits of TQM principles could be realized. Combined with low-cost capital procurement and philosophy that favoured long-term gain of market share over the maximization of short-term profitability, post-war Japan was a manufacturing miracle waiting to happen.

Difficulties with Japanese and western cultures

Nothing, however, is perfect. The Japanese, despite their loud protestations to the contrary, have a problem with fundamental innovation and creativity and a tendency to become obsessive about detail. That, perhaps, is a price they pay for a culture which stresses conformity, tradition and consensus. In the West, by contrast, there are problems with status, greed and short-term thinking, a price we pay for a culture that stresses individuality, hero-worship and competition.

Each culture has its benefits and limitations. The diligence and application of the Japanese make western notions of a protestant work ethic seem positively frivolous. The Japanese obsession with detail, quality and flexibility has created the phenomenal output and economic growth witnessed during the past 40 years. However, there is no guaranteed formula for perpetual economic success; markets are incredibly complex and fundamental changes are inevitable. Every successful management strategy is merely a temporary solution, applicable to the current state of affairs but not necessarily to those that will exist in the future. Also, any successful formula is capable of being driven beyond the boundaries of practical utility. Obsessions, even obsessions with aspects of quality, can be counter-productive. The following example is pertinent.

In February 1993 Nissan Motors announced the closure of its Zama factory near Tokyo with the loss of some 5000 jobs, almost a tenth of its workforce. There are a number of reasons why this closure became necessary. The downturn in Japan's home market and the lack of foreign growth markets capable of absorbing excess production both played their part. But a more fundamental reason can, surprisingly, be attributed to the Japanese obsession with flexibility and product variation. Taken as a basis philosophy, flexibility and product variation make marketing sense: up to a point. Product variation requires design flair, flexible manufacturing and access to a wide range of parts and raw materials. Flexible manufacturing is something the Japanese excel at. However, there inevitably comes a point where economic factors must be considered. Product variation does not come free of charge, and the more variation there is, the more it costs.

In 1933 only a few of the 11 Japanese vehicle producers were making a profit and leaders such as Nissan and Mazda were perilously close to the bottom-line.[2] Apart from the market difficulties cited above, analysis suggests that the proliferation of models and model variations, which has become something of an obsession with many Japanese car manufacturers, has contributed significantly to the problems many companies have experienced. One Nissan model for example offered 86 different variations of steering wheel and Toyota has offered 32 types of sound systems in cars it has exported to the USA.[3]

Combined with the Japanese's strategy of focusing on increasing market share through minimal profit margins it is clear that the costs incurred in maintaining such high levels of product variability inevitably become prohibitive at some point. It appears that this point has been reached. product variability is a viable strategy *only within the parameters of market satiability and bottom line profit margins,* unless one wants to produce motor cars at a loss. It seems that in the cases cited above this economic point was crossed because of an *internal* drive, i.e. company generated, towards excessive product variation without careful analysis of market demand and overall profitability. It is well to remember that customer satisfaction is a necessary but not sufficient determinant of organizational viability; customer needs must be met cost effectively.

There is a very real danger that elements of TQM philosophy can assume the mantle of dogma and be applied automatically rather than strategically. There must be a balance between what is possible and what is prudent. In the same way that moral philosophy asserts that we cannot derive an *ought* from an *is*, we also, in terms of economic sense, cannot derive a *should* from a *can*. Because a manufacturer can provide 86 different variations of steering wheel it does not automatically follow that it should do so since market characteristics must be the ultimate arbiter.

It seems therefore that an obsession with a general principle of quality, product variability, was taken too far in this particular case. Product variability, alongside other factors such as technical excellence, must be geared to market requirements if organizations are to remain financially viable. The difficulty, and the art, of course, is in deciding where the stop sign is.

In contrast to the situation that exists in Japan, the UK has a fundamental problem with class divisions and underinvestment. The traditional dichotomy between 'management' and 'workers' is still widespread. Status symbols seem to be as much an obsession with many British managers as they are anathema to the Japanese. In many cases the manifestations of this work-based apartheid, such as reserved parking, superior dining facilities, special concessions and plush offices, seem mundane. But in reality they cut deep, deeper, I firmly believe, than dissatisfactions caused by differentials in levels of remuneration, although these too are commonly ludicrous. They cut deeper because they are symbolic of a caste system more fundamental than that conducted purely at the economic level. They imply that management is culturally superior to workers: that it is somehow better than them.

The overwhelming majority of first- and second-line staff I have interviewed in the course of researching this topic have been scathing regarding institutionalized divisions of this type. Management must understand that all work increasingly requires a considerable element of *voluntarism*; only machines can be made to operate to their limits. Management cannot legislate for successful TQM: *people must want to do it or it simply will not happen,* and people are acutely sensitive to symbols of assumed superiority. This fairly obvious fact of life seems to elude the majority of management pundits. I firmly believe that organizations would take a massive leap forward in releasing the knowledge and talent that undoubtedly lies dormant within our organizations if they were to eliminate unnecessary and demeaning divisions of this type.

The reluctance to invest

During my initial training as a mechanical design engineer the plant maintenance office of the company in which I was employed sported a metal plaque that was constructed from various brass and copper components manufactured in the factory. It was both ingenious and exceptionally well engineered. However, it is the well-recalled message contained upon it that is pertinent:

COMPANY MOTTO

NEVER SPEND IF YOU CAN MEND
NEVER BUY IF YOU CAN WELD
BUT IF YOU MUST BUY—BUY SECOND HAND

They lived by it too. At the time (1967) when Germany and Japan were successfully developing and utilizing state of the art numerically controlled machine tools we in this particular manufacturing organization (long since defunct) were working with equipment that had seen its best days during the Second World War.

We often appear to have a national obsession with things antique and a pathological aversion to notions of obsolescence; we want things to be 'like they were' rather than 'like they could be'. This is both endearing and lucrative in terms of the tourist industry but it is tantamount to suicide in any other. The concept of long-term investment seems to be *persona non grata* to the majority of British management, particularly investment in people.

Exhortations from the great and good continue to rain down upon our 'captains of industry' urging them to invest in training their workforce. Politicians and pressure groups continuously harangue the government on its pathetic record in providing real training opportunities for this country's disgracefully abandoned mass of unemployed talent. Yet nothing of much consequence happens. There is no excuse whatever for this; it is real bare-bones stupidity.

Conversely, this failure of vision on the part of much of British management and government is a godsend to the foreign manufacturers who come here in their droves. They recognize that the British workforce has been underutilized and underequipped for years. Britain is first choice in Europe for American and Japanese companies. In 1991 53 per cent of all direct Japanese investment in Europe came to Britain, Germany attracted only 9 per cent and France even less. And they are not coming just for cheap labour, they could get that even cheaper in Ireland, Greece, Portugal or Spain. They come here because they recognize the existence of an enormously underutilized resource, British workers. Properly trained and equipped British workers have proved as good as the world's best. Professor Garyl Rhys of the Cardiff Business School asserts that productivity in Nissan's Sunderland plant is bettered by only two other plants in the world. The message of these transplant factories is obvious. The talent is here: investment pays.

It is clear that we must change many of our basic assumptions and attitudes if we are to become a real contender in the markets of the 21st century. What worked previously is not working any more. Our major weaknesses are in areas of strategy and application. We tend to muddle through from day to day rather than developing a clear vision of where we want to be, articulating that vision to everyone within the organization and acting on it. And when we do manage to make a reasonable job of vision definition we are often woefully inadequate at seeing it through. I believe that these difficulties can be overcome with effort and that an understanding and application of TQM concepts is the central way forward.

Common problems in the marketing of quality

Although I firmly believe that the application of TQ concepts and techniques offers the only viable route to long-term survival, an important point needs to be made. The word 'quality' is, if not already dead, at least dangerously ill. The majority of managers and workers are sick and tired of hearing it. It has become, to use Tom Peters' disparaging term, the domain of the 'technofreak'.[4] The responsibility for much of this can be laid at the door of those who have jumped on the quality bandwagon without a great deal of commitment or indeed understanding of what the central concepts imply and appear to view the whole thing as a PR exercise. Organizations who have fallen for the glitz and glimmer approach have invariably hit difficulties. This approach trivializes the whole process and positively encourages ridicule and derision.

I believe strongly that the term must be used sparingly and that we must focus on real change rather than on slogans and exhortations. The idea of quality can be used as an extremely effective organizing philosophy to foster initial understanding and commitment to action but we must be aware of the very real dangers of overexposure and trivialization as time passes.

People are not fooled by false slogans and banal statements telling them that the customer is king. The vast majority of sloganizing and poster exhortations produced to date has been insulting to the intelligence. My favourite example is the major software company that decided to incorporate a 'gosh isn't that clever' series of slogans as part of its quality campaign. One gem in the series consisted of a poster carrying a simple statement that said:

QALITY–THE ONLY THING MISSING IS 'U'

Unfortunately the company issued the poster a few days prior to announcing that its customary Christmas bonus would be substantially reduced that year. Within hours a rival poster was being faxed everywhere, it said:

CHRISTMAS BONS–THE ONLY THING MISSING IS
'U' TOO!

Another large organization employs the slogan 'Organizing For Quality' to describe its approach. This is commonly shortened to 'O For Q'. Say that quickly and see what you get. And, as if that isn't enough, the next stage is to be called 'O For Q 2'!

One of the most potentially damaging challenges to the successful implementation of TQM is the attack on credibility that will, almost inevitably, be mounted by the organizational cynics. Every organization has its quota and, if nothing else, these people can spot an opportunity for ridicule a mile off. Great care has to be taken with the use of terms such as 'mission statement' (commonly subverted to 'missionary position') and designations such as programme 'champion' (the wonder horse), etc.

One of the best produced exhortations I have come across to date simply said:

Quality. We don't have to do it, survival is not mandatory.

The initial stages of any drive to improve organizational effectiveness will benefit from some form of easily remembered, unifying, rallying call and 'quality' meets this requirement well. However, there comes a stage when any rallying call begins to wear thin and there is a point at which it can become counter-productive. My own experience strongly suggests that the most effective method by far of marketing the quality message is through positive action. And the higher up the organization that action occurs, the more powerful the message will be.

If TQM is to be truly successful then many people will be required to do many things differently from the ways they have done them in the past. This is where the major difficulties arise. People are extremely adept at ignoring the fact that things they are comfortable with need to be changed. However, the mere fact of *knowing* that things need to change will produce psychological tensions and these tensions must be dissipated in some way. One obvious solution, of course, is to simply go ahead and make the changes which are required, but this is rarely easy. Force of habit is an extremely difficult adversary, particularly when such habits have been established over a substantial period of time. Ways of thinking and behaving become virtuallly automatic with the passage of time and most people have a tendency to create 'comfort zones' in which to operate. The term comfort does not, however, necessarily imply pleasure or ease. Comfort zones are simply established patterns of thought and behaviour within familiar contexts. In some cases change may be resisted even though it will improve the individual's lot in an objective sense. Thus the manager who has become habituated to perpetually rushing here and there may nevertheless resist changes that actually reduce the necessity to do this.

If behavioural changes are not made, however, psychological tension will remain and the individual will need to deal with it. One very effective way of relieving this tension is through laughter. This is an excellent remedy for stress; clinical studies have confirmed this fact and some successful stress-release and creativity enhancement techniques utilize laughter as the underlying basis of their whole approach.

Making fun of threatening or unwelcome ideas has been a classic problem-avoidance strategy throughout history. Smokers, for example, faced with mounting evidence of the irrationality of their habit, may find release from tension by laughing at statements such as 'Stopping smoking doesn't help you live any longer, it just feels like it' and so on.

The changes required by TQM will create psychological tensions for many people but these tensions are to be welcomed; they are a necessary prerequisite for real change to occur. We must ensure, however, that they are channelled into positive action rather than being dissipated through easy targets for derision and ridicule. Established attitudes and behaviour patterns are highly resistant to change and this is the principal reason why TQM implementation is so difficult to achieve. There is no quick and easy remedy for this: no 'fast track' to quality. However, important lessons can be learned from those who have attempted to implement TQM and change the nature and culture of the organizations they work for. The remainder of this book describes the most important human challenges that such initiatives present.

I will begin with the area of general understanding. Although much has been written about TQM concepts and principles, a good deal of confusion still exists in many areas. My feeling is that this is primarily due to the fact that TQM has its roots in manufacturing and has often been presented as a highly 'technical' branch of knowledge. It is technical in the sense that certain elements of TQM involve the use of quite difficult mathematical theories, particularly in the fields of probability and statistics. Quality control methods used in manufacturing, for example, often involve highly complex techniques such as probability distributions, factorial experiments and the analysis of signal-to-noise ratios. The work of Genichi Taguchi, the Japanese expert who introduced the concept of quality improvement through statistically designed experiments, is a classic example of the highly technical nature of some areas of quality control.

Fortunately, however, TQM is not just about quality control (quality control is an element of TQM), and it does not require that every manager becomes a skilled mathematician! What it does require is a sound understanding of the fundamental concepts involved, including certain aspects of probability and systems theory. Most importantly, TQM requires managers to develop their appreciation and understanding of the inherent nature of processes and to *use* this understanding in carrying out their day-to-day responsibilities.

The vast majority of managers do not operate in the rarefied atmosphere of probability theory and multiple sampling scenarios; they deal with the practical difficulties involved in simply getting things done. What follows therefore is a discussion of the central concepts and principles of TQM with particular reference to general management responsibilities.

2

The keys to quality

'The meaning of a word is its use.'

Ludwig Wittgenstein

'But what is this stuff all about ... really?' This question was asked towards the end of a three-day intensive course that focused on the application of TQM principles within the service sector. It is an interesting question and it emerges from time to time during introductory level quality training sessions. I welcome its appearance because it indicates that the disparate elements of TQM theory are beginning to be perceived as forming a cohesive whole.

However, when the TQM penny does begin to drop, different people tend to see the implications in different ways. Some see the likelihood of increased work loads, others see opportunities for personal growth; some see substantial benefits accruing from flexible working relationships, others fear job losses; some see empowerment, others see power-stripping; some see it as liberation, others as manipulation, and so on. Quality is an emotive as well as an intellectual issue and the way that quality concepts are introduced and explained at early stages of a quality improvement programme has a major influence on the chances of successful implementation.

It seems that a number of common difficulties emerge during these early stages and that these difficulties can be usefully considered as falling into one of the three following categories.

1. Some level of confusion concerning concepts and principles.
2. A tendency towards overcomplication or oversimplification.
3. Difficulty in applying TQM techniques in non-manufacturing contexts.

In order to tackle these problems effectively it will be necessary to provide some information regarding historical development and to explain some fundamental principles. However, I do not wish to cover ground that has been dealt with extensively in other publications dealing with quality topics. Rather, I will focus on the areas of practical difficulty and confusion that have emerged during TQM awareness training sessions, in confronting real life obstacles to TQM implementation and through discussions with managers and facilitators involved in quality development projects.

Now that quality has evolved beyond the 'fad' stage in many areas we are in a better position to appreciate the practical limitations of certain aspects of theory and to address some of the common difficulties that have arisen in various contexts. What follows therefore is a brief history and description of the key concepts of TQM together with an analysis of the associated conceptual and operational problems that commonly arise.

Quality control: the roots of TQM

The fundamental basics of TQM have evolved from quality control techniques pioneered by Walter Shewart, a statistician at the US Bell Laboratories in the 1920s. Shewart realized that quality control depends entirely on process control and he developed techniques that enable process stability to be monitored. One of the most important of these techniques is the control chart which will be discussed in detail in a later section.

Quality control techniques have evolved primarily within manufacturing contexts and there is a simple reason for this. Quality control employs the use of statistical principles and techniques that rely on an ability to quantify critical variables with a considerable degree of accuracy. Quality means measurement. Modern measurement techniques, as applied in most high-volume manufacturing contexts, are extremely accurate and reliable and they form the bedrock on which quality control techniques can be built. Accurately measuring the diameter of a microscopically fine wire or the resistance of an electronic component too small to be seen with the naked eye is, in the trade, a fairly straightforward process.

However, this reliance on accurate measurement poses severe problems when we attempt to apply quality control techniques in non-manufacturing contexts. Accurate measurement is much more difficult in such contexts because in many instances we are dealing with vague ideas and human judgements. How, for example, should we approach the quantification of such critically important success factors as 'empathy' (in the case of a medical doctor), 'ambience' (in the case of a restaurant), 'approachability' (in the case of a manager), 'patience' (in the case of a teacher) or 'service' (in the case of a hotel)?

It is a considerable challenge but it is a challenge that must be faced if we are to gain the undoubted benefits that TQM can bring to non-manufacturing areas. There are enormous potential gains to be made in applying quantitative statistical techniques and although these are very early days progress is being made. In the following sections I will outline a number of approaches to these and other challenges and suggest ways in which further progress may be achieved. As a first step it will be necessary to clarify some fundamental quality concepts and to examine some major difficulties that commonly arise.

So what is quality . . . precisely?

This is another common question! The generally accepted wisdom is that quality can only be discussed in relation to the needs of customers. The 'Quality Revolution' therefore has attempted to focus attention on determining and meeting these customer needs.

The traditional method of providing goods and services, so the quality argument goes, has been (and still is) predominantly 'supplier-led' rather than 'customer-driven'. In a supplier-led environment goods and services are designed and delivered in ways that are biased towards the needs and requirements of the supplier rather than the customer. Technical standards, levels of functionality, delivery times, scheduling and pricing are predominantly set by the supplier rather than being influenced effectively by the customer.

Examples of the reality of this situation, though much diminished in recent years, are still abundant. The quality of service in hotels and restaurants varies enormously, many public services are a disgrace, finding a competent builder or plumber can be a nightmare, personal computers and electronic equipment are usually difficult to understand (can you programme a 14-day video timer?), the instruction manuals that accompany them are commonly useless, the reputation of banks is at an all time low, faith in the effectiveness of the police and the judiciary system is eroding rapidly and the privatized monopolies are widely perceived as being rip-off artists. Customers, in short, are somewhat less than delighted.

The silver lining to this cloud of course is the opportunity to shine in the midst of a general gloom. Staff your hotel or restaurant with courteous, well-trained people; produce electronic equipment that is easy to understand and use, and write instruction manuals in plain English; set your prices at a level that corresponds with customer perceptions of value and so on. This in effect is the central selling point of the whole quality message: the customer is king and quality is what the customer says it is. The route to success therefore is to know your customer's requirements and arrange your business in order that you can meet, or better still *exceed*, these requirements while making a viable return on your investment or, in the case of public services, a cost-effective use of public money. It is a devastatingly simple idea with flawless logic; the challenge is making it work in the real world. I will now discuss a number of common difficulties in translating theory into results.

Who are the customers?

In many instances customer identification and product/service development is (theoretically) a relatively straightforward process. Market research and trend analysis can be used to identify groups or individuals who would be likely to react positively to the general type of product or service we intend to provide. Some fictional examples may be illustrative:

1. Single young people aged 21–27 with £3000+ p.a. disposable income.
2. Recently retired people with unmet academic aspirations.
3. Lone parents with literacy/numeracy needs.

In TQM terms these groups of individuals can be considered as being 'target customers' (we will consider some of the difficulties of using such terms in non-traditional 'market' contexts later). By gaining detailed information from representative samples of each group we can generate invaluable data concerning specific requirements and critical mistakes to avoid.

For example we may find that our first group of customers (singles, aged 21–27) are interested in activity-based holidays with near equal divisions of sexes and some links with New-Age philosophies. Our newly retired group may be interested in on-campus university-based short courses specializing in arts and humanities during the summer months. Our single parents may be concerned about adequate child-care provision and require learning materials that reflect their adult interests and be keen to learn with others in similar economic circumstances.

Of course the above points are pure guesswork but armed with genuine information of this sort we can (at least theoretically) design and deliver a product or service that is closely matched to customer needs and priced at a level which represents excellent value for money. Bingo! Quality. Naturally it is not always quite so straightforward in practice but it can and is being done in very diverse situations. The procedure outlined above, clear identification of customers and accurate specification of needs, is the archetypical quality development process and in markets such as consumer goods and services it can be utilized to great effect. The reader will appreciate that the whole process is dependent on our ability to clearly identify the customer in the first place. When we move from traditional consumer markets, however, this is not always as straightforward as the above cases imply.

Who, for example, is the customer of the prison system and what therefore should a quality prison service look like? Similar questions may be asked about compulsory and post-compulsory education, the health service, training organizations, central and local government, the police and a host of other providers. The answers given to these questions will influence the type and structure of provision offered but the nature of the problem is such that it may generate a number of differing views and, consequently, a range of responses.

The education system is a prime example. It is fair to say that there is no single unifying notion of who the customer of the education system is, what education is for and, therefore, what it should set out to achieve. The government has its views and priorities, so do individual parents and children; employers and local authorities have theirs and the views of managers, lecturers and teachers will also vary between and within particular schools, colleges and universities.

This lack of cohesion of vision will almost inevitably lead to some disagreement at the operational level. Disagreement in terms of curriculum content and design, assessment of progress, teaching methods, disciplinary issues, staff assessment and development needs and so on.

Although there are no straightforward solutions to conundra of this type, one of the most significant outcomes of the quality movement has been the increasing tendency to ask such fundamental questions about the nature and purpose of public and private organizations. What this analysis has shown is that there are commonly a *number* of different types of customers involved in the production and supply of goods or services. This range of customers can usefully be divided into two distinct types: *direct customers* and *indirect customers.*

Direct customers

Direct customers form the target group that the supplier consciously aims its products or services at. Direct customers are those who consume and/or pay for the goods or services provided. In many cases the consumer and payer are one and the same; the individual who buys and reads a newspaper, eats and pays for a meal in a restaurant or purchases a ticket to travel on an aeroplane. In other cases the consumer and payer may be different; the adult who picks up the children's tab at the hamburger store, the parent who foots the bill for dance classes and the organization that settles its employee's hotel expenses.

Let us briefly consider the implications of these different classifications of customers. In the former instance (consumer-payer) the customer has complete control over purchasing decisions and an absolute veto as far as quality is concerned. The supplier must therefore understand the customer's requirements along a range of critical variables and provide cost-effective goods or services which satisfy or exceed these requirements.

In the latter instance (consumer–nonpayer) the paying customer is not the consumer and therefore a conflict of interests may arise that the supplier must be aware of. Product and service quality must reflect the consumer's requirements but pricing decisions must be made with the payer, rather than the consumer, in mind. The vast majority of children are expert at judging hamburger quality but they are usually ignorant (and unconcerned) of the relative price of a hamburger and fries bought at one restaurant compared with another or indeed from a supermarket, but the adults are not! Similarly, parents may compare the cost of tennis lessons with those for swimming, horse-riding or gymnastics. Business hotels must keep in touch with fluctuations in general corporate policy regarding levels of subsistence, allowable extras and so on.

It is clear therefore that the latter instance is more complex than the former because two *levels* of direct customer are involved. To remain successful the supplier must balance the needs and requirements of both. The McDonald's organization provides an excellent example of this balancing act in operation. Its core products, style of premises and service delivery meet the needs of many children and teenagers, its main group of direct customers. As my own children are exceptionally loyal to McDonald's I spend a considerable amount of time and money on their premises. In contrast to my children, however, I abhor fast food, so what do they offer me? An analysis is instructive.

1. Their prices are not cheap but not excessive.
2. Service is quick and always courteous.
3. They provide an acceptable cup of tea.
4. The decor is not exactly to my taste but it is not unpleasant.
5. The occasional special offers, promotions and 'free gifts' seem very good value.
6. I have only once seen a dirty or badly equipped McDonald's toilet (I always look, in the hope, I must confess, of catching them out).
7. They seem to have been mortified by the rain forest scare and now, I am sure, are 'greener than green'.
8. The nutritional literature they provide helps to reassure me that I am not ensuring that my children grow into blubberous, unfit lumps.

Apart from items 5 and 7, none of these factors is of the slightest interest to my children.

I am confident that all of this has been accomplished by design rather than chance: someone has done the sums. Of course this does not mean that McDonald's will continue to be successful. That will depend on whether they maintain their standards and, more importantly, deal with the challenge of current, emerging and not yet conceived competition; time will tell. The point is, however, that they understand the *stratified* nature of their direct customer network and attempt to balance product and service dimensions accordingly. We will return to this topic later.

Indirect customers

Indirect customers are those individuals, groups or organizations who are affected or potentially affected by the activities of a supplier even though they do not deal directly with them. For example, if you live near a McDonald's and you are a committed fast-food-hater you will nevertheless be liable to the potential disruption, noise, litter, etc. that the organization's activities may generate. If McDonald's does not consider your needs and those of your neighbours seriously then they are quite likely to give themselves operational problems.

With regard to the notion of customers therefore (this is another word that is wearing thin) in TQM terms a customer can be defined as *any individual, group or organization that is actually or potentially impacted by the design, production or delivery of goods or services.*

It is clear therefore that different operations will generate different networks of direct and indirect customers. If you are producing hand-knitted pullovers in an isolated Shetland croft and selling them by mail order you will have a negligible network of indirect customers. If, however, you are producing electricity by means of nuclear fission you have a very wide potential network indeed. Standards of operational safety and requirements for waste disposal and pollution emission are consequently set extremely high and are constantly monitored by representatives of both the direct and indirect customer networks. As with the case of direct customers, indirect customers will also be subject to stratification. The following examples may clarify the point further.

The Ford Mondeo, launched in 1993, was the first mass-produced car marketed in Britain to feature a driver's-side air bag as standard issue on all models (no doubt it will not be the last). This is a major selling point; air bags have proved effective in reducing serious head and facial injuries in low to medium speed impacts, there is therefore an immediate potential benefit to the drivers of these cars. However, using the notion of direct and indirect customer networks we can analyse the *overall* effects that such a change may have. Studies such as this can help organizations clarify the wider implications of potential product and service innovations and identify possible areas of difficulty that may arise from the sometimes conflicting interests of direct and indirect customers. Some form of grid is useful in summarizing this type of information and Table 2.1 is offered only as an example. The abbreviations DC and IC refer to direct customers and indirect customers respectively.

Table 2.1   Summary of direct/indirect customer information

Customer	Potential benefits	Potential costs
Driver (DC)	Reduced head/ facial injuries	nil
Driver's relatives (IC)	Reduced head/ facial injuries	nil
Driver's employer/ business (IC)	Reduced head/ facial injuries	nil
NHS/private health insurance	Reduced head/ facial injuries	?

As we can see from this analysis, the major potential benefits accrue to the direct customer, the driver. Also, his or her relatives, business/employer and health providers, all indirect customers, will benefit from the possibility of injury reduction in the event of an accident. However, this is not the whole story; the potential costs column for NHS/private health insurance must remain problematic until the total consequences of introducing such a change are evaluated. As we will see in later sections change, even when seemingly minor and innocuous, can have far-reaching implications that are not readily apparent prior to implementation. In the case of the introduction of driver air bags we must consider any non-obvious possibilities which may materialize.

Psychological research has indicated that increasing perceived driver security may lead to an increase in the tendency to drive recklessly. The introduction of compulsory seat belts in Britain, for example, has resulted in a reduction in fatalities for people in cars but a rise in deaths among cyclists and pedestrians and research in the USA has shown that go-kart drivers drive faster when the kart is equipped with a seat belt. Thus the introduction of the driver air bag may increase perceived driver security and lead, in some cases, to an increased level of reckless driving. Balanced against the benefits to the driver therefore are the potential losses to other drivers and pedestrians, their relatives, businesses and health providers. A more complete grid (Table 2.2) must therefore include the indirect customers.

Table 2.2 Customer-network information summary

Customer benefits	Potential	Potential costs
Passengers in car (IC)	nil	?
Other drivers (IC)	nil	?
Pedestrians (IC)	nil	?
Relatives and businesses/ employers of passengers, other drivers and pedestrians	nil	?

We can see via customer–network analysis therefore that a seemingly welcome safety development involving a direct customer could also result in negative consequences elsewhere in the network, better for a few and perhaps worse for many. A possible solution to this difficulty could be to ensure that the bags are maximally effective at speeds below 40 mph.

We can compare this situation with another in which a mass-produced car is provided with a device that maintains its stability in the event of a front tyre blow-out at legal speeds. It is clear that this innovation is different from the previous example; it is of no benefit in the event of a crash, all it can do is help prevent one should a tyre blow out while driving. The customer-network analysis in this case is shown in Table 2.3.

It is clear from this example that such a safety innovation is designed to be proactive rather than reactive; it is there to prevent

Table 2.3 Customer-network information summary: potential costs vs potential benefits

Customer	Potential benefits	Potential costs
Driver (DC)	Reduced injuries	nil
Passenger(s) (DC)	Reduced injuries	nil
Driver's relatives (IC)	Reduced injuries	nil
Driver's employer/ business (IC)	Reduced injuries	nil
NHS/private health co. (IC)	Reduced injuries	nil
Other drivers (IC)	Reduced injuries	nil
Pedestrians (IC)	Reduced injuries	nil

accidents rather than increase the chances of surviving them. Also it is as much a benefit to passengers and others as it is to the driver. As such it may positively influence attitudes to shared responsibility for safety and ultimately affect driving in a constructive way also: a truly virtuous cycle.

I have not used the above examples in order to denigrate the introduction of driver air bags but to illustrate the potential benefits of understanding the complexity and interdependence of direct and indirect customer networks.

Markets and stratified customer networks

One of the most damaging potential (and actual) dangers in adopting TQM practices is that techniques may become ends in themselves rather than being the means through which the requirements of markets, and therefore customers, may be effectively met (witness the 86 varieties of steering wheel). It is easy to forget that TQM is in fact *a means to an end* and that end is the cost-effective satisfaction of customer needs within particular market contexts.

In order for any providing organization to be a viable entity, be it a supermarket, a cinema or a hospital, there must be a demand or at least the possibility of a demand for the goods or services it offers, in other words, a market need. The notion of customers and markets is essential to TQM philosophy and practice; however it is true that such concepts apply more obviously and easily in some situations than they do in others. A major obstacle in extending the field of application of TQM arises from the use of terms such as market and customer. While I can understand the initial discomfort associated with the introduction of these terms in some areas we must not let this be a major barrier to the productive use of TQM techniques in non-traditional contexts.

It is clear, however, that market needs will vary dramatically from situation to situation. The ultimate aim of the supermarket for example is to maximize its selling space and sales turnover, likewise the cinema will aim to maximize its seating capacity and throughput. It is clear, however, that in the case of a hospital we are dealing with a very different type of 'market' indeed.

The hospital will not aim to *maximize* the use of its facilities and equipment but rather to have *adequate* facilities and equipment available to meet the fluctuating demands of its customers. Whereas an ideal situation in terms of the supermarket and cinema is to have every till working at capacity and each and every seat filled, such a situation is not the case with the hospital. Hospitals do not *aim* to have every bed filled and every conceivable piece of equipment used to its maximum capacity on the maximum possible number of occasions; the situation is entirely different.

Having made this point, however, the notion of customers and customer networks is as pertinent to the hospital as it is to the supermarket or cinema. Hospitals do have customers, direct and indirect, and an analysis of these customer networks can help ensure that the overall *effectiveness* of hospitals is maximized.

In order that we may deliver quality products and services we must first understand the nature and composition of the markets we are aiming to serve and our current approach to those markets. Every provider is, to a certain extent, required to focus on particular sectors of the markets they operate in. Thus most supermarkets focus on meeting the requirements of low- to middle-income families and individuals rather than the wealthy. The large chain cinemas (via the film industry) mainly target young people between the ages of 14 and 35 rather than the over 60s and most hospitals are equipped to deal with the less exotic of ailments and accidents. A certain amount of customer focus is therefore inevitable if organizations are to remain viable, but customer network analysis can indicate areas where further specialization may be warranted.

Markets are incredibly complex systems in a state of continuous flux and organizations must respond to market trends if they are to remain viable. Consider, for example, the market for consumer electronic goods such as personal computers and home video and entertainment systems. This market is predominantly driven by research and development in microchip design and capability and component miniaturization. Innovations in areas such as these are rapidly utilized in the development of new products or the upgrading of existing products. It is a dynamic and highly competitive market in which you are either quick or dead. The scale of innovation and structural change is immense and appears to be accelerating exponentially. In this market there are no certainties and, as organizations such as IBM have found to their cost, past success is no guarantee of future security.

In IBM's case the problems can be attributed to the fact that its customer's requirements altered dramatically during a period of 7 or 8 years. This shift in customer requirements has largely been a consequence of the development of powerful minicomputers (later followed by powerful personal computers) and the concurrent emergence of systems which allow databases to interlink. These developments have led to a dramatic reduction in demand for the large, expensive, and high service cost mainframe computers that have been the chief source of IBM's income for the past 30 years or so.

Analysis of IBM's plight seems to indicate that signs of this fragmentation were not detected, or at least not acted upon, in time to adjust accordingly. While it is extremely easy to manage an organization in retrospect it does seem to be the case that IBM continued to devote the majority of its attention to a customer segment (mainframes) that was declining while ignoring (relatively) an emerging segment (minicomputers, PCs and integrated database systems) that was growing.

I will not delve further into the relative demise of IBM at this point, interesting though it is, but use the example to clarify the notion of stratification within a particular market. Prior to 1985 or thereabouts IBM had focused its attention primarily on its mainframe customers, in other words it had *prioritized* them, with great success. Their difficulties appear to stem from an inability to respond effectively to changes of preference within that customer segment.

Prioritization, or customer segmentation, is a key factor in the delivery of quality. It is extremely difficult, if not impossible, to deliver quality goods and/or services to a highly differentiated customer base; there inevitably comes a point where we become unable to satisfy widely differing requirements. Many organizations have learned this fact at considerable cost.

Quality means knowing customer requirements in great detail but an excess of diverse requirements can result in systems overload. Organizations must therefore focus their efforts and resources on meeting the needs of *specifically targeted customer segments* if they are to be successful in future. Excellence requires focus, precision and close attention to detail; there are, however, a number of important points to consider in regard to these requirements. The reader will see that these requirements suggest that organizations must become specialists. I think that this is in fact happening in many areas and that it will become more widespread in future. Developments within the motor car industry are a case in point. The classic vertically integrated car plants once epitomized by General Motors and Ford have been superseded by factories which outsource the majority of their production requirements to specialist suppliers of raw materials and component parts. A great deal of the motive force behind this development has been the success of Japanese car manufacturers who rely on a huge tiered network of component suppliers to provide them with the materials and parts required for final assembly of their cars. Japan's Ministry of International Trade and Investment reported that a Japanese car manufacturer can have up to 13 500 firms involved in the supply of component parts for final assembly.[5]

There is an increasing tendency for organizations to concentrate their efforts on the core of their products or service and, where possible, to source raw materials and support services from external providers. This change in direction has been facilitated by the emergence of specialist suppliers offering products and services with quality and cost parameters not achievable in-house. Markets are fragmenting into tinier and tinier slivers of excellence-centred providers.

Every organization must therefore analyse its customer networks and focus its attention on those segments it is best able, or needs bound, to serve. Again there are major differences between for-profit market suppliers and others such as hospitals. It is clear that a hospital cannot in many cases simply choose its customers although many hospitals specialize in dealing with certain forms of accident or disease (e.g. burns, spinal injuries, AIDS, eye injuries). Although every hospital will have certain elements of service in common we would expect there to be differences in provision between a hospital serving the needs of a town such as Eastbourne where there is a significant proportion of elderly people and one serving the needs of a city such as Milton Keynes where there is in all probability a somewhat higher incidence of childbirth and child-related medical services required. Market analysis and customer-segment targeting are therefore essential to the delivery of quality goods and services. We cannot be all things to all customers.

3

Creating quality: understanding and meeting customer needs

Operational problems with definitions of quality

When we have identified and targeted our customer segment(s) we can then begin to consider the form that our quality products or services should take. This again raises a number of practical difficulties (no one said that achieving quality would be easy!).

First, we need to generate a working definition of quality in order to have some form of yardstick by which we can measure progress. The established quality gurus offer the following range of alternatives:

'Conformance to requirements.'

Philip Crosby

'A predictable degree of uniformity and dependability at a low cost, suited to the market.'

W. Edwards Deming

'Full customer satisfaction.'

Armand V. Feigenbaum

'Fitness for use, as judged by the user.'

Joseph M. Juran

The above definitions are a beginning in clarifying what we mean by quality. Quality is a function of customer perception; it is what the customer perceives it to be in relation to his or her personal requirements. It is clear therefore that the above definitions of quality beg a number of awkward questions in terms of operational reality. These are questions such as:

'How do we determine the requirements we will need to conform to?' (*re* Crosby)
'How do we determine what will be suited to the market?' (*re* Deming)
'How do we determine what will fully satisfy customers?' (*re* Feigenbaum)
'How do we determine what the user will judge as being fitness for use?' (*re* Juran)

We can only begin to answer these questions if we have comprehensive knowledge of our customer's wants, needs and expectations. Obtaining this knowledge can be difficult, however. A major problem arises from the fact that customers are often vague about specifying their requirements prior to a transaction; they tend to judge after the fact. As far as quality goes it is often more difficult to describe it than to experience it, as one delegate remarked in relation to service quality: 'It's hard to pinpoint exactly what it is, but I know it when I see it'.

The bottom line, however, is that there is no substitute for hard data as far as customer requirements are concerned. The more we understand about our customers the better equipped we are to make decisions about the design, production and delivery of goods and services. The only effective way of obtaining this information is through our customers and if, as we have already noted, they find it difficult to tell us precisely what their requirements are then the problem belongs to us; we are obviously not going about it in the right way. If standard techniques such as questionnaires and customer surveys are not working effectively then we may need to develop more innovative procedures for obtaining the information we require.

Let us, for example, consider the problem of excessive queuing time, a source of extreme irritation for many customers. How do we find out how long a person is prepared to wait in a queue before he or she becomes irritated? The question as it stands is of course unanswerable: it depends on the person, the context and the time of day. Someone who has left their car parked on double yellow lines will become agitated more quickly than someone who is out for a morning's leisurely shopping; people queuing during their lunchtimes will become more easily agitated than at other times and so on. How can an organization deal with these ranges of expectations?

The first step is to realize that they exist and then begin to establish baselines from which to act. We are then faced with our original problem: how can we establish a baseline acceptable waiting time? There is little to be gained by approaching this problem through customer response surveys: they do not know any more than we do. The only way of obtaining reliable data is to correlate customer satisfaction indicators with actual waiting times. Thus one large American bank video recorded customers in queues and measured the amount of time it took for them to display behavioural indicators of irritation (a controlled experiment). A number of studies of this type, carried out at different times of the day, enabled the bank to install electronic sensors (measuring queue length) beneath the carpeting which indicated when extra tellers were required at the counters.

Quality variables cannot, however, be established with one hundred per cent certainty or indeed with any long-term validity. If we could, then fame and financial security would inevitably follow. All we can find out with any degree of certainty is what satisfies the majority of customers *at the present time.* But as all goods and services must respond to changing requirements if they are to survive in the long term, we must constantly compare our standards with the shifting requirements of our customers and the service levels provided by our competitors and adapt accordingly. If we fail to do this we will inevitably find ourselves in difficulties; again witness the recent woes of IBM.

This point highlights a basic difficulty that much of the current literature on quality overlooks: quality is inevitably about approximation. We cannot determine—with one hundred per cent certainty—that what we intend to do will in fact conform to customer requirements, be suited to the market, fully satisfy our customers or be judged to be fit for use by them.

It is important to acknowledge this point because it prevents us from being seduced into believing that TQM is a guaranteed formula for business success; it is not, nothing is. This point is important because it is almost inevitable that, sooner or later, an organization which has been exalted as a paragon of TQM practice, will find itself in economic difficulties or worse. The cynics will then pounce on it with the ferocity of a pack of wolves and declare that the whole TQM philosophy is therefore proved defunct.

As stated earlier, customer satisfaction is the central principle of TQM but customer satisfaction alone does not guarantee sustainability; we must also have an extremely prudent attitude towards other key variables such as costs. Lauding currently successful organizations as exemplars is an extremely precarious business, and this is why *In Search Of Excellence* is interesting reading in 1994!

TQM is not 'the answer' or 'the formula' because there is no answer and no formula guaranteed to produce results. There can be no answer because too many unknown variables are at play. Whether the customer judges us to have provided quality goods or services depends not only on what we do but also on what our competitors do, on technological developments, political developments, social developments and a host of other factors that will shape the future. The answer is unknowable in detail because the future is unknowable in detail: there are no absolute certainties. There are, however, powerful TQM techniques for monitoring and reducing costs and keeping in touch with shifting trends and volatile markets.

The only way to keep abreast of change is to be sensitive to early indicators and take appropriate action as soon as possible. This of course is a double-edged strategy: the earlier an indicator appears, the less reliable it is, but the sooner we act the better chance we have of capitalizing on an emerging trend. Again, that is the nature of the game.

Many (perhaps most) organizations are woefully inadequate at generating hard data on quality variables and monitoring changes in customer requirements and preferences. Many tend to assume that if the books are full today and everyone is busy then things are basically OK: maybe, maybe not.

Identifying customer priorities

One of the key factors involved in the delivery of quality is the recognition that customers tend to form their judgements of goods and services through the assessment of critical characteristics. In other words, when they judge quality, customers pay more attention to certain aspects of goods and services than they do to others.

In many instances, however, the customer is not able to make an accurate assessment of the actual capability of goods or service providers and consequently resorts to the use of 'proxy variables' in order to make decisions about quality. For example, a patient's perceptions of the effectiveness of doctors and surgeons (something most of us do not have the capability to assess objectively) has been shown to correlate positively with the quality of pre- and post-treatment explanation given and the possession of developed interpersonal skills in the doctor or surgeon concerned. Similarly, people form opinions of the effectiveness of lawyers and solicitors through variables such as the time taken to reply to a telephone call or respond to a written query.

A Japanese car manufacturer sent senior design engineers to live in wealthy areas of California for a 6-month period to become familiar with the lifestyles of potential customers for its proposed range of luxury cars. Some extremely useful information was generated as a result of this research, including the realization that seemingly innocuous characteristics such as the particular sound that the doors made on being closed and a certain smell of leather were in fact critical to customer's perceptions of quality in the luxury car market.

Psychological research has shown that there is a major difference between factors which cause dissatisfaction and those responsible for enhancing customer's perceptions of goods and services. A good deal of this knowledge is based on the work of Frederick Herzberg, a psychologist who investigated motivation at work. Herzberg's central discovery was that many of the factors which caused dissatisfaction at work were different in type from those that generated high levels of motivation. Herzberg called the dissatisfying elements 'hygiene factors' and the motivating elements, not surprisingly, 'motivators'.

Hygiene factors at work include such variables as working conditions, quality of supervision and, surprisingly, pay. Herzberg's research showed that when these factors fell below acceptable levels they caused demotivation. However, he also concluded that their effect in generating motivation was limited; once hygiene factors were brought to an acceptable level they removed the previous dissatisfactions but did not, in most cases, provide a reliable source of potential motivation. Thus an ineffective heating system in a factory or office will generally lower people's motivation to work while an effective system will not necessarily stimulate people to make any extra effort, consequently, 'Let's do it for the effective heating system guys!' is not a rallying call to be recommended. Neither, according to Herzberg, is 'Let's do it for the pay!'

Hygiene factors therefore are only capable of generating or eliminating dissatisfaction and Herzberg made the important discovery that the opposite of dissatisfaction is not motivation, but merely non-dissatisfaction. While we must take care not to overgeneralize from psychological studies such as those carried out by Herzberg (a danger I will discuss in detail in a later section) such findings have important implications for providers of goods and services. They suggest quite clearly that providers should maintain the hygiene characteristics of goods or services at acceptable levels (but no more) and concentrate their key efforts and resources on identifying and providing those characteristics that act as motivators. In other words: *Providers must clearly identify the performance characteristics that have the greatest impact on customer perceptions of quality and focus monitoring and improvement efforts on these characteristics.*

These critical characteristics may be related to aspects of the goods or services provided, e.g. technical excellence, reliability, style, flexibility etc., or they may be related to characteristics that are 'bolted on' to the goods or services. For example, it was not that many years ago that certain makes of motor car were judged to be 'better cold starters' than others (even when brand new models were compared), and therefore were perceived to have an advantage on a critical characteristic. Nowadays, however, all makes of motor car are expected to start readily in adverse weather conditions and this 'advantage' has therefore been eliminated (a motivator has become a hygiene factor in this instance). As the core performance elements of goods and services begin to equalize, as they have done significantly in markets such as cameras, televisions, household electrical goods and VCRs, manufacturers are focusing attention on 'bolt on' characteristics such as finance, free gifts, extended guarantees and comprehensive support and after-sales service facilities.

The reader may have noted the fact that I have not included any examples of competing service sector providers whose core performance levels have equalized. This is simply because I am unable to think of any. Variation in competence is endemic to the service sector, a fact that reinforces the argument for the urgent application of TQM techniques.

It is clear therefore that in order to supply quality goods and services we must have detailed knowledge of our customers and the aspects of our products that are of most significance to them. We can begin to assess our current position in regard to these objectives by asking three critical questions.

Assessing customer focus

This assessment can be based on three critical questions. Every provider of goods and services should, as an absolute minimum, be able to answer the following question:

- *How many new customers have we attracted* in the past 6–12 months (or whatever timescale is appropriate) and why *specifically and in detail*, did they choose us rather than any of our competitors?

Many (most?) organizations cannot answer this question effectively yet the potential information it contains is priceless and the source of this information is right with us. All we need to do in this case is ask the question effectively, and it is a question that is well worth asking. The fact that we may currently be attracting a healthy quota of customers tells us nothing, of itself, about the inherent quality of what we offer. Customers may be coming to us because there is no viable alternative, or for trivial reasons such as the fact that we happen to be conveniently positioned, or simply because we are the slight leaders in a generally terrible field. Factors such as these may be getting people through the door at present but they will not foster customer loyalty or lead to customer recommendations and long-term sustainability. Seemingly 'healthy' organizations can go under in double-quick time when effective competition capitalizes on the seething customer discontent bubbling away beneath the surface. This is what happened in the case of the British motorcycle industry, which managed to go from domination of its many markets to oblivion at the hands of the Japanese in only 25 years. If customers are coming to us we need to know why and know it in detail.

Moving along one level of difficulty the next question we should be able to answer is:

- *How many actual customers have we lost* in the past 6–12 months (or whatever timescale is appropriate) and why, *specifically and in detail*, did they choose to go?

When, as sometimes happens, a customer complains or makes a 'dramatic exit' we are presented with a golden opportunity to gain information that will help us decide whether action is necessary and if so what action to take. Every customer complaint should be dealt with courteously and investigated thoroughly but it does not necessarily follow that change needs to be made in every instance; it depends on the nature and validity of each particular complaint. As we will see in a later section one of the key strategies in providing quality goods and services is to ensure that we attract only those customers whose requirements we are capable of satisfying.

Research has indicated, and common sense and experience supports the fact, that most dissatisfied customers do not make a formal complaint to the particular organization concerned but simply take their business elsewhere. This poses a more complex problem as it may be difficult to identify or trace customers (excluding major customers of course) who have left because of unvoiced dissatisfaction. It is quite difficult for a large supermarket to gain information of this sort for example but less so for a small corner shop. Nevertheless, random sampling can be carried out in an attempt to identify customers who have defected, perhaps, for example, as they leave rival supermarkets. When we do identify these customers, however, we usually receive comprehensive and detailed information on their reasons for choosing to go!

The last question we should be able to answer is more difficult than the previous two:

- *How many potential customers have we lost* in the past 6–12 months (or whatever timescale is appropriate) and why, *specifically and in detail,* did they choose not to come to us?

Again this poses difficulties of access in many situations but it is not an insurmountable problem. There are three reasons why we will have lost these potential customers and the root causes of each of these reasons will be increasingly difficult to determine accurately. The three reasons are:

1. Because they were unaware of our existence as suppliers or were unaware of some or all of the goods or services we are able to supply.
2. Because they went to a competitor offering a better quality (in

their view) product or service of the same type as our own.
3. Because they decided against a product or service of our type and chose an alternative course of action.

An analysis of the underlying causes of reason 1 can provide us with information that will enable us to identify weaknesses in our marketing efforts. Type 2 information can provide us with indicators of specific areas we need to improve on. Type 3 information can indicate the emergence of new forms of competition and may alert us to fundamental changes in the markets we serve.

It is clear from the above that in order to provide quality goods and services organizations must:

- Clearly identify the priority market segment(s) they intend to serve.
- Understand the important characteristics of the customers who make up the market segment(s).
- Understand the general requirements of the customers who make up the market segment(s).
- Understand the key product or service characteristics that customers use to assess quality within the market segment(s).

4

The management of variance

Once we have established the market segment(s) we intend to focus on, the general requirements of customers who make up the segment(s) and the key characteristics these customers use to judge quality, we must convert this information into operational strategies and systems for delivering the goods or services required.

As noted previously, we cannot specify acceptable quality standards with complete accuracy, a certain amount of approximation is inevitable. There are two major problems we must avoid if we are to be successful: we must not set our quality standards too low or too high. The consequences of each of these errors will be different. If we set our standards too low we will lose customers; if we set them too high we will incur unnecessary costs and make continuous improvement more difficult; it is a delicate balancing act.

One method of establishing baseline standards is comparative benchmarking, a technique pioneered by Xerox, in which stringent comparisons are made between self-performance and the performance of recognized 'best in class' operators across a range of key characteristics. Thus Toyota is currently a benchmark organization in terms of Just-in-Time (JIT) manufacturing systems; Virgin Atlantic in airline customer service; Sainsbury's in store hygiene; Nordstrom, a US fashion retailer, in retail customer service, Intel in microprocessor design and manufacture, Apple Computer in user friendly software, Kwik-Fit in terms of exhaust and clutch service and so on.

Apart from specialized areas such as those mentioned above organizations will be judged on generalized characteristics from non-competing providers also. In this way an organization's performance in areas such as reception, telephone manner, courtesy and speed of service may be compared with the performance of similar functions within organizations that are not competing in terms of core goods or services offered. Queuing for 10 minutes in the bank will be compared with a maximum wait of 3 minutes in the supermarket and so on. In this way organizations can establish internal and external quality performance standards by comparing their own procedures, processes and results with those of recognized best in class organizations. For example a manufacturer of specialized castings may benchmark its invoicing system on that of a mail order company, its recruitment procedures on a computer manufacturer and its customer care policy on an insurance broker.

Once appropriate quality performance standards have been quantified it will be necessary to introduce limits of acceptability about an ideal target value because some level of variation is inevitable. Quality characteristics such as time waiting to be seated at a restaurant, for a lecture to commence, for the telephone to be answered, for a loan to be approved, for the results of a medical test to come through and so on will inevitably vary from instance to instance but they must be contained within acceptable limits. No one expects the phone to be answered on the first ring every time, or the lecture to begin to the second on every occasion, for each person's steak to weigh the same to within one-tenth of a gram and so on. However, we are not impressed by the company that lets the phone ring 20 times before answering it, the lecturer who arrives 15 minutes late or the steak that is visibly much smaller than those of our fellow diners. Maintaining variation within acceptable limits is one of the key elements of quality.

Variation in processes

In order that we can maintain variation in quality characteristics within acceptable limits it is necessary to understand how such variations arise. The first step in achieving this goal is the recognition that quality characteristics are the outcomes of particular processes and in order to manage variation in outputs we must understand and manage the underlying processes which produce them.

In order to achieve this it is necessary to understand process capability, process variation, process cycle time and a range of other concepts and techniques that allow us to influence process outcomes. This is a vast subject in its own right and I will deal only with the most important aspects of process management in the sections that follow. Readers who are interested in furthering their knowledge in this area are directed to the further reading at the end of this book.

Process capability

Organizational processes take an input, modify it in some way and deliver it to a user or customer (often another process). Processes are designed to add value to inputs by changing them in some positive way. Thus the value of raw cast ingot is enhanced when it passes through the machining process that turns it into an engine component; the value of a pressed steel car body is enhanced when it passes through the rustproofing and painting process and the value of a purchase order is enhanced when it passes through the authorization process and so on.

However, the value-added potential of all processes depends on their ability to modify inputs in a prescribed way. The cast ingot will only have its value enhanced if the machining process alters it according to the design specifications required for a functioning engine component. The car body will only be value-added if the painting process meets the specifications required for sale and the value of the purchase order will only be enhanced if the authorization process satisfies the requirements for it to be acted on. Mistakes can occur at any stage in these processes which may result in a non-functional output, for example, a scrapped engine component, a car body requiring a respray or a purchase order returned for countersigning. When processes fail to deliver their outcomes to prescribed specifications they add cost, in the form of wasted effort, rework and scrap, rather than value.

The proportion of outputs that are within prescribed specifications can be said to constitute the capability of the particular process that produces them. Because we expect non-conforming outputs (e.g. scrap and rework) to be the exception rather than the norm, process capability is commonly expressed in terms of the percentage of conforming outputs that a particular process will be likely to generate. It is clear therefore that process capability will be dependent on a number of key variables; these are:

- the quality of inputs to the process
- the degree of precision required of the process outputs
- the design of the process

- the stability of the process.

It will be useful to consider these variables in some detail.

Process inputs

It is clear that if they are to do what is expected of them processes must have inputs that are capable of being transformed into the required outputs, for example, we can't make a Rolls-Royce from Ford Fiesta components. Similarly if our process is designed to produce engine components from raw castings then these castings must be within certain limits regarding size, metallurgical composition, machineability and so on. Our unpainted car body must be welded effectively and thoroughly de-greased and our purchase order must conform to requirements in terms of basic detail, design, etc.

These input conformance requirements also apply to human resource processes such as training and development; these will only be effective if the quality of personnel selected to undergo training (i.e. the selection process) is appropriate to the type of outcome required. Processes can be designed to accept a certain amount of variation in the quality of their inputs but this again must be held within acceptable limits. The capability of any process therefore cannot exceed the capability of the process(es) that provide its inputs.

Degree of precision required

Some degree of variation is inevitable in the output of any process, therefore process capability will be inversely proportional to the degree of precision of output required. For example, wood nails with a target length of 25 mm and a permitted variation of 1 mm in either direction will be much easier to produce than nails that have a permitted deviation from target length of only 0.1 mm in either direction. A manufacturing process that is currently 100 per cent capable of producing the first type of wood nail may only be 10 per cent capable of producing the second type (i.e. only 10 out of every 100 nails produced would be within the tighter specifications) and it may be only 1 per cent capable of producing nails with a permitted length variation of only 0.05 mm in either direction (i.e. only 1 out of every 100 nails produced would be acceptable).

As we tighten the specifications for outputs we must adjust the existing process in order to meet the new requirements, e.g. by taking greater care in setting up, monitoring the process continually, maintaining all parts of the process effectively and so on. However, if we continue to tighten output requirements we will approach the absolute capability of the process concerned. When absolute process capability is achieved any further adjustments to the process will result in an increase in variation of process outputs. In other words, when a process has reached its absolute capability it is producing the best results it possibly can and tampering with it will only make things worse.

Once a process has reached its absolute capability further improvements in outputs (in terms of quality or consistency) can only be obtained by making fundamental changes to the process itself, e.g. by using faster, more accurate or more reliable equipment, obtaining better quality raw materials, training staff in more effective methods, changing the working environment or working practices and so on.

Process design

Once we know the degree of precision required of our outputs we can begin to design our process. There are two key points to consider here:

- The process must be designed in accordance with the limitations and capabilities of its component functions. If human beings are involved in the process, for example, we must ensure that they are not required to do more than they are capable of doing. Many processes fail because of excessive demands being placed on particular functions at particular times. For example, a number of catastrophes and near catastrophes have resulted from the fact that electronic data systems can generate information at speeds and levels of complexity far greater than people are capable of assimilating. Similarly with machinery and equipment, processes should be designed so as to avoid repeated excessive demands (i.e. demands close to, or at, the equipment's absolute capability to function effectively). In an ideal situation process capability should exceed or match maximum possible demand. Although this is an admirable aim, practical realities and limitations frequently mean that such a situation cannot be achieved.

- The process should be designed to minimize unnecessary effort and wasted resources. In other words it should aim to maximize the value added content of each component function of the process. This can be greatly assisted by careful consideration being taken of workplace layout, type and positioning of equipment, materials flow, key stage bottle-necks and so on.

It is clear that to maximize effectiveness in producing consistent outputs a process must be both capable and efficient. An important point must be made here, however. The mere fact that a process is capable and efficient does not, of itself, guarantee that its outputs meet with customer requirements.

Processes stability

As we have already noted, all processes are subject to variation over time and no two outputs of any process will be exactly the same in all respects; variation is inevitable. However, the causes of variation in outputs can be very different and these differences have important consequences for the effective management of processes. Let us consider the following situations as examples of differing causes of variation in process outputs.

Imagine that we visit a particular restaurant for the first time and find the food to be excellent and the service superb. We decide to return and on our next three visits we are again delighted. We recommend the restaurant to our friends and decide to take an important business client to dinner there in order to negotiate a vital contract. Prior to the visit we extol the virtues of the restaurant to our client, a gourmet.

To our immense embarrassment, however, we find that on this occasion the food is average but not commendable and the service is, if anything, surly. We see the manager discreetly and complain about the sharp drop in standards. He apologizes profusely and informs us that Tuesday (the very day we are there) is 'Andre's day off'. Andre is head chef. It is clear from this example that Andre is a key component function in the process of producing excellent food and service, i.e. no Andre, no excellence.

The cause of variation in output in this case can be attributed to the presence or absence of Andre; in process terms we can say that this variation in output is due to an *assignable cause*. Therefore process stability (to provide excellent food and service) is dependent on an identifiable cause, Andre, or to be more precise, it is dependent on the presence of someone with his capabilities. If no one is capable of substituting for him then the process of preparing and serving excellent food will not be stable over time. To bring it into a stable state the management would need to train a substitute chef to Andre's standards or not allow him any leave or, failing this, to close when Andre is not available. Process stability is an extremely important aspect of quality; customers are often more satisfied with a service that is consistently good than one that is periodically excellent and periodically average.

Let us now imagine that, chastened by the experience, we ensure that clients are taken to dinner only on days other than a Tuesday. All is well for some time but on one instance the quality of the meal drops again. We enquire as to the reasons for this and the manager emerges to inform us, with gushing sincerity (for we are regular customers) that:

- Andre is 'not himself' owing to difficulties of a romantic nature.
- They have just discovered that the temperature in the ovens fluctuated, due to a drop in gas pressure, during the cooking process.
- The quality of fresh vegetables and herbs was affected by a temporary breakdown in chilling equipment at the suppliers.

Assuming that our manager is telling the truth it is clear that the cause of variation in this instance is different in type from that previously considered. This is essentially a random or *chance cause* of variation in process output. It is sheer bad luck that all three things occurred simultaneously.

Chance causes of variation in output are part of all processes, it is impossible to control every single factor that can contribute to variation and in some instances minor fluctuations combine to produce variations in output that are beyond designated limits. The consequences of these fluctuations can be positive as well as negative of course. If on our next visit to the restaurant Andre's love life is particularly good, gas pressure is absolutely constant and all the vegetables are dew-fresh then it is 'give my special compliments to the chef' time.

The reliability of goods and services is therefore dependent on the stability of the underlying processes which produce them. Process stability is in turn dependent on the presence of assignable and chance causes of variation. Assignable causes of variation in process outputs can be identified and, in theory, eliminated. When all assignable causes of variation in process outputs have been removed, all that will remain are chance causes. When this situation has been achieved the process is said to be stable or to be in statistical control.

Characteristics of stable processes

Stable processes display a number of important characteristics. Probably the most important of these characteristics is the fact that *variation in the output of stable complex processes is predictable.* Stable processes display a particular pattern of variation in their outputs, this pattern of variation is called a normal curve of distribution.

The normal curve of distribution

The normal curve of distribution, or bell curve, is shown in Figure 4.1. The curve has a number of special mathematical properties; the most useful of these (in terms of quality) are the properties of *average* and *range*. The average of any normally distributed variable (such as the petrol consumption of a particular model of car, the height of adult men and women or their IQ) is represented by the central position on the normal curve; this is the average value of the variable under consideration. The range of a normally distributed variable is a measure of how much spread exists between the highest and lowest values of the variable concerned. Different processes may produce outputs which have the same average but very different ranges. This situation is shown in Figure 4.2.

As can be seen from Figure 4.2 each process is stable (each generates a normal distribution in terms of its output) and the average value of the variable concerned is the same for each process but there is a vast difference in the amount of variation from the mean that each process generates, in other words each process has a different range. If the variable in consideration is the petrol consumption of three different types of motor car we can see that

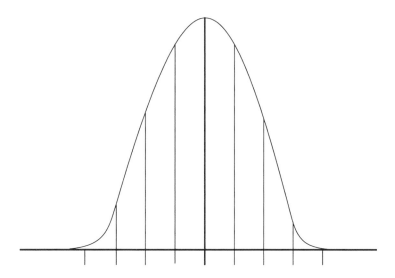

Figure 4.1 The normal curve of distribution

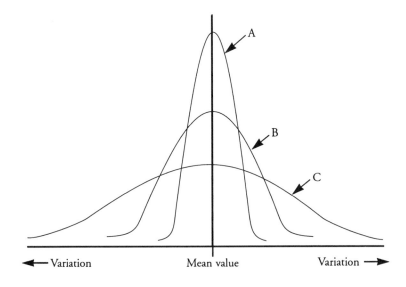

Figure 4.2 Normal curves of distribution with the same mean value but different degrees of variation

the cars produced by process A have a very small variation from an average value, those produced by process B show much more variation about the average and those produced by process C are more variable still. Each type of car has the same average petrol consumption but there are different levels of variability between individual models in each range. If we were to purchase a car produced by process A we would be more certain of its petrol consumption than we would with cars produced by process C. Until we assign values to the average and range of each distribution, however, we are not in a position to make judgements about the marketability of either motor car. If, for example, the average value for petrol consumption for cars produced by process A and process C is 25 mpg and the range of variability for process A is plus or minus $^1/_4$ mpg and for process C it is plus or minus 1 mpg neither car would have a mass market. Conversely if the average mpg of cars produced by both processes was 95 mpg with process A having a variability of plus or minus 5 mpg and process C plus or minus 10 mpg, both would have a mass market.

The important point to note here is that *process stability and consistency of output are meaningless until they are linked to some form of standard or requirement.* Consistency of output is a necessary but not sufficient factor in the production of quality goods and services. Focusing exclusively on consistency of process output is one of the possible quality traps that must be avoided. It is pointless to have stable processes churning out consistent outputs that are no longer in line with market requirements.

Probabilities of variance

The single most important quality of the normal curve of distribution is that it allows us to calculate the probability of variation from a process average. All normal curves of distribution can be described in terms of their average value and the range of variation (or deviation) from this average. The mathematical properties of the normal curve are such that probabilities of variation from the process average can be predicted. These probabilities are shown in Figure 4.3.

All normal curves of distribution exhibit these qualities. This means that for any stable process we can calculate the average value of its output and the expected range of variation from this average.

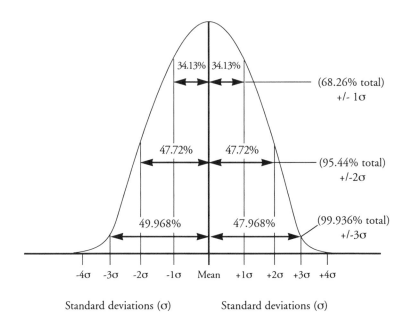

Figure 4.3 Probabilities of variation from the mean within the normal curve of distribution

We can also calculate the probability that a particular output will occur. In Figure 4.3 we can see that variation can be measured in terms of standard deviations from the average value. Standard deviations are a property of normal curves and they allow us to calculate the percentage of deviations expected from the average value. Figure 4.3 shows that 68.26 per cent of all values of stable process outputs will be within plus or minus one standard deviation from the average (34.13 per cent in each direction), 95.45 per cent will be within plus or minus two standard deviations from the average (roughly 47.72 per cent in each direction, third place decimals are not shown) and 99.9936 per cent of all values of the process output will be within plus or minus three standard deviations from the average.

Using established formulae it is possible to calculate the average and standard deviation for any variable that is normally distributed. To use a practical example we will consider the average and standard deviation of output of a machining process that produces gearbox shafts. On taking an adequate sample of shafts produced by the process (assuming of course that it is stable) we find that the average diameter of shaft produced is 1.00 inches and that the standard deviation (SD) is 0.0005 inches. Using this information, and assuming that the process remains in a stable state, we can predict the following from a random sample of 100 shafts produced:

- 68 will have a diameter between 0.9995 inches and 1.0005 inches (plus or minus one SD from the average)
- 14 will have a diameter between 1.005 inches and 1.001 inches (between plus one and plus two SDs from the average)
- 14 will have a diameter between 0.9995 inches and 0.9990 inches (between minus one and minus two SDs from the average)
- 2 will have a diameter between 1.001 inches and 1.0015 inches (between plus two and plus three SDs from the average)
- 2 will have a diameter between 0.9990 inches and 0.9985 inches (between minus two and minus three SDs from the average).

There is roughly one chance in ten thousand that a shaft will be produced that is more than three SDs from the average. It is clear from this example that if the required specification for the diameter of an acceptable shaft was that it measures between 0.9980 inches and 1.0020 inches then the process is capable of consistently meeting this requirement *if it remains in its present state*. But even if the process remains stable it is still susceptible to chance variations, the variability inherent in all processes. Difficulties may arise if the range (spread of variation) increases significantly or if the average value shifts too far in a particular direction. A robust process would be designed to accommodate chance fluctuations of this sort and still produce acceptable shafts. As we have previously noted such a process would be said to be in statistical control.

It is clear that a process that is not in such a state will be completely unpredictable and therefore the outputs of such a process will be unpredictable also. One of the key aims of TQM therefore is to bring processes into a state of control (where only chance factors influence variation). One major technique employed to this end is known as Statistical Process Control (SPC). SPC has tended to be associated chiefly with control charts (see below) and complicated statistics and many practitioners believe that the use of formal SPC techniques is an essential component of any successful TQM programme. While I do not believe that this is necessarily the case (my local butcher, for example, delivers a consistently excellent service without ever having heard of TQM or SPC), I do believe that an understanding or 'feel' for process dynamics is of significant benefit to any provider of goods and/or services.

The above use of a manufacturing example is indicative of a major reason why TQM techniques have been developed primarily within manufacturing contexts and are only slowly permeating into the service sector. It is a great deal easier to control and quantify the processes involved in the manufacture of shafts than it is to control and quantify the processes involved in the delivery (manufacture) of services such as education, training, health care and management.

Control charts

The distribution curve for a particular process can be likened to a snapshot of what the process is producing at a given point in time. Because chance fluctuations will still be present in stable processes the shape of this distribution curve, although remaining normal, will fluctuate over time. Figure 4.4 illustrates this point; we will use the gearbox shaft process described previously.

As we can see, at 9.00 am the process distribution has its average in the centre of the desired specifications and its range (spread) is well within design limits; this is an ideal situation. At 11.00 am we find that average value has shifted significantly to the left but the range has decreased and we are still producing shafts well within design limits. At 2.00 pm the distribution average has returned to the mid-point of the specification but the range has increased significantly although we are still within specifications. At 4.00 pm we see a major shift of the average and although there has been some reduction in the range we are likely to produce a percentage of shafts outside of the lower design specification if the process average and spread remain in this configuration over a period of time.

It is clear from this example that the critical aspects of any stable process are the average value of its key output(s) and the range of variation from this average. We do not therefore need to plot the whole distribution curve on each sampling occasion; we merely need to calculate the average and range and plot their values on a suitable chart. This type of chart is known as a control chart and it is a very powerful way of monitoring processes and deciding what action is necessary to *prevent* defective outcomes from occurring.

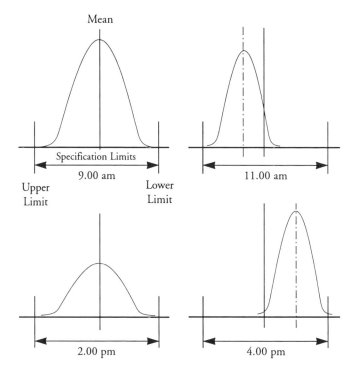

Figure 4.4 Variation in a stable process over time

Most importantly control charts can tell us when to:

- leave the process alone
- increase sample size or sample frequency
- adjust something
- do something different
- stop doing something
- shut a process down.

One of the most important benefits in the use of control charts is that they focus attention on 'real time' monitoring of an organization's key processes rather than simply measuring the outcomes of these processes (when it is often too late). This means that attention is directed towards the prevention of defective outputs rather than their detection and rectification. Control charts are constructed on statistical principles that are relatively straightforward to understand and some excellent books are available on this topic (see Further reading). Although an in-depth analysis of the mathematical concepts involved is beyond the scope of this book, I have found that it is useful to understand the fundamentals and these are outlined below.

Control charts for variables

The most common type of control charts are used to monitor some form of variable such as the diameter of a machined shaft, the temperature of a baking oven, the demand for electricity supply and so on. Control charts are constructed to monitor the variation in the average value (usually called the mean (X)) of the variable concerned and the range (R) of variation from this mean value. The mean and range are calculated by taking a sample from the stable process at given times. Using standardized formulae it is then possible to determine the expected variation in mean and range over time, assuming of course that the process remains stable or in control. As we are measuring the process in real time we will be able to detect sudden changes in process output or to identify a trend toward process failure; this information will allow us to take corrective action. Control charts are therefore constructed to have warning and action limits as shown in Figure 4.5.

In general terms stable processes will exhibit predictable patterns of output that may be represented visually on a control chart. If a process is in control we can reliably expect that:

- No mean or range value will lie outside of the calculated action limits
- There will be no incidence in which two consecutive mean or range values lie within the same warning zone
- There will be no incidence in which more than six consecutive mean or range values lie above or below the expected average
- There will be no incidence in which more than six consecutive mean or range values continuously ascend or descend
- On average no more than 1 in 40 values will lie in warning zones.

Control charts therefore provide a clear visual representation of ongoing process dynamics and enable process decisions to be made. Figure 4.6 is a typical control chart for a stable process.

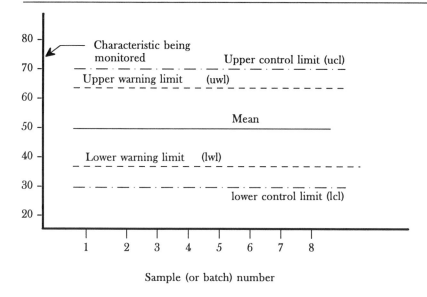

Figure 4.5 A typical control chart with warning and action lines

Control charts for attributes

Attributes differ from variables in that they are either present or absent, OK or not OK, while variables are present to a certain degree. In terms of a motor car, for example, it either does or does not have attributes such as power steering, a cassette player, a phone, whereas its petrol consumption will be somewhere on a particular scale, as will its acceleration, interior and exterior finish and so on.

Whereas variables are measured, attributes are counted and classified; that is, attributes may be present or missing, present and OK or present and not OK (you may for example have a coffee-maker in your hotel room but it may not work). Attribute control charts are designed to monitor defects in process outputs. There are three types of commonly used chart: the p–chart, the np–chart and the c–chart.

The p–chart is designed to monitor the percentage of defective units in a product or service (a unit is a discrete element of a product or service) the np–chart monitors the number of defective units and the c–chart monitors the number of defects in the units (elements) of a product or service. For example, a customer's satisfaction with a hotel will be influenced by a number of factors such as price, service,

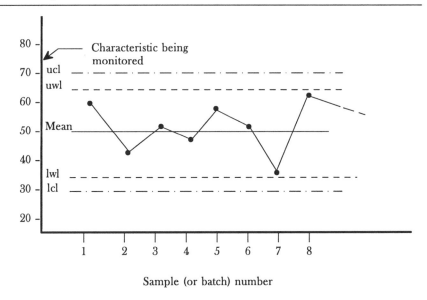

Figure 4.6 A control chart showing typical variation in a stable process

quality of food and the quality of the hotel's rooms. Each room can be considered as a unit of the hotel's service and the hotel will aim to maintain standards in each room according to its marketing promises. Thus it may be that certain items should be present in each room, items such as a daily menu, writing materials, soaps/ bathroom utensils, coffee/biscuits and so on. If these items are designed to be replenished on an on-going basis then it is of course possible that some may be overlooked; when this occurs the room can be considered to be a defective unit of service.

A p–chart could be used to monitor and control the percentage of the hotel's rooms that do not meet the prescribed standard. An np-chart could be used to monitor and control the number of defective rooms present (obviously a defect rate of 5 per cent has different ramifications in a hotel with only 20 rooms (1 room not up to standard) compared to one with 500 rooms (25 rooms not up to standard). A c–chart could be used to monitor the number of defects in each room (while the absence of only 1 item renders the whole room defective we may wish to monitor the total number of defects per room). Of course the ideal situation would be to have no omissions whatever but as we have already noted no process is perfect and variation will occur over time.

A similar situation occurs with the processing of an invoice, a claims form or a stock control sheet. It is necessary to supply all the required information correctly and legibly, do any necessary calculations correctly and obtain any mandatory countersigning, etc. A failure to meet requirements in any one or more of these attributes will result in a defunct form.

It is important in terms of quality, however, to recognize that in many situations customers will place a different emphasis on different attributes of a product or service. Thus in the context of a hotel we may be more forgiving of the fact that our biscuits have not materialized than we would be if there were no towels in our bathroom. Similarly with a payment order, we may be more forgiving of an untidy form than one in which a mathematical error costs the organization money.

This is an extremely important point in terms of the implementation of TQM in organizations. Many organizations have rushed headlong into the application of techniques such as SPC and have attempted to measure anything and everything that varies irrespective of their relative impact on customer satisfaction. For those of a mathematical inclination, SPC techniques can be both interesting and great fun, however, we must not lose sight (as some organizations unfortunately have) of the fact that the whole purpose of applying TQM techniques (particularly in the early stages of implementation) is to *monitor and control those processes that have a major impact on customer satisfaction*. Attempting to measure and control everything is as sure a route to bankruptcy as deciding to measure and control nothing.

Implications for stable processes

As we have already noted, the properties of the normal curve of distribution are extremely useful in relation to the management of quality. The question we must ask ourselves, however, is: why do so many different sorts of quantities conform to a normal curve? Why is it, for example, that when we look at such diverse measures as age-specific height or weight, scores on IQ tests, electricity consumption on a particular day, apple sizes, number of emergency medical calls on a particular day and so on that we find very close conformance to a normal distribution? The answer is to be found in a mathematical construction known as the central limit theorem.

Central limit theorem

In essence the central limit theorem predicts that the average value of a set of measurements will follow a normal distribution even if the individual measurements themselves do not.

This may seem a little confusing at first but a practical example will clarify the point. Imagine that a machine produces electric light bulbs and that due to a random fluctuation in the machine's workings it either produces a super-bulb that has a lifetime of 1000 hours or a dud that will fail after 10 minutes. Because the machine's fluctuations are random we cannot predict what type of bulb will be produced at any given instant. However, after running the machine for some time we find that its output is stable at around 70 per cent super-bulbs and 30 per cent duds. The question is: can we predict with any certainty what the average life of a box of say 40 bulbs produced by this machine will be? The answer, surprisingly, is yes. Although the life of the particular bulbs that comprise each box is not normally distributed the average life of a box of bulbs will in fact follow a normal distribution. In this particular case the average life of each box of bulbs produced by the machine will be about 700 hours and we will see the expected percentage variation from the mean characteristic of a normal distribution (as shown on p.50).

The central limit therorem states that the average result of a number of randomly fluctuating factors will be normally distributed. Let us consider for example the heights of 13-year-old boys. A cursory examination of a random group (say 10) of 13-year-olds will in all probability show a considerable variation in height from individual to individual. This variation will be due to such factors as genetic endowment, quality of nutrition, exposure to serious illness and so on which is extremely varied between individuals. However, if we were to work out the average height of this group we would find that it approaches the average height for 13-year-old boys, and the larger our random sample, the closer we will approach the mean. Although the individual heights in any number of randomly selected groups will not be normally distributed, the average heights of randomly selected groups will be.

We can see therefore that when a particular measure (height, weight, IQ, electricity consumption, etc.) is the result (or average) of interactions between a number of other factors, this measure will be normally distributed.

We can apply this principle in order to understand variation in the effectiveness of individuals, teams, departments and organizations. It is clear that the outputs (products and services) of any organizations, be it motor cars, TVs, loans, healthier people, effectively trained people or whatever, will be the result (average) of the interactions between a large number of factors within the organization concerned. As such we can expect that these outputs will also be normally distributed. This situation will also apply to the outputs of particular departments within these organizations and to the teams and individuals within these departments.

Individual performance level

Individual performance can also be understood as being the result (average) of a number of interacting variables (these variables comprise the 'system' in which individuals work) and can therefore also be expected to be normally distributed. Once we are aware of this fact it is possible to determine the mean and range of variation in output that can be expected from such a system, provided it remains in a stable state.

Implications for management

This concept has considerable implications for management. If we take the view that a department, section or team is in fact a stable system then it follows that variation in performance (output) between individuals working in that system will be due largely to chance factors only. As the reader will no doubt appreciate, this poses some interesting questions in terms of performance-related pay systems!

Let us consider the point in more detail. It is suggested that, in the majority of instances, an individual's performance level in a particular job (be it management, sales, training or production) is best understood as being the resulting sum or average of a large number of factors operating in the individual's environment. In other words, in the majority of instances variation in individual performance levels is more to do with the system in which individuals operate than the individuals themselves.

Ability/motivation

The reader may at this point complain that I have omitted the most vital determinants of performance, i.e. individual ability and motivation. It can be (and usually is) argued that good performers are good because of their particular abilities and/or motivation levels and that poor performers are poor because they have less of one or both of these variables.

Let us consider this argument further, first in relation to ability. Ability is simply realized potential; therefore if an individual is recruited or promoted into a post for which he or she does not actually have the capability, then responsibility lies with the selection process and not the individual. If a previously capable individual becomes incapable of performing his or her duties over time (assuming that he or she is doing their absolute best) then a number of factors may be involved. It could be that the problem is one of ineffective training and development or it may be related to fluctuations in the individual's capability (which may have temporarily deteriorated through illness or detrimental personal circumstances). Of course it may be the case that work demands have reached a level that exceeds absolute potential (they are beyond the individual's ability to cope).

What, then, of motivation? Again, if we are recruiting demotivated people then the recruitment system is at fault. This is rarely the case, of course; people become demotivated over time through such organizational factors as their boss's perceived attitude to them, a failure to resolve critical differences, their changing working conditions, lack of training or learning opportunities, lack of support in dealing with personal and work problems, a perceived unfairness in the promotion system, having to take responsibility for outcomes that are influenced by factors largely beyond their control and so on.

Of course individual performance is influenced by individual ability and motivation *but these in turn are largely determined by the vagaries of chance interactions between the multitude of organizational factors that influence them.* In the same way that an organization's output of goods and services will be normally distributed, its output (or its creation) of capable and motivated people can also be expected to show a normal distribution. In other words, within the expected limits of variation, it is pointless to either praise or blame the majority of individuals for their particular level of performance. *It is virtually nothing to do with them*: such differences are totally predictable within a stable system, they are due to chance factors only.

The reality of chance

Many people find this notion difficult to swallow (more difficult if they are successful, less so if they are not). The idea that chance or luck has probably played a very significant role in the majority of individual and organizational success stories is anathema to many of our cherished notions of the excellent company, the perfect strategy and the brilliant leader. The reality, however, is often very different. Let us consider a few notable examples.

- In the middle of the great depression in the US, IBM was virtually bankrupt with massive quantities of unsold punch-card accounting machines stacked in vast warehouses. There seemed no possible way of finding a market for them and the situation was dire. Then, at almost the last possible moment for IBM, the US government passed the Social Security Act of 1936. This Act created an instant and immense market for accounting machines and IBM survived.[6]
- In 1959, the fledgling McDonald's fast food company was in serious financial difficulties. It was facing lawsuits that totalled 20 times the company's net worth and could see no possible way of generating the funds necessary to avoid appearance in the bankruptcy courts. One of the co-founders of McDonald's later admitted that the situation had almost driven him to suicide. After a massive internal effort that raised only a quarter of the funds needed, McDonald's approached the larger institutional investors. They got nowhere. Then, acting on a tip, they contacted a medium sized life assurance company on the premise that they were seeking investors for expansion (they did not, however, mention their difficulties). The president of the insurance company ordered a financial investigation that did not uncover the company's financial problem. They invested an amount that saved McDonald's.[7]
- In 1950 Akio Morita, the founder of Sony, had produced a pioneer tape recorder which he marketed furiously to Japanese

consumers, businesses and universities. He even loaded them on a truck and gave public demonstrations. Many people liked them but no one wanted to buy. The research and development costs sunk into the venture made its success vital to the small company and after a period of time with no sales whatever, Morita was totally perplexed as to an appropriate course of action. Then, in his own words, 'a fortunate chance incident' shifted his viewpoint on marketing the recorder and he subsequently sold it to law courts and schools.[8]

- Between 1943 and 1949, an American patent attorney named Chester Carlson peddled the prototype of a new device he had developed for duplicating documents and drawings to the major high-tech firms in the USA. During this 6-year period he visited, and was turned down by, IBM, NCR, 3M, DuPont, Kodak and many others. He had almost given up the ghost when he finally approached a small, struggling New York company named Haloid, who decided to take a risk on the new gadget. Haloid is now better known as the Xerox Corporation.[9]

I am of course not suggesting that chance is the only factor influencing success. IBM, McDonald's, Sony and Xerox continued to be successful because of the sustained and developed quality of their products and staff. The point to be made, however, is that all organizations (and individuals for that matter) are, particularly in the early stages of growth, highly likely to be subjected to random crises that will only be weathered with a little good fortune. Or, as in the case of Haloid, good fortune is self-booted out of the opposition's arms and into your own. It is a statistical certainty that, for some at least, the toast will land butter-side up.

Readers who are particularly intrigued by these notions will find further examples and a rigorous scientific analysis of the evolutionary effects of chance happenings in current literature devoted to the study of the newly emerging sciences of complexity and chaos theory.[10]

The key elements influencing process variation

We have already noted that the variability in outputs of a process will be predictable if the process remains stable. In other words, if the process elements that have a critical impact on desired process outcomes (the key elements) remain stable, then variation in process outcomes will follow a normal curve of distribution. This is easy to understand in terms of the production of goods and services. To produce consistent quality we must ensure that five key elements remain stable. These five elements are:

- employees
- equipment
- materials
- methods
- environment

If these key elements are kept constant over time (that is they are subject only to random fluctuations) then the process is stabilized and the output from this process will be predictable. Unpredictable outputs will only occur if one or more of these key process elements is changed in some way. Using the example of a restaurant such changes could include:

- The appointment of a new chef
- A new oven being installed
- A different supplier of meat and vegetables being used
- Different cooking methods being experimented with
- Major changes being made to the kitchen environment.

Changes such as these will be highly likely to alter the normal curve of distribution of process outputs. For better or worse, the mean and range of variation of outputs will change.

It is clear from this identification of key process elements that the only one capable of self-generated positive change is the human element, the employees. The remaining elements, equipment, materials, methods and the environment will only be likely to undergo beneficial change if they are acted on by human beings. However, they will be highly likely to undergo detrimental change if they are left to themselves. Equipment and the environment deteriorate if not maintained, and materials and methods become obsolete. The whole process therefore is dependent on people, and people have two crucial and somewhat conflicting roles to play. These roles are:

- To control the process in such a way as to maintain existing levels of quality and consistency (predictability) of outputs.
- To change the process in such a way as to improve the quality and/or consistency of outputs.

In terms of the distribution curves for the processes concerned, the first (maintenance) challenge is to control the five key elements in order that the existing mean and range of process outputs remain within existing limits (assuming of course that these are acceptable to customers).

The second (improvement) challenge is to reduce the range of variation of process outputs and/or shift the mean in the direction of improved customer satisfaction. Of course due attention must be paid to the costs of achieving these improvements, as we noted earlier (86 steering wheel example) gains in customer satisfaction must be made in a cost-effective manner. Figure 4.7 (a), (b) represents these two forms of process management.

The reader will no doubt observe that there is a major difference in applying SPC techniques in manufacturing and non-manufacturing contexts. In manufacturing contexts control charts are used primarily as a means of monitoring variation from a desired perfect state (the target value or mean of the process concerned). In such cases points outside of the upper and lower warning lines on the chart indicate the possible failure of the process to continue delivering usable outputs and that corrective action is necessary. Also, as we have seen, certain other indicators such as seven consecutive points to one side of the mean or a run of seven points in a particular direction also give warning that something is amiss.

In non-manufacturing (service) contexts, however, this situation may not apply. There is, for example, no perfect customer satisfaction target: customers are constantly revising their expectations as they experience the service levels of differing suppliers. Also, of course, there is no upper limit in terms of customer satisfaction. This being the case we can use control charts as a diagnostic tool to help stabilize and improve service delivery processes. The following case study illustrates a possible application of the technique.

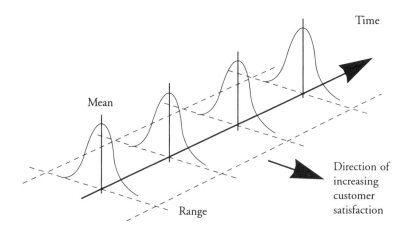

Figure 4.7(a)

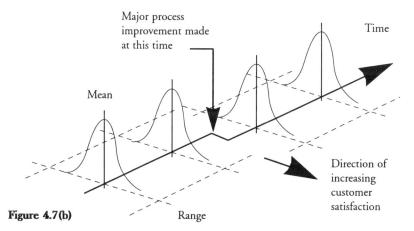

Figure 4.7(b)

Figure 4.7(a)   Process outputs over time showing acceptable control of variation but no improvement in customer satisfaction. (b) Process outputs over time showing acceptable control of variation combined with improvement in customer satisfaction due to fundamental process changes

Case study: Quality Hotels plc

Let us imagine that the management of Quality Hotels plc is committed to the philosophy and principles of TQM. Being such an organization they have of course established procedures which monitor customer satisfaction levels on a continuous basis. Customers are asked to rate critical aspects of the hotel's services against those of other hotels in a similar class. This is achieved through the use of customer rating scales. Customers rate key services on a scale from 10 to 100, where 10 represents woeful comparative inadequacy and 100 represents stratospheric superiority. Experience to date has shown that overall customer satisfaction ratings are normally distributed about a mean value of 68 points with an average range of 18 points. These scores are obtained by taking a random sample of six customer evaluation sheets every other day, adding together each individual category score and dividing by the number of categories measured. This data is then used to plot points on a control chart. These scores represent the hotel's overall capacity to meet the various requirements of its customers. While aggregate measures such as these are useful in monitoring the stability of the system as a whole they are of little practical use in identifying priority areas for change as they are too general. However, they are of immense potential in establishing parameters for *internal benchmarking.*

As already noted, average customer satisfaction ratings such as these represent the overall capability of the organization concerned. Taking the whole organization as a single system, these ratings indicate the effectiveness of that system and its processes. If the five key process elements (people, methods, materials, equipment and environment) remain in a stable state then we can predict with some certainty that aggregate customer satisfaction will also remain stable. This data could therefore be used to construct a control chart and monitor process capability over time. Figure 4.8 is such a control chart.

It is clear from this control chart that the process is stable. As we noted earlier, however, average scores are likely to be normally distributed due to the effects of the central limit theorem and that underlying measures may not be normally distributed (as with the heights of 13-year-olds in our previous example). However, once we have established some baseline data on the overall capability of the system we can then focus on individual components of that system and compare their effectiveness with this overall standard. Let us imagine, for example, that we continue to take overall random samples of customer responses but that we also decide to monitor the response scores achieved by discrete elements of the hotel's provision such as room service, breakfast or reception.

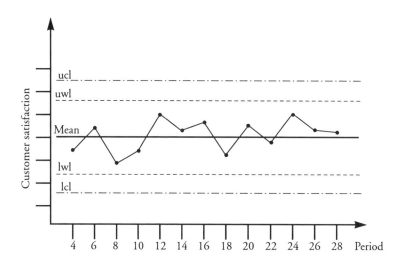

Figure 4.8   Control chart showing average customer satisfaction scores, Quality Hotels plc.

Using the parameters calculated for our service overall, we can now plot data from our study of discrete elements of service onto the control chart. A fictional result of this study is given in Figure 4.9. It is clear from this exercise that breakfast service is in control with respect to the overall capability of the hotel but that reception and room service are out of control. In a manufacturing context both of these situations would warrant investigation and alarm. However, in a service context such as this the situation is different. Service provided by reception is out of control in a negative sense (the vast majority of points are below the mean value). Room service, however, is out of control in a positive sense (all points are above the mean value).

This is where service applications of SPC techniques differ from manufacturing. In manufacturing there is no difference between transgressions on either side of the control chart centre line; both are bad news. In the service context, however, they mean different things. Negative (below the centre line) transgressions are, as in manufacturing, an indication that remedial action is necessary. Service levels are below those that can be expected from inherent variation only, special causes are at work and they must be sought and eliminated. However, the positive transgression (above the

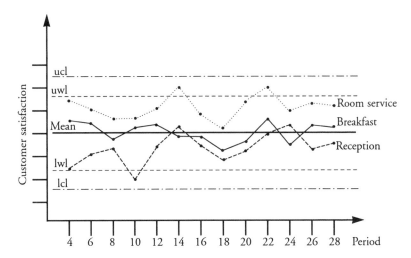

Figure 4.9 Control chart showing their performance of three discrete elements of service

centre line) by room service means that it will be in our interest to identify the special causes of variation and attempt to duplicate them elsewhere. Reception is faring worse than the overall system would predict but room service is achieving results above that expected. Room service is therefore beating the overall system with results consistently superior to those we could expect from chance variation only.

5

Using control charts to improve performance

This case study, although fictional, allows us to explore a number of important principles and techniques in TQM. First it is based on the collection of customer-focused data and the application of statistical techniques. Second, it is used to provide management with important and actionable information that can form the basis of a quality improvement initiative.

Let us briefly consider the information available from the collection of these data and the construction of a control chart. It is clear that we have established a baseline figure for the level of overall customer satisfaction provided by the organization in terms of critical service functions. This in itself can tell us a great deal, particularly when data clarifies our position in relation to our competitors. The control chart constructed from this information can be used in a number of ways:

- To determine the mean performance level for the system as a whole. This then becomes the baseline performance level for all functions.
- To identify functions that are performing consistently to baseline performance level: these functions will be in control on our control chart (evenly distributed about the average).
- To identify functions that are performing consistently below baseline performance level: these functions will be 'negatively' out of control (predominantly in the bottom half of the chart).
- To identify functions that are performing consistently above baseline performance level: these functions will be 'positively' out of control (predominantly in the top half of the chart).

When we have established this information we need to find the special causes of variation that lead to performance levels consistently below or above baseline. Because we are taking the view that performance variation is primarily influenced by underlying processes and systems we need to search for the root causes of performance differentials within these processes and systems. In using this information we have two prime objectives:

1. To bring negative functions up to baseline performance level.
2. To use functions that are 'positively out of control' as internal benchmarks for improvement activities.

The reader will see that this approach involves both *control* and *improvement* of business processes. There are a considerable number of advantages in using this technique but it must be managed effectively. First, because we are using control charts with appropriately constructed limits we can better separate consistent performance from the sporadic variety. Sporadically effective or ineffective performance can create images in managers' minds that are difficult to shift, particularly when they are extreme. Consider the control chart shown in Figure 5.1 for example which tracks the performance of two teams of sales staff.

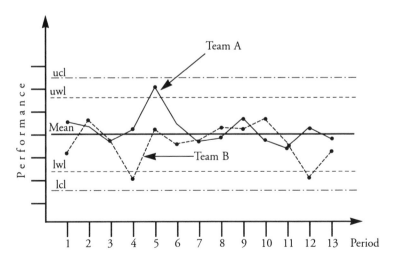

Figure 5.1 Control chart showing the performance of levels of two teams which vary significantly in certain periods.

As can be seen from the chart, the performance levels of both teams remain in control over the period monitored but two major 'blips' appear for each. Team A experiences a positive blip in periods 4 and 9 while team B experiences negative blips in periods 3 and 12. Such dramatic variations in performance can have far-reaching consequences. It is highly likely for example that both teams will 'internalize' the aberrant results. That is, they will be likely to see themselves as having, to some extent, caused them, particularly in the case of the positive figures. There may of course be some element of truth in this; they may have indeed contributed to the variations in performance but these performance levels are still within the limits predicted for the process as a whole. In reality their contribution to the aberrant figures (both high and low) may be insignificant compared with the influence of other factors within the process. The problem is that spectacular deviations such as these tend to stick in managers' minds and, because they have no idea whatever as to the natural variation inherent in their business processes, promptly dish out accolades or threats.

When running training courses and seminars on TQM this particular idea, that many aberrant performance levels are primarily due to the system, usually meets with a good deal of incredulity. This reaction is understandable because, as we have already noted, there is a strong tendency in western cultures to equate success or failure with individual competence levels. In Britain particularly there is the culture of the Hero and the Failure and even of the Heroic Failure. 'Successful' managers and entrepreneurs are exalted as possessing some form of secret ability that is lacking in mere mortals such as ourselves. It may be the case that they do but I personally doubt that such abilities are completely independent of situational factors. For example, Sir John Harvey-Jones did a good job of managing ICI but he did not actually do it completely alone and he was operating in the middle of a boom. We will of course never know whether the same results would have been achieved with different management support staff (or even, dare I say it, with different front-line workers, I imagine that their efforts contributed something) or in a different economic climate. We do seem to have a debilitating desire to explain success and failure in terms of specific individuals. This inevitably involves an element of simplification because individuals operate within systems and processes that are complex, incredibly interrelated and subject to fortuitous and unfortuitous machinations.

This fact has not been lost on the therapeutic community. In recent years there has been a marked shift of emphasis in therapy away from the notion of individually focused interventions to one that recognizes the crucial role of the family system in generating (and indeed sustaining) psychological disorders in individual members. As John Donne rightly said, 'No man is an island'. I believe that it is high time that our approach to understanding variation in performance standards also accommodates a wider, systems, perspective.

Determining causes of performance variation

Let us return to the example in Chapter 4 (Quality Hotels plc): our study reveals stable baseline performance from breakfast services, consistent overperformance on behalf of room service and consistent underperformance from reception services. Although each of these functions operates within the same overall system (the hotel itself) it is highly likely that each will have developed an individual 'microsystem' within this larger system. Our task therefore is to understand how such microsystems produce consistently positive or negative variation. Initial analysis must focus on the fundamentals of all processes, the five key process elements identified above (p.63), and an Ishikawa or Fishbone diagram (Figure 5.2) can be used as a heuristic tool.

As can be seen from the Ishikawa diagram each of the five key process elements is broken down into a number of component parts and each of these parts examined for possible contribution to consistent variation. In many cases this can be based on a standard procedure, an example of which is given below.

A primary analysis of key process elements

Is consistently positive or negative variation in process outputs significantly influenced by the five key process elements?

- *The employees* Through:
  Recruitment and selection methods
  Recognition and reward systems
  Training and development programmes
  Personality factors

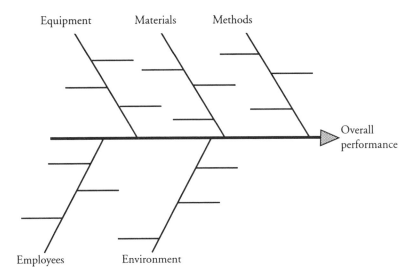

Figure 5.2 Ishikawa or Fishbone diagram used to analyse the factors that may contribute to consistent performance difference.

    Skill factors
    Educational factors
    Previous experience
    Group cohesion
- *The working environment* That is:
    The physical environment
    The psychological environment
- *The methods used* Such as:
    Operating methods
    Problem-solving methods
    Planning methods
    Resource allocation methods
    Process design methods
    Process monitoring methods
    Process improvement methods
    Work allocation methods
    Goal-setting methods
    Quality assurance methods
    Communications systems
- *The materials used* Through:

Suitability
Cost
Control of quality
Availability
Specialization
Storage systems
Delivery systems
Procurement procedures
● *The equipment used* Through:
Suitability
Cost
Availability
Effectiveness
Capacity
Maintenance
Specialization

This analysis of key process factor elements is not exhaustive and may be different in different contexts but the technique of analysing underlying processes is essentially universal. The reader will no doubt appreciate that this approach is quite different from traditional management approaches to understanding differences in levels of performance which, in the overwhelming number of cases, have tended to focus primarily on the assumed capability differences of individuals or groups.

Comparative benchmarking

A good rule of thumb in TQM is to assess performance through the use of comparative information rather than attempting to create measures from scratch, hence the usefulness of internal and external benchmarking techniques. The study of Quality Hotels plc, for example, used the notion that underlying microsystems are primarily responsible for differing performance levels. Once we have analysed and quantified the key process elements in our chosen benchmark area therefore they can act as baseline measures and be used in comparative studies. In this way we should be able to identify similarities and differences in the underlying processes involved in different microsystems and isolate those that contribute most to the differences in levels of performance.

In most organizations the first stage of an improvement programme is best focused on the task of bringing underperforming areas up to baseline performance levels by comparing the underlying microsystems of each. For reasons of sensitivity and morale it is unwise to refer to underperforming areas as such and therefore benchmarking documentation and data should use non-evaluative descriptors wherever possible (such as 'standard' area). An example of a structured analysis framework is given below. The number and type of comparisons used is, of course, not exhaustive or prescriptive.

A framework for the structured analysis of key process elements in benchmark and standard areas

Element 1   Staff

• *Staff recruitment and selection processes*   How do staff recruitment and selection processes (including promotion) operate in internal benchmark and standard areas (or, in the case of external benchmarking, between external benchmark and internal standard areas) in terms of: the effort devoted to preliminary R&S activities (time and financial). For example detailed preparation of person and role specifications, analysis of potential employee market, design of appropriate advertising and process for deciding where advertisements are placed, criteria for shortlisting candidates, planning for selection interviewing including composition of panel (where appropriate) pre-briefing and proposed structure of interview, criteria for final selection.

Who carries out search, advertising, shortlisting and interviewing? What relevant qualities, experience and training do such personnel have? How are R&S activities perceived by staff? What are the critical differences between R&S activities in both areas? As a result of this comparative study can specific changes to existing R&S activities be identified for standard areas?

• *Recognition and reward systems*   What recognition and reward systems operate in benchmark and standard areas, official and unofficial, financial and non-financial? How are they perceived by staff? What are the critical differences between recognition and reward systems in each area? As a result of this comparative study can specific changes to existing recognition and reward practices be identified for standard areas?

• *Training and development activities*   What training and development activities (formal and informal) are carried out in benchmark and standard areas? What is the duration of training per employee? How are training and development activities designed, structured and delivered? How are they perceived by staff? What are the critical differences between training and development activities in each area? As a result of this comparative study can specific changes to existing training and development activities be identified for standard areas?

• *Personality characteristics*   What are the personality characteristics of staff in benchmark and standard areas? Are personality characteristics appropriate to role responsibilities? Are certain personality characteristics actively recruited? Are appropriate personality characteristics encouraged? What are the critical differences between the personality characteristics of staff in each area? As a result of this comparative study can specific personality characteristics be identified for staff in standard areas?

• *Skills*   What skills do staff in benchmark and standard areas possess? Are skills appropriate to role responsibilities? Are certain skills actively recruited? Are overall skill levels adequate? How are appropriate skills developed? What are the critical differences between the skills of staff in each area? As a result of this comparative study can specific skill requirements be identified for staff in standard areas?

• *Educational characteristics*   What educational characteristics do staff in benchmark and standard areas possess? Are educational characteristics appropriate to role responsibilities? Are educational characteristics taken into account at recruitment? What are the critical differences between the educational characteristics of staff in each area? As a result of this comparative study can specific educational requirements be identified for staff in standard areas?

• *Prior experiences*   What prior experiences do staff in benchmark and standard areas possess? Is prior experience appropriate to role responsibilities? Is specific prior experience a factor in recruitment? What are the critical differences between the prior experiences of staff in each area? As a result of this comparative study can specific prior experiences be identified for staff in standard areas?

● *Group cohesion* What level of group cohesion exists among staff in benchmark and standard areas? Is the level of group cohesion appropriate to responsibilities? Is an appropriate level of group cohesion encouraged? What are the critical differences between group cohesion levels in each area? As a result of this comparative study can specific changes to existing group cohesion levels be identified for standard areas?

Element 2   The working environment

● *Physical environment* What are the characteristics of the physical environment in benchmark and standard areas in terms of: space, light, ventilation, heating, hazards, location, cleanliness, attractiveness, state of repair, access to amenities? What are the critical differences between the physical environment in each area? As a result of this comparative study can specific changes to the existing physical environment be identified for standard areas?
● *Psychological environment* What are the characteristics of the psychological environment in benchmark and standard areas in terms of: levels of trust, open communications, sense of teamwork, sense of individual purpose, sense of belonging, sense of freedom to act, sense of job security, sense of value to the organization? What are the critical differences between the psychological environment in each area? As a result of this comparative study can specific changes to the existing psychological environment be identified for standard areas?

Element 3   Operating methods

What operating methods are used in benchmark and standard areas in terms of: specified standards, standardized operating procedures, systematic problem-solving techniques, effective planning and scheduling techniques, identification of key processes, design of key processes, monitoring of key processes, continuous improvement of key processes, standard setting, quality assurance techniques, communication systems? What are the critical differences between the operating methods used in each area? As a result of this comparative study can specific changes to existing operating methods be identified for standard areas?

Element 4   Materials used

What materials are used in benchmark and standard areas in terms of: suitability, cost, specialization, consistency, ease of use, availability. What are the critical differences between the materials used in each area? As a result of this comparative study can specific changes to existing materials be identified for standard areas?

Element 5   Equipment used

What equipment is used in benchmark and standard areas in terms of: suitability, age, cost, speed, specialization, maintenance considerations, energy considerations, ease of operation, safety considerations, reliability, availability? What are the critical differences between the equipment used in each area. As a result of this comparative study can specific changes to existing equipment be identified for standard areas?

When the major differences between the underlying process elements in standard and benchmark areas have been identified we can institute a programme of changes aimed at reducing these differences. If the analysis has been accurate and the change programme effective, underperforming service areas should be brought into statistical control. When this has been achieved for all underperforming areas (that is none are negatively out of control on our control chart) we can then turn our attention to functional areas that are producing results consistently (but not too dramatically) above baseline performance and apply our comparative analysis once more. These areas now become our new benchmark (our new control chart mean) and the whole system is then recalibrated about this mean and new control limits are calculated.

The reader will no doubt realize that while internally-focused improvement activities such as these can produce significant results we must not be seduced into the belief that all is therefore well. Ultimately we will be judged in relation to our competitors and it will also be necessary of course to gain information which indicates our performance in relation to them.

Some practical considerations

It is clear from the outline given above that a detailed study of this type will involve a considerable amount of time and effort. This fact alone is often sufficient to turn off many managers and organizations. This is unfortunate and stems from an erroneous assumption concerning many TQM techniques (an assumption exacerbated by a number of TQM evangelists).

Many managers, when exposed to general principles such as these, rightly see them as being totally unworkable in terms of the constraints and pressures of their particular organizations. Some common responses are: 'That's fine if you've got nothing else to do' or 'Tell me how to get the three or four extra staff I'll need to do it'. These responses, coming as they do from managers working in the real world, are both pragmatic and correct. However, this is mainly because such general descriptions often represent *a very mature example of the technique concerned*. There are very few organizations capable of doing all of it, from scratch, in a short time period. But this is not necessary. TQM does not have to start with a big bang. Indeed my own experience tends to suggest that this is not the optimum way to proceed even if an organization has the resources to do so (unless the competitive situation makes it imperative). In many instances TQM can start off as an experiment, a different way of looking at things and a willingness by management to try different approaches to managing. The rate of progress required to achieve a full-blown TQ culture depends entirely on the nature of an organization's customer base, its current structures and personnel, the rate of innovation and development in the markets in which it operates and the quality and strength of competition (which essentially means their stage of TQM development). True, many organizations such as Xerox, General Motors and Ford, implemented TQ procedures in double-quick time but this was out of pure necessity. In each case Japanese competition was threatening to see them off for good.

There is a widespread and mistaken idea that TQ techniques such as SPC, comparative benchmarking and customer satisfaction surveys are, by definition, grand and complex undertakings appropriate only to the Rank Xeroxs, General Motors and Fords of this world. Nothing could be further from the truth. But the preconception that quality improvement initiatives must be dramatic is one of the reasons why many quality initiatives fail. Followers of one or other of the currently fashionable 'Gurus' have often sold the quality idea not only as being a revolutionary approach (which is the case for most organizations), but also that it requires a revolutionary pace of change (which is not necessarily the case). Revolutionary change is certainly required in many instances but revolutions result from growing internal unrest rather than dictatorial imperatives and are commonly incremental in nature until they reach a critical momentum. The dramatic revolutionary uprising is not caused solely by the events of the day in question but through the cumulative experiences of time.

When writers on quality make the important point that TQ initiatives can only succeed with support from the very top, they sometimes overlook the fact that a vital element of this support must be for the initial minority (and they will be a minority) of 'revolutionaries' within the system who genuinely take TQ ideas and practices on board at an early stage. In the vast majority of instances time will be needed for these revolutionaries to become the recognized role models for appropriate organizational behaviours and senior management must support, recognize and regard their 'aberrant' activities, particularly in the early stages of quality improvement programmes.

Despite the claims of many packaged-answer merchants there is no set way of achieving TQM; no 'master plan' guaranteed to bring results. TQM can start big or it can start small; it can be achieved through evolution as well as revolution. Implementation depends entirely on the existing structure and culture of the organization and the environment in which it operates. But it has to start somewhere and its development must be nurtured.

The common tendency to view TQM as a dramatic 'all or nothing' affair is symptomatic of western management's predilection to, in the words of the Japanese quality expert Masaaki Imai, 'worship at the altar of innovation'. We in the west have a strong preference for immediate, dramatic action, 'the big shake up' (preferably led by a charismatic, lone and rugged hero). The eastern approach to quality improvement is characteristically quite different (I consciously use the term eastern rather than Japanese in order to reflect the fact that Japan is no longer a lone pioneer of quality improvement in eastern Asia). The eastern approach, encapsulated in the Japanese word 'Kaizen' (improvement) is exemplified by the undramatic, gradual and constant movement towards absolute perfection (which, of course, can never be attained).

Imai contrasts the traditional western approach of progress through abrupt change and innovation with the Japanese preference for continuous improvement as being akin to the difference between a stairway and a gradual slope. In the western model (the stairway) dramatic events such as mergers, acquisitions, shake-outs, restructuring and technological breakthroughs occur at intervals and move the organization onto an improved level of performance where, in theory, it remains until the next form of breakthrough emerges. Imai, however, contends that what really happens after breakthrough is that performance gradually and inevitably declines over time thus precipitating the next period of upheaval. The Kaizen approach is quite different and stresses the cumulative benefit of gradual refinement and improvement. Dramatic progress through breakthrough and innovation is not ruled out also but the prime focus remains one of day-to-day incremental development.

There are a number of important ramifications to this philosophy. As Kaizen is about the identification and implementation of small step improvements to processes and procedures there is no necessary requirement that such improvements should result from large research and development efforts. Anyone can contribute to Kaizen activities. In a Kaizen culture the level of improvement necessary to engage management's attention and support is commonly quite minute. In Nissan's Tochigi plant, for example, any suggestion that promises to shave at least 1/100th of a minute (0.6 seconds) from an operating process is taken seriously by management.[11] This is certainly quality through evolution as opposed to revolution. In fact the similarities between Kaizen activities and those of evolution by natural selection are striking.

Consider the evolution of complex organs such as the eye. It is clear, unless one is a creationist, that eyes did not spring into existence at a single stroke. Somewhere in the far history of sighted species a genetic mutation will have equipped an ancestor or a number of ancestors with a membrane that was bluntly sensitive to light and shade. This chance mutation will have endowed such ancestors with a minute advantage in avoiding predators and locating food. Given this advantage these early 'seers' would be more likely to survive and produce offspring with, through hereditary mechanisms, similar or perhaps enhanced sensitivity to light. Slight chance improvements such as these which occur continuously over the millenia ultimately culminate in the complex and specifically refined organs of current species. Of course each process is fundamentally different in that Kaizen is a purposeful activity which has perfection as its ultimate (though unattainable) goal while biological evolution has no ultimate goal whatsoever.

I again stress the point that constructive TQ activities can begin anywhere and at any level within an organization and that the key role of management is to facilitate and reward progress wherever it occurs. Facilitation is the prime activity here, unless managers are prepared to really support TQ activities (as opposed to paying lip-service) and to change existing systems and confront existing barriers to improvement then very little, in my experience, will ensue. To do this managers must begin to think from a process perspective rather than the traditional linear 'cause and effect' perspective.

Similarly, fundamental TQ activities such as the collection of customer satisfaction data need not imply vast expenditure on surveys and questionnaires. Raising front-line staff awareness of the need to satisfy customers and perhaps making it possible for them to ask randomly selected individuals for their opinions is a beginning. When leading training courses and seminars on TQ, I always stress these points because they are important. Introducing the principles and techniques of TQ does not require that the organization has its back well and truly up against the wall (although, sadly, this is too often the sort of prompting that is needed), or that profound organizational changes must occur in short periods of time. I often use the analogy of TQ development as being akin to the growth of a snowball: if top management continues to push it (through personal commitment, support, recognition and reward), it will get bigger, and the perfect place to start pushing is where there is plenty of fairly fresh snow! In other words do not focus too much attention on the cynics or those with a vested interest in maintaining the *status quo*.

The effective application of TQ techniques will improve the performance of *any* organization; as a medical friend of mine asserts—you don't have to be ill to get better! I hope that I have convinced the reader by this stage that TQM is not some specious academic theory that looks good on paper but falls flat in the real world. TQM is the real world. By definition, any organization that currently has satisfied customers and is making an acceptable return on investment, is, however vicariously, practising the tenets of TQM.

However, there may be considerable room for improvement and much may have been achieved through luck alone. Also, if it is to succeed long term the organization will need to monitor its performance as perceived by its customers and to reduce unnecessary waste.

In the final analysis, all that TQM aims to achieve is that luck is converted into judgement and that business success is achieved by systematically and cost-effectively generating superior levels of customer satisfaction. The whole point of the techniques, philosophy and processes so far discussed in this book is that they be used to satisfy the customers that organizations have now and hope to attract in the future. If we can continuously achieve this aim then we will prosper. The customer is therefore the whole point of the organization's existence and any and all information we can obtain which helps us clearly understand the critical needs and expectations of our customers the better placed we will be to meet them. We must get better at obtaining critical customer data; there is absolutely no way around this. Of course many organizations now accept this fact but that does not mean that they are therefore successful at doing it. Because customers are vital we have to exercise care in our dealings with them. In Chapter 6 we will examine a number of important points regarding the collection and use of customer-focused information.

6

Gathering and using customer-focused information

Like most important business activities, attempting to gather customer-focused information is not without its potential difficulties. The form and style of methodology used to 'get closer' to customers needs careful thought. For example, in their eagerness to 'listen to the voice of the customer' a number of organizations have fallen foul of the 'How are we doing?' type of approach to the collection of customer information (a colleague describes this as 'death-wish research'). Such an open-ended approach, in my experience, encourages respondents to focus on the negative, to use absolute criteria in their evaluations and to judge services and products against theoretical perfection rather than practical achievability. 'How are we doing compared with . . . ?' is a better approach and encourages respondents to think deeper and in a more balanced way about the issues involved and to base responses on actual experiences rather than idealistic (and frequently unrealistic) expectations. Comparative data also makes action more likely if only because of the fact that they are based on achievable results (by definition, if we are benchmarking, someone else is doing it).

Many organizations have also discovered that surveying customers can be a pretty demoralizing affair unless it is structured effectively. Many people work hard at their jobs (most people believe that they do) and although a great deal of the effort many people have to expend is probably created unnecessarily by ineffective systems, to be given a list of critical customer comments at the end of a hectic day is somewhat less than cheering. This is why the inclusion of survey questions such as 'What do we do well?' also provide necessary cerebral and emotional information. What is clear, however, is that some form of ongoing performance measurement of customer satisfaction is absolutely necessary. After all, if we are in danger of losing touch with customer requirements we are in danger of losing market relevance, and without market relevance all the quality procedures, standards and awards in the world have absolutely no validity whatsoever.

Financial information versus customer information

It is a source of constant amazement that organizations large and small would not dream of operating without some form of financial control and monitoring system and yet they commonly have no coherent strategy for effectively monitoring the opinions of the very people who supply the 'raw materials' (i.e. the incoming money) that is the *raison d'être* for the whole financial monitoring circus in the first place. Ask any organization to identify those staff who are totally or significantly involved in financial control and monitoring and a list (usually quite long) will be forthcoming. Ask for a list of those staff who are totally or significantly involved in customer satisfaction monitoring, however, and a very different response commonly ensues. Why is this? There are a number of common reasons.

First, customer satisfaction monitoring is not mandatory: organizations do not have to do it. No one, for example, will refuse an organization a loan because they do not do it or are not seen to do it effectively (unlike the situation with financial systems); no external body will audit it and the company report does not (as yet) require it. Next there are the simple pressures of day-to-day work. Then there is the view that measuring customer satisfaction is essentially a waste of time because nothing can or will be done about adverse comments. There is also the cynical view that, as most customers have no idea how difficult it is to run the sort of business we are in, they will inevitably make stupid remarks and we will then have to explain the stupidity of them. Many managers and organizations are *afraid* to do it. As one senior manager confessed during a training session, 'To be honest I'd rather not know, I've got enough problems as it is'.

Also of course there is the question of who coordinates the whole process, who actually designs the system, collects the data and interprets the results. And when they have been interpreted, what happens next? In practice, very little usually. Because customer data is frequently aggregated it becomes so broad that specific responses are difficult to formulate. This is particularly true of information collected via questionnaires and postal surveys. Ideally customer information should be gathered primarily by first-line staff but all levels of management should increase their contact with customers. The key to success in this venture is that everyone from the top down recognizes that obtaining customer information, positive and negative, is the single most important activity any organization can undertake.

Organizations must be particularly aware that customer information can be threatening to many first-line staff and their management and that there is a natural tendency to look for good news and to suppress bad. This is understandable given the traditional management tendency to search for guilty parties whenever the stuff hits the fan. If staff understand, and most importantly *believe*, that management appreciates that their performance level is greatly influenced by the systems in which they have to operate they will be less likely to act from knee-jerk personal defence and be much more likely to engage in open constructive dialogue. We must develop the attitude within businesses that, as far as customer information goes, any news, 'good' or 'bad', is good news. To this end we must ensure that no individual or group is fearful of being punished for revealing negative customer information otherwise this vital information will be 're-engineered' or simply buried and, ultimately, so will the company.

John Akers, the deposed CEO of IBM, made an eerily prophetic statement on the disparity between the internal IBM view of the company's products and services and the one which he was repeatedly getting elsewhere when he said, 'I am sick and tired of visiting (IBM) plants to hear nothing but great things about quality and then to visit customers who tell me about problems'. The true voice of the customer must permeate the organization and when it does, it must be capable of being translated into positive action; in other words, it must create an impact. Unless customer satisfaction data impacts on staff in some manner it will inevitably be doomed to irrelevance. But impact alone is not enough; on whom in the organization the information impacts is also critically important. A systems approach would counsel us that the impact must be felt by those who have the organizational clout necessary to influence the systems and processes that produce the outputs about which customers are giving us their opinions, i.e. management. Some companies understand this point very well. Rank Xerox for example mails 10 000 customer satisfaction surveys every month and bonuses related to the results of these surveys account for 3.5 per cent of income for line staff but a massive 35 per cent for executives. The company also incorporates a 'bottom up' as well as the traditional 'top down' performance appraisal system. (This is further explained in Part 3.)

This is sound TQ logic. After all, in quality terms, line staff are the internal 'customers' of management and who better to inform an organization of the effectiveness of internal suppliers than their internal customers. Upward appraisal is one of the inevitable consequences of applying the TQ principle of supplier–customer networks logically and robustly throughout the organization. And it is a process that is catching on: W. H. Smith and The Body Shop also employ upward appraisal as a tool for continuous improvement. However, changes of this magnitude are not without their reverberations. Vern Zelmer, Rank Xerox's UK managing director, described upward appraisal as being a 'life-threatening experience for the old command-and-control managers'.

TQM heresy

Some words of caution! Orthodox texts on quality effectively counsel that 'the customer is king'. This, like all maxims, can be taken too far. A more useful maxim would be that 'the customer whose needs we are capable of satisfying is king'. This point is sometimes lost in the quasi-religious, customer-obsessed fervour that accompanies much of the literature and training in the field of quality. An effective quality development programme must consider the rights of *suppliers* as well as customers (this is particularly true with respect to 'internal' customers and suppliers). Some customers have wildly unrealistic requirements and many are somewhat less than considerate in registering their discontent when these requirements are, inevitably, not met. An effective quality development programme will recognize the fact that some customers have requirements that are simply beyond the capabilities of the processes available to deliver particular goods and services. It is vitally important that management recognizes this possibility and does not simply knee-jerk into the attitude that customer complaint automatically means delivery failure. We simply cannot please all of the people all of the time and to attempt to do so is to invite disaster. The ideal situation is that we arrange things so that we only attract those customers whose requirements are commensurate with the capabilities of our processes. This, of course, is easier said than done and in some circumstances it is practically impossible. However, it is well to remember that customers come in various hues and that some are better avoided if possible and that not all customer complaints should be treated as if they are tablets of stone.

Why quality is not going to go away

Quality is not going to go away for two principal reasons. The first is that it is simple common sense that any provider must satisfy its customers (we will assume henceforth that these are bona fide customers) in a cost-effective manner if it is to survive, and the second is that no provider will be free from competition in the future. If you don't do it, someone else will. Whatever the immediate effect, all organizations must get closer to their customers, both internal and external. Because many organizations have traditionally avoided such a process it can, at first, be both uncomfortable and threatening. There is no viable alternative, however.

The emergence of quality-conscious competitors such as the Japanese have changed the nature of the competitive context for good. Customers have now experienced the benefits of value-for-money goods and services that are tuned to their specific requirements and they are not going to go back to the old 'take it or leave it' days. This fact alone has forced many established providers out of the complacent stupor in which they have operated for many decades. And, ultimately, if they are able to adopt quality practices themselves, it will be in everyone's interests.

The situation is similar to that which occurs in political life. It is a maxim of democratic politics, for example, that the absence of an effective and credible opposition actually weakens government. Without the critical analysis and perceptive probing of a hostile and effective opposing party, decisions inevitably become sloppy and standards fall. This situation was clearly the case with the Thatcher government of the 1980s and its ineffective Labour opposition. Also, devoid of any external challenge, internal dissent becomes a mere nuisance to be ignored or dealt with through disparaging terms such as 'wet'.

A very similar situation existed in the British motorcycle industry until the early 1960s. Because of the absence of competition British manufacturers could afford to ignore the relatively few customers (myself included) who felt strongly enough to complain about shoddy workmanship and appalling design. Along with this, the absence of competitive products and services also tends to set customer expectations at unrealistically low levels which further reduces any pressure for improvement from providers. Those days, however, are gone for good and the pressures which destroyed the British motorcycle industry and have revolutionized the world of manufacturing are relentlessly and inevitably permeating service and public operations also.

Whatever an organization decides to call its operating principles, be it Quality, Value, Excellence or if indeed it calls them anything at all, a fundamental truth must be faced. Every organization must satisfy its customers' needs in a cost-effective manner if it is to survive in the future. This is the real bottom line.

Quality certification and quality awards

The reader will no doubt register that I have so far avoided any reference to quality certification or quality awards. There are a number of reasons for this. First, the only people who can confer a meaningful quality certificate on any organization are its customers. Second, the general rush for registration to BS 5750 in this country is, I believe, primarily the result of subtle coercion and pressure marketing rather than being driven by a genuine desire for enhanced customer satisfaction.

Quality certification

Personal research indicates that many organizations apply for registration simply because others in their sector have done so and they consequently feel it is necessary if only to avoid being outmarketed by the competition. Others register primarily in order to be one of the first in their field to get it. As one manager recently told me, 'As far as I am concerned BS 5750 is basically a photo-opportunity'. I do not, however, wish to deride the need for effective documentation of critical processes, this is essential, but I do believe that the BS 5750 bandwagon is driven by hype and fear rather than desire. Small businesses in particular are fearful that without BS 5750 they will be automatically excluded from the race in terms of bids for contracts from large companies and government departments. In such instances BS 5750 is simply a necessary ticket to get into the game.

The take up in Britain has been high in comparison with the continent where the equivalent standard ISO 9000 has fared less well. Approximately 25 000 British companies are registered through BS 5750 with about 400 new applications being processed every month. In contrast to the British Standards Institution who administer the 5750 award, its German equivalent the Deutsche Institut fur Normung, suggests that the continental take up has been meagre. France leads the way with a mere 480 ISO 9000 registered companies while Norway and Austria can manage only 34 between them.

Does this suggest that we in Britain are therefore more quality conscious? I very much doubt it. I feel that one important reason (in addition to those indicated above) stems from a basic lack of confidence in our own abilities and a psychological need to be 'stamped OK' by some external examining body. However, my experiences in management and teaching have led me firmly to the belief that examinations of all sorts (and BS 5750 accreditation is an examination par excellence) leads primarily to 'examination learning', i.e. get it then forget it. This was brought home very clearly to me recently when I asked a front-line assembly employee of a large electrical goods manufacturer what he knew about BS 5750 (which the company had achieved very early on). He knew very little other than the fact that BS 5750 inspections were preceded by a great deal of activity that did not occur, as he put it, 'when we're working normally'.

Some companies have also in some instances tended to give the impression that the possession of BS 5750 implies that their products and services are superior to those provided by organizations who do not possess the award. This is not the case. BS 5750 is a procedural management system. It says nothing about the quality of a company's products or services, it merely addresses their consistency. They may, of course, be consistently unacceptable. As a representative of the BSI's legal services department admitted, 'We spend half our life telling people that the statement 'products are BS 5750 certified' is meaningless'.[12] Official certification of quality standards can provide an organization with a valuable opportunity to examine their existing systems and clarify procedures and processes. The danger is that the process of certification becomes an end in itself rather than a means to an end and when it is over people may feel that quality has 'been done' and that products and services are therefore guaranteed to meet customer needs and expectations. This, of course, is not necessarily the case. Perhaps the last word on certified quality standards belongs with the condom-dispensing machines which sport the BSI kitemark and the statement 'Approved to British Standards', to which is commonly added the comment: 'So was the *Titanic!*'

Quality awards

As with quality certification, quality awards can have a double-edged effect. As well as inspiring people to strive for certified excellence they can deflect an organization from its primary objective of satisfying the needs of its real customers, i.e. the people who actually pay the wages, if, as can easily happen, they become ends in themselves. Apart from this, the effort, data collection and organization required to meet the standards of a prestigious award such as the Deming Prize, the Malcolm Baldridge National Quality Award or the award of the European Foundation for Quality Management can exert considerable strains and incur substantial costs. As was suggested at the beginning of this book, there is a very real danger that TQ initiatives can become something of an obsession if not managed effectively, i.e. kept within the bounds of sound business sense. A number of documented cases already exist. For example, James Broadhead, who became CEO of the much vaunted TQM paragon Florida Power and Light Company shortly after it won the Deming Prize, found it necessary to dismantle the 'quality bureaucracy' that had mushroomed into existence during the preparatory stages and called a halt to the extensive overuse of statistical charts and ineffective problem-solving techniques. It was also discovered that achievement of the award had cost an estimated $1 285 000, a cost that the Florida Utilities Commission would not allow the company to pass on to the customer.

Another startling example is that of Wallace Company, a US family-owned pipe and valve distribution business operating primarily in the chemical and petrochemical industries. Wallace Company was the first small organization (280 employees) to win the Baldridge Award in 1990. In late 1991 they filed for Chapter 11 bankruptcy protection. The consultant who was ultimately called in by the board of directors concluded that the effort required to achieve the award had diverted vital management attention away from critical areas of corporate strategy necessary for survival in the market-place.[13]

It seems clear from these and other examples that the most pressing danger involved in seeking to achieve prestigious quality awards is that they can divert attention from the basic business of business, that is, satisfying customer needs. Organizations can fall victim to an ego-driven desire to join the 'Quality Elite Club', to be 'In'. However, if customers find that they can obtain better service and value for their money through a competitor then possession of all the quality awards attainable will be of no avail. Ultimately, the only quality club worth getting into is the one run by your customers.

SUMMARY AND KEY POINTS

- Quality and Total Quality Management are simply terms describing sound business principles of customer orientation and cost effectiveness.
- Traditionally, organizations have been internally rather than externally focused and this has resulted in a tendency to be 'supplier led' rather than 'customer driven'.
- Some suppliers, notably the Japanese, have successfully implemented TQM techniques and dominate many manufacturing markets. These techniques are now permeating service and public sectors.
- People are the key to TQM. Traditional organizational barriers and class distinctions work against quality and they will need to be removed.
- Implementing TQM is not easy and it requires understanding and genuine commitment from the very top of the organization.
- Customers are a key concept in TQM. An organization's customer base may be complex and involve direct and indirect customers.
- Organizations cannot satisfy the needs of an over-diverse

customer base and therefore some form of stratification and focus is necessary.

- When judging quality, customers pay greater attention to certain elements of a service or product than they do to others. Organizations must be able to identify the key variables affecting customer perceptions of quality in their particular areas of operation.

- When organizations have identified the key factors influencing customer perceptions of quality they must establish standards of performance that meet these requirements.

- Key performance standards are determined by underlying key processes. All processes are subject to variation and therefore the outputs of these processes will also be subject to variation. Organizations must engineer their key processes in order that they are capable of delivering key performance standards within limits that are acceptable to customers.

- Variation in process outputs result from special or random causes. Special causes of variation can be identified and removed. When all special causes of variation have been eliminated the process is said to be stable and variation in outputs will be due to random or chance causes only.

- A stable process cannot be improved through tinkering. If an unacceptable percentage of outputs from a stable process do not meet customer requirements then fundamental changes must be made to the process itself.

- Stable processes generate predictable outputs that conform to a normal curve of distribution. Using this information it is possible to construct control charts that enable us to monitor processes and determine whether or not they are likely to remain stable. In this way processes can be adjusted or stopped before defective outputs are produced.

- Performance levels are determined largely by the underlying systems and processes in which individuals operate. Variations in performance levels therefore are best understood as being the result of underlying process differences.

- Performance improvement programmes are best thought of as process improvement programmes. Internal and external benchmarking can be a valuable tool for identifying the differences between fundamental aspects of the microsystems that lead to differences in levels of performance.

- Traditional western approaches to management and improvement have tended to take a revolutionary rather than evolutionary perspective. Eastern approaches, in contrast, focus on gradual systematic improvement. The ideal situation is an integration of both.
- There is no fixed method for introducing TQM into an organization. The principal determinants will be the current structure and culture of the organization, the strength of competition and the desire for improvement.
- Customer information is the key to quality improvement and long-term viability. Care must be exercised in structuring customer surveys and a number of common errors need to be avoided. The collection and use of customer information must be seen as being vital to the future of the organization. As such, customer information must impact on individuals who have the authority to influence internal systems and processes.
- The achievement of quality certification and quality awards can be useful in focusing the organization's attention on systems and procedures. However, there is a danger that awarding bodies may become the 'preferred customers' of the organization, with potentially damaging results.

Concluding remarks

In this section I have attempted to clarify the central philosophy and fundamental principles of TQM and to highlight some of the implementation difficulties that must be faced. I hope that the reader will concur with the view that the philosophy of TQM is based on simple common sense. The basic assertion of TQM is that organizational success (in the public and private sectors) can only be achieved through the cost effective delivery of goods and services that meet, or indeed exceed, customer expectations. In order to achieve this, TQM principles counsel that we must know our customer's requirements in detail, engineer our processes in such a way as to guarantee consistency of acceptable output, minimize unnecessary cost and continually refine and improve all that we do.

The fundamental principles of TQM are therefore shown to be logical, rational and desirable. Given these points, the question we must ask ourselves is: why is TQM so incredibly difficult to implement? The remainder of this book seeks to provide some answers.

Part II

The enemy within

'We have met the enemy, and he is us.'

Walt Kelly.

'Systems die; instincts remain.'

Oliver Wendell Holmes Jr.

The first part of this book concluded with the question: why is TQM so difficult to implement? As there is no readily apparent flaw in the basic philosophy, and given that achieving operational success is desirable, it follows that the application of TQM principles is an eminently rational course of action. Despite the seeming infallibility of this conclusion, however, organizations consistently fail in their attempts to make TQM an operational reality (official estimates put the failure rate of quality programmes as being in the region of 80 per cent). Why?

My own experience of working within organizations, of attempting to help teams implement some form of quality development programme and of running seminars and training courses on quality related topics has convinced me that the problem is a human one, i.e. the difficulty lies within ourselves.

If we are to truly understand the challenges we face in implementing TQM within organizations then we must examine some fundamental aspects of human thought processes and social behaviour. Having made this suggestion, however, I fully appreciate that it is likely to be greeted with something less than explosive enthusiasm by many managers. This is the fault of the topic, and some of its enthusiasts, and not the managers. A great deal of damage has been done to the credibility of psychology in business through exaggerated claims about the efficacy of certain theories and approaches. The disparaging term 'crapology' has been warranted in some instances, particularly with respect to the completely idiotic acts that have too frequently been perpetrated in the name of 'management development'. Also, the often disappointing results that followed many early attempts at implementing the ideas of the so-called 'Humanistic Movement' have left many managers extremely disillusioned. All in all the application of psychological theories to business has had a pretty bad press.

There are a varied number of reasons why this has occurred but a good deal of the responsibility can be laid at the door of consultants and trainers. Many management consultants and management trainers appear to have simply jumped on a particular psychological bandwagon without fully understanding the strengths and limitations of the theories they have too often peddled as facts.

Human thought processes and human interactions are extremely complex. Psychological studies can offer us insights into the silent machinations that underpin our thoughts, feelings and actions but these insights cannot be considered as immutable truths. They are ultimately generalizations because the greater part of psychological knowledge (particularly the really interesting bits) is fundamentally probabilistic.

A few practical examples will help to clarify the point. It is reasonably well established that some personality types are more prone to high blood pressure and coronary disease than others. These personality types, known as Type A, are characteristically time-conscious, excessively competitive, preoccupied by deadlines, prone to do several things at once, are insecure about status and need the admiration of others in order to feel worth while. Many studies have indicated a link between the possession of such traits and a propensity towards coronary diseases. But it does not follow that every person displaying these personality characteristics will in fact succumb to some form of coronary heart disease; it is simply more probable that they will. Similarly with psychometric testing, it is by no means an infallible method of selecting candidates for particular jobs, but it is better than most.

Psychological knowledge is therefore not infallible, but in business not much is, however, it is usable. Problems commonly arise when psychological theories are peddled as facts and it is implied for example that every individual will respond to 'theory Y' management (à la McGregor), that everyone is striving to become 'self-actualizing' (à la Maslow) or that everyone considers money to be a 'hygiene' factor rather than a 'motivator' (à la Herzberg) and so on. This may be true in very many instances, but there will inevitably be exceptions.

That being the case, however, we are still left with the basic fact that the success of TQM depends on people more than anything else. As very many organizations have found to their cost, the hype, rhetoric and mechanical application of quality tools and techniques does not matter one iota if a *genuine commitment* to implement the changes that are necessary for TQM to work is missing, and that commitment can only come from people. We must understand the critical reasons why TQM initiatives fail with such monotonous regularity, and there is one fact we can rely on, it is not the techniques and procedures. I have never met an individual who said that TQM failed in their company because someone discovered that Pareto Analysis does not really work or that Statistical Process Control was fundamentally flawed. The techniques and procedures work. In fact, as far as the successful implementation of TQM is concerned, they are practically irrelevant. TQM does not fail or succeed because of techniques. TQM fails or succeeds because of people.

The comments frequently made about failed TQM initiatives are indicative and they occur repeatedly, for example, 'After a while things just fizzled out'. 'We had to postpone it (TQM) to deal with an emergency and we never really got it going again'. 'Manager A was never really behind it'. 'It caused more arguments than it was worth'. 'The people who were really enthusiastic just gave up trying in the end'. These are 'people reasons'. Similarly with the successes, the beneficial effects of successfully implementing TQM are predominantly seen as being changes in the way people work together. Managers are seen as more approachable; there is less of a 'them and us' situation and more of a team spirit; people feel they are more respected; there is a different atmosphere; there is more open communication, and so on.

The critical factors influencing the outcome of TQM initiatives revolve around the ways in which people think and act, both individually and collectively. It is necessary therefore that we are aware of what is known about such things as individual and collective decision-making processes and the ways in which organizational structures influence attitudes and behaviour. It is to these topics that I will now turn.

7

Individual irrationality

Barely 36 hours after his inauguration as President of the United States, Bill Clinton found himself in the middle of a serious political storm. What was the reason for his difficulties? Zoe Baird, his nominee for the prestigious and powerful post of attorney-general, the chief law enforcement officer in the US, had admitted to employing a Peruvian couple, both illegal aliens, as live-in servants for the best part of 2 years. Worse still she admitted that she had also neglected to pay the required Social Security contributions for the period in question. She was immediately de-selected as prospective attorney-general.

In a similar vein, some months earlier and 3000 miles to the east, David Mellor, a British politician was obliged to resign his ministerial post as a direct consequence of press revelations, recounted in great and embarrassing detail, that he had conducted an improper liaison with an unemployed 'actress'. The seeming ease with which the British press obtained embarrassingly detailed evidence of the liaison would indicate that its perpetrator was somewhat less than cognitively gifted. Nothing in fact could be further from the truth. Like his American counterpart, Mr Mellor is a highly intelligent, well-educated and ambitious politician. We must therefore ask the question: why on earth did they do it?

If we ignore the somewhat banal reasons, we are left with an intriguing problem: why should two successful, highly ambitious and intelligent individuals behave with such monumental stupidity? In attempting to understand such acts as these (and the reader is no doubt aware that there are literally thousands of other well-documented instances of equal and greater stupidity recorded) we must appreciate two important aspects of human behaviour that have far reaching implications for all our endeavours:

1. People frequently act in ways that directly threaten their freely-chosen long-term aims.
2. The more threatening an activity, the greater the tendency to ignore or underestimate its possible consequences.

The combination of these tendencies presents us with a considerable problem, and is not limited to the effective running of organizations; it extends to the long-term survival of the human species itself. The first was originally described by Freud; he called it Thanatos or the 'death instinct', people's desire to engage in self-destructive behaviours. Whether this is in fact the case is actually neither here nor there, the reality is that people repeatedly engage in extremely risky activities.

The second tendency can be described as wishful thinking and it is extremely common. The most dangerous manifestation of this type of thought is the irrational belief that nothing really bad will happen irrespective of the actions we take. it is the 'I am a charmed individual, nothing bad will happen to me' technique of problem resolution (which essentially amounts to problem denial), i.e. not thinking clearly about the possible consequences of our actions or indeed not thinking about them at all. Clearly Ms Baird and Mr Mellor succumbed to both with disastrous results. I use these examples purely to underscore the fact that *we do not always act in ways that are likely to help us achieve our aims and aspirations.*

I offer a final example. Very few people wish to contract painful fatal diseases yet many people continue to smoke cigarettes when the risks involved are well documented. They deal with these considerable risks largely through the employment of strategy 2 above, or by refusing to be influenced by threatening information. Indeed one smoker is reputed to have commented that reports of research into the damaging effects of smoking had frightened him to such an extent that he had stopped reading the newspapers!

Irrationality in action

In an excellent and extremely readable account, Stuart Sutherland, Professor of Experimental Psychology at the University of Sussex, has surveyed a broad spectrum of human irrationality. His book, '*Irrationality—The Enemy Within*', should be required reading for all managers and decision makers. In the sections that follow I will refer to some of the more common manifestations of irrationality described by Professor Sutherland. If forewarned means forearmed then some understanding of the causes of irrational behaviour can help us avoid acting irrationally in future. However, there is more to the problem than this. The avoidance of irrational behaviours on one's own account is only a single factor in the TQM success equation; the potential irrationality of others must also be considered.

If TQM is to become an operational reality within organizations then it is a fundamental requirement that people are genuinely prepared to cooperate with each other in the interests of long-term security for all. Such beneficial cooperation is, of course, rational, but it requires that a high level of trust is established between people and that there is a genuine commitment to put the long-term interests of the whole organization above those of a particular group or individual. This is easier said than done. The rhetoric of shared responsibility and a common desire for long-term security is severely tested every time a group or an individual is required to *voluntarily* disregard an opportunity for short-term gain in the interests of long-term security for all. Voluntary cooperation is in fact a complex psychological problem and it bears scrutiny if we are to avoid many of the common difficulties that TQM initiatives must overcome. The following exercise hopefully illustrates the point.

The manager's dilemma

Imagine the following situation. Two intelligent and highly ambitious middle managers who work for Justin Thyme Manufacturing Inc. are summoned to the company president's office. The president, something of an amateur psychologist, presents them with the following scenario.

A very senior quality management appointment is to be made in the near future. The post is seen to be of critical importance to the continuing success of the company and the president has three candidates in mind. They are the two middle managers concerned and someone from outside of the company. The president tells both managers that he is convinced the post requires a person who combines a strong sense of self-belief with decisiveness and an ability to foster genuine cooperation between company departments. He then informs them that he has devised a unique selection procedure which he will use to identify the right person for the job. Each manager is then taken to a separate room and told that one of the following options must be chosen:

Option 1. To nominate herself (or himself) for the job.
Option 2. To nominate the other manager for the job.

However, being diabolically clever and desiring some light relief, the president (who knows that both managers hate each other but hate the thought of an external candidate getting the job even more) adds the following consequence to the decisions to be made:

1. If each manager nominates herself (or himself), the job will automatically go to the external candidate.
2. If one manager nominates herself and the other nominates her also, the president will give her the job.
3. If they nominate each other there will be a further set of selection procedures but the external candidate will be eliminated.

Clearly the best strategy would be for the managers to collaborate and nominate each other. This would give each a further shot at the job and also eliminate the external candidate. But neither can be absolutely sure of what the other will in fact do. To nominate the other manager is dangerous since if she nominates herself, the president will give her the job.

This problem is a variation of the 'The Prisoner's Dilemma' which has been much used and much discussed by psychologists and philosophers alike. It is designed to test whether or not individuals are prepared to act collaboratively in uncertain situations. The dilemma facing each manager is whether or not to trust the other to 'do the decent thing'. To put the problem in general terms, there are three possible outcomes:

1. If both act in their own interests and nominate themselves then the outcome will be *lose-lose.*
2. If one acts in his or her own interests and the other acts collaboratively then the outcome will be *win-lose* (with the selfish individual winning).
3. If both act collaboratively then the outcome will be *win-win* (both remain in contention for the job).

Although this situation is hypothetical, the basic problem is far from being so. Let us consider a number of real-life examples.

At present we discharge vast quantities of noxious gases, a major cause of the greenhouse effect, into the upper atmosphere. If we continue with these levels of emission it is highly probable that our actions will jeopardize the future of the planet. Reducing noxious gas emission is expensive, but if no one does anything about it then in the long term everyone will lose, including countries that have contributed virtually nothing whatsoever to the problem *lose–lose*. If all the industrialized countries (the major culprits) do reduce emissions significantly then everyone on the planet will ultimately benefit *win–win*. However, if a few selfish countries do not act to reduce emissions while the majority do, these countries will obtain short-term rewards. First they will not incur the expense involved in reducing their own emission rates, and second, they will obtain the vicarious benefits of an overall reduction in the greenhouse effect which results from the unselfish actions of those countries that do reduce emissions *win–lose*.

A similar situation exists in relation to the production of nuclear weapons, in meeting water purity requirements, in providing adequate environmental and economic protection for workers and in the provision of training and development opportunities in organizations. In each case there is the opportunity to gain short-term benefits by failing to invest for the future. If other countries act to reduce the production of nuclear weapons, thus making the world a safer place, there is a short-term opportunity to make your own country more powerful by not doing so. If you refuse to abide by agreed international water purity standards, as the UK has, then you have the opportunity to make bigger profits now and possibly benefit from the future development of purification plant technology in other countries. If you refuse to accept international proposals regarding the social and economic rights of workers, as the UK government has, then in the short-term you benefit from lower wage costs, higher profit margins and greater flexibility in dismissing staff than your competitors. If you do not train and develop staff within your company then you benefit in the short term from lower fixed costs, higher profit margins and, as long as somebody does it, a pool of trained labour to be poached as the need arises.

It is clear, however, that these benefits are indeed short term. Not playing your part in reducing noxious gas levels merely postpones the inevitable, and international disapproval may ultimately cost you more than the outlay you have saved. Similarly, other countries will not simply stand by while you increase your cache of nuclear weapons; indeed you may find that in the long term international sanctions weaken your economy to such an extent that it collapses or internal unrest forces a change of government.

Refusing to meet agreed recommendations on water purity brands you as a backward, unsafe society, which will influence future international investment decisions and also affect industries such as tourism. Failure to comply with agreed employment rights creates an unmotivated, uncommitted workforce and in the long term you lose more than you gain. Failure to invest in training and development means failure to create a learning culture within the organization; in the end you also lose.

Such problems of cooperation permeate everyday organizational life and they are of vital importance with respect to TQM. If management decides to trust the 'workers' what guarantee is there that they will not take advantage of that trust for their own ends? And if the 'workers' decide to trust the management, how can they be sure they will not be exploited? If, as a manager, I commit myself to open communication and admit I have departmental problems, what guarantee is there that my colleagues will not conceal theirs and score some points? If, as a middle manager, I embrace the principles of TQM, what guarantee is there that I will still have a job in 2 years? These are the questions that people seldom ask openly, but they are major concerns. In reality there are no cast-iron guarantees that managers or workers will not abuse trust or that open communication will prevail or indeed that jobs, in their current form, will survive a TQM drive. But all of life is without cast-iron guarantees. If TQM is to work then people must be encouraged to take the risk of cooperating in the interests of security for all.

Of course if everyone acted responsibly the world would be a safer place for everyone, the water would be fit to drink everywhere, everyone's fixed costs would be comparable and therefore competitiveness would be based on quality, people would not be subjected to unsafe working environments or morally indefensible employment practices and society would derive enormous economic and social benefits from the skills of a well-trained and highly motivated workforce. This being the case we must ask ourselves why it does not happen. The basic answer probably has its roots in our evolutionary history.

The whisperings within

Of all the major survival strategies employed by our distant ancestors, speed of action was probably one of the most effective. Speed of action commonly decided the outcome of early man's two principal survival issues, dinner and death. Act too slowly in one particular situation and you didn't get to eat, act too slowly in another and you got eaten. In order to stay alive our early ancestors could not afford to spend a great deal of time deliberating on potential courses of action and they were not, perhaps literally, predisposed to look a gift horse in the mouth. Rapid, decisive action was the key to survival and much of that action did not require conscious thought; it was simply instinctive, i.e. sidestepping today's threats and pouncing on today's opportunities. As far as they were concerned, if indeed they were capable of being concerned at all, tomorrow would have to take care of itself. And that philosophy worked fine—50 000 years ago.

However, many of these ancient survival instincts are potentially lethal in a world that is fundamentally different. We cannot simply act according to primitive internal programmes and expect productive consequences every time. Our ancestors benefited from these actions because they had very little control over their future, which was commonly brief, largely random and highly dangerous. Their immediate actions were unlikely to affect this future in any dramatic way. Our future, by contrast, is considerably longer, more predictable and much more likely to confront us with the consequences of our previous actions. Despite these changed circumstances, however, primitive survival responses do remain with us to this day. To demonstrate this fact simply creep up behind another human being, burst a paper bag and watch the reaction. Such a reaction is completely adaptive in a world populated with hungry predators, it is somewhat less appropriate in an office.

To return to the situation described earlier. It may be the case that Ms Baird and Mr Mellor fell victim to the ancient human tendency to act in response to immediate opportunities without considering the long-term possibilities of such actions. I am absolutely sure that given the chance to take the decisions again each would act completely differently.

Short term, long term

It seems clear therefore that it would be in our interests to resist the innate tendency to act impulsively when such action is likely to harm our long-term aims. Again this is easier said than done. But in order to dissuade the reader from feeling that such control requires managers whose personal attributes would constitute God's job description, it will be useful to consider the following, very different, case histories.

The rise and fall of People Express

People Express was the first airline to be established as a result of deregulation in the US airline market. In the 5 years following its establishment in 1980 People Express grew to occupy fifth place in the league of US carriers. Its growth in this period was phenomenal, from 3 airplanes to 117 and from a turnover of less than $38 million to nearly $1 billion. Yet in 1986 it made a loss of $300 million and was taken over by Texas Air Corporation. Ironically, People Express was a victim of customer satisfaction.

The initial success was founded on a number of radical approaches to business involving structuring, pricing and employee involvement. There were only four levels of management in the company. There was universal stock ownership for employees, a highly innovative approach to personnel development that involved extensive cross-training and job rotation, a clearly focused client group (budget travellers), extremely friendly and well-motivated flight personnel, innovative pricing (baggage handling and meals were extra) and low overheads (on some routes flying with People Express was cheaper than going by bus).

As a result of this total approach People Express boomed, demand escalated and the company expanded rapidly in order to keep up with its ever-increasing share of the market. But in doing so it laid the seeds of its own destruction. As it expanded to meet demand there was little time for training and developing personnel; recruitment became a difficulty and the numbers of part-time employees increased; a broader range of customers, attracted by some features, were dissatisfied with others; pressure of volume meant that service standards slipped; other companies began to compete on price; customer dissatisfaction grew; People Express's stock price fell which further demotivated staff and pushed falling service standards even lower. This downward spiral led to the company being dubbed 'People Distress'; customers deserted en masse and the company went under in 1986.

In hindsight (always an easy way to manage a company) a number of lessons are clear. Expansion in carrying capacity was not accompanied by a commensurate investment in maintaining critical quality standards. Simply knee-jerking into an expansionist reaction to customer demand ignored the fact that the nature of the customer base was also likely to change. Innovative approaches to human resource development became counterproductive as the emphasis shifted towards a volume-based strategy, and so on.

It is clear that People Express's tendency to spontaneously 'say yes' to a continuously expanding number of customers was its undoing. It is, however, an understandable tendency; it takes a very brave person to turn away a paying customer, and in this case it involved thousands of them! It is understandable but it still led to the demise of the company. Ultimately it is far better to satisfy the vast majority of your 2000 customers per week than it is to satisfy only 60 per cent of 4000. Still, you may say (and you would be right), turning them away is a very difficult decision in the real world of business. It is difficult, but not impossible. A number of personal, but most importantly structural, factors are involved. We will consider the structural factors a little later on; first let us examine some of the personal ones.

The rise of the Sony Corporation

In 1955, Akio Morita, chairman and co-founder of Sony, was in New York doing the rounds of prospective retailers for his fledgling company's prototype transistor radio. At Bulova, a famous retailer and producer of electrical goods, he was presented with a considerable opportunity.

Following trials, the man in charge of Bulova's purchasing division informed him that they liked the radio very much and wished to make a purchase of 100 000 units. The value of this order represented several times the then capital value of Sony Corporation. Morita turned it down. He turned it down because the purchaser had stipulated one unacceptable condition: that the name Bulova, not Sony, was to appear on the radios. In Morita's view the establishment of the Sony brand name, then totally unknown outside of Japan, was critical to the long-term future of the company. Taking the deal would bring considerable short-term benefits but threaten the long-term aim. In explaining his reasons to the incredulous purchaser he said that he could not accept the condition because '... I am now taking the first step for the next 50 years of my company'.[14] Mr Morita continues to consider this decision as being the best he has ever made.

Not long after this incident a large US retailer with a chain of approximately 150 stores asked Morita to quote prices on quantities of 5000, 10 000, 30 000, 50 000 and 100 000 radios. The quote he received astounded him. The price for 5000 radios would be Sony's regular price and for 10 000 there would be a discount: so far so good. However, at 30 000 radios the unit price actually increased. It increased again for 50 000 and the unit cost quoted for a purchase of 100 000 radios was much higher than Sony's regular price! Baffled, the retailer asked what the logic was. Mr Morita explained that his company was geared to the production of under 10 000 radios per month. To increase this would mean larger premises, more equipment and, most importantly, more people. He felt that the bigger the order, the greater was the risk to his company and to the long-term security of its employees, particularly if it proved to be a one-off. The increased costs therefore reflected these factors. Again thinking in the long term he reasoned that it was better to grow steadily than to leap on one big opportunity only to find later that you are grossly overcapable and cannot sustain your capital costs. The purchaser also saw the logic, and ordered 10 000 radios.[15] It is clear from this account that Mr Morita acted rationally when one considers his overall aims, i.e. the long-term future of Sony and a commitment to employee security. It is also clear from these cases that each company was managed from completely different perspectives. Managers at People Express reacted to short-term demand by expanding at a rate which precluded the maintenance of service quality standards that had established their success in the first place. Akio Morita acted in accordance with a long-term vision of what he wanted his company to become.

The mismanagement of risk

Given the basic information in each of the above case studies (and not knowing the companies involved or the outcomes) managers have a strong tendency to consider that refusing the large order (as happened with Sony) is more risky than expanding facilities to meet growing demand (as happened in the case of People Express). The reasons for this difference in perception are fairly obvious. In the case of Sony, management is actually turning business away whereas the approach taken by the management at People Express is essentially 'the answer is yes, we'll sort the details out later'. These are totally different management responses to situations that have a great deal in common, which indicates that they stem from radically different management philosophies. A number of extremely important questions are raised by the differences between each response and an analysis of the underlying factors which contributed to each decision will be useful. I believe that these factors are primarily psychological in nature and are related to the ways in which people manage risk. Risk management is a critical factor influencing business success and the more we understand about the psychological processes involved the better equipped we will be to use them to our advantage. Again a few practical exercises will illustrate the points most effectively. Consider the following hypothetical situation.

A wealthy and somewhat eccentric philosopher who enjoys engaging people in problems of logic and risk presents you with the following challenge. She asks you to choose between the two options described below:

Option 1. You can accept £100 with certainty.
Option 2. You can have the chance of winning £200, or winning nothing, on calling the correct outcome of the flip of a fair coin.

Which of these options would you choose?
Now consider the next proposition:

Option 1. You can accept a certain loss of £100
Option 2. You can have the chance of losing £200, or losing nothing, on calling the correct outcome of the flip of a fair coin.

Which choice would you make in this situation?

Research shows that the majority of people choose the first option in the first situation and the second option in the second situation. In other words they are more willing to take a risk in the second situation than in the first. Why is this? In the first situation we are certain of receiving £100 with option 1 but we have a 50:50 chance of ending up with nothing if we go for option 2, so most people take the certain £100. In the second situation we will lose £100 for certain if we accept option 1 but there is a 50:50 chance that we will lose nothing if we take a risk on option 2 and most people go for that risk. It seems clear from these and other studies that *people are more prone to take risks in order to save losses than to make gains.*

This tendency can be seen quite clearly if we look at the outcome of the exercise described below.

Imagine that a group of terrorists is holding 600 men, women and children hostage in a large hotel. They have threatened to kill them all and time is running short. You are in charge of the rescue operation and after careful study and expert advice you are faced with a choice from one of the two following options whose outcomes are known:

Scenario 1
Plan A. It is certain that 200 lives will be saved.
Plan B. There is a 33 per cent chance that 600 lives will be saved.

Which option would you choose?

Now consider the following scenario:
Scenario 2
Plan A. It is certain that 400 will die.
Plan B. There is a 66 per cent chance that 600 will die.

Which option would you choose?

It is clear when one has access to both scenarios that the situations involved are identical, the options are simply expressed differently in each case. Despite this fact experimental evidence shows that the majority of subjects choose option A if they are presented with Scenario 1 and choose option B if they are presented with Scenario 2. Remember that these options involve exactly the same probabilities in each case. The fluctuation in choice has been caused by *the manner in which the problem is presented.*

When we consider the point above, that we are more likely to take risks to avoid a possible loss than to make a possible gain, the change of decision becomes clearer. In scenario 1, where the problem is defined in terms of certain and possible gains, the less risky option is preferred. In scenario 2, where the problem is defined in terms of certain and possible losses, the riskier option is preferred, In scenario 1 it may be the case that we are less prepared to take a risk because we are guaranteed 200 lives saved, and after all 'a bird in the hand ...'. Whereas in scenario 2 we are faced with a certain loss of 400 lives but a 33 per cent chance of saving everyone. It is not known with any certainty why people tend to behave in this way. It may be purely emotional in that scenario 1 uses positive terms such as lives saved for certain while scenario 2 talks of numbers dead for certain. It may be that when the situation is described negatively (in terms of certain deaths) we feel that action could result in saving some of the 400 who would automatically die if we choose option A. Or, as Stuart Sutherland speculates, it may be that as described in scenario 2, a possible 600 deaths does not seem that much more than a certain 400 given that there is a 33 per cent chance of saving everyone, and the risk therefore seems warranted.

One of the important findings of studies such as these is the realization that people's readiness to take risks can be influenced by the way a situation is presented. Professor Sutherland points out that this is irrational and, of course, he is correct. It is irrational, but we may be able to use such irrational tendencies for the benefit of organizations, a topic that will be addressed later.

Returning to the study of People Express and Sony, it is clear from the information available that, due to customer pressure, each organization was faced with an important strategic decision. For People Express this meant a decision about the pace of expansion. In the case of Sony it was a decision about the philosophy of brand-name exposure. It is important to recognize that each company stood to lose revenue if it did not adapt to these pressures. The point to consider, however, is whether or not each company *perceived* their possible courses of action in identical ways. Broadly speaking there are two ways of viewing the situation, from a short-term perspective or from a long term perspective.

An organization that is focused primarily on the short term would be highly likely to perceive the situation primarily in terms of the *immediate losses* that would result from a failure to capitalize on existing opportunities. However, an organization that is focused primarily on the long term would be highly likely to consider the impact that any short term decision would have on long term aims. Such an organization may therefore perceive this type of situation as one in which the long term gains achieved by taking difficult but appropriate decisions now would far exceed the short term losses incurred.

We may speculate therefore that managers at People Express opted for rapid expansion in order to avoid the immediate perceived losses that would be incurred if they turned customers away. We may also speculate that the management at Sony opted to turn customers away in order to secure longer-term gains. The important point to note is that both courses of action involved risks. As was mentioned earlier, however, when presented with the bare facts of each case the majority of managers view the Sony decision as being far riskier than that taken by the managers at People Express. However, as we will see below, the reality may be quite different.

Why is it that so many managers see the decisions in this way? The central reason is probably related to the fact that in the case of People Express the decision to expand meant that immediately available revenue would not be lost. In the case of Sony, however, the decision to turn custom away meant, in effect, that the company would immediately lose revenue that was in its power to accrue. These losses were accepted against the possibility of greater but essentially unquantifiable gains sometime in the future. What influences most managers is the fact that the immediate revenue is real and the future revenue is uncertain. Consequently, the decision to turn the certain revenue away appears to be the riskier option by far. However, this is only the case if one takes a purely short term view. Let us look at the situation in greater depth. Psychological research of the type described above suggests that when people act in order to avoid losses (as may have been the case with People Express) *they are likely to take more risks* than they do when they act in order to secure possible gains (as may have been the case with Sony).

Although I do not have access to the precise details concerning the decisions taken at People Express the subsequent result of those decisions, i.e. bankruptcy, indicate that they involved considerable risks indeed. It may be that those risks were not adequately considered at the time or that the strategy for expansion was ill-conceived. In contrast to this situation, however, we have seen that psychological research indicates that people are *less likely to engage in risky behaviour in order to secure possible gains*. It may therefore be the case that the decisions taken by Akio Morita, in the pursuit of long term gains, were subsequently more rational.

Naturally this is pure speculation in terms of what actually happened in each case. However, the evidence concerning the demise of People Express strongly indicates that it fell victim to an understandable temptation to capitalize on short term opportunities. In doing so, the basic infrastructure which brought initial success was fatally undermined. It seems clear that the long term risks involved in expanding so rapidly were not adequately considered.

The research outlined above has considerable implications for the management of organizations. First, it suggests that companies that operate from a short term perspective will be likely to perceive expenditure that does not guarantee a return, and any missed opportunity to accrue short term revenue, as losses. And they will consequently take action to avoid such perceived losses. We have also seen that action of this type is biased toward risk. In contrast, companies who operate from a long term perspective are more likely to view certain expenditure as *investment* if it accords with long term aims and they are less likely to take serious risks in order to make short term gains.

The difference in perspective can be seen clearly when comparing international attitudes to financial investment. It is a serious failing of both the British and American financial systems that there is little appetite to invest for the long term, a critical factor in Japan's continuing success. This excessive financial short termism has resulted over the past few years in British companies which are barely profitable being obliged to pay continuously large dividends in order that they remain within the grace and favour of the City. This money has to come from somewhere and it is primarily sourced from deferred investment and vicious cost-cutting. However, it can be argued that the recessionary cycle of an economy is precisely the time when organizations need to invest in effective restructuring and preparation for upturn. If financial investors will not commit for the long term then managers will continue to act in ways that jeopardize the continuing future of organizations. Contrast this situation with the recent dramatic changes of fortune of two 'British' companies,

Rover and ICL. Both Rover and ICL have benefited enormously from Japanese investment. ICL, which is 80 per cent owned by Fujitsu, has shown remarkable progress during a period of savage price cutting within the industry while Rover, which has a 20 per cent cross shareholding with Honda, has made tremendous improvements to the way it designs and manufactures motor cars. Both, however, have gained most from the nature of the commitment involved which is primarily non-directive and most importantly long term, and neither company is pressurized to show large profits in the short term. Unless a similar change of attitude occurs among British and US investors then programmes such as TQM which are by their very nature essentially long term, have little real chance of succeeding.

8

Deep thought

A company's future is primarily dependent on the strategy it decides to adopt. Strategy is part science and part intuition. No strategy is certain to succeed but some have a much higher probability than others. There are three stages involved in the development and implementation of a strategy they are:

1. Strategic decision-making
2. Formulating a plan of action
3. Making the plan a reality

It is clear that the first stage in this process, decision-making, is vital. If we go wrong here then everything that follows is inevitably doomed to failure. Decisions are taken by people and we have already seen that there is a common human tendency to act impulsively and to think irrationally. This does not auger well for the quality of human decisions. Much of our difficulty, however, can be overcome with effort; we must learn to think more effectively in order to make better decisions. This can be achieved through understanding the avoidable causes of irrationality, by improving our ability to estimate probability and by ensuring that we invest (that word again) an adequate amount of mental energy on the important decisions we have to make. In a nutshell we need to think more deeply.

In this section I will describe a number of situations that require the reader to consider some concepts in statistics and probability. I hope that this is not an overly daunting prospect although I am sure that it will not be a welcoming one; and this is a symptom of a major problem, i.e. the general aversion to thinking mathematically. One of the greatest strengths of TQM lies in the fact that it is based on data and techniques of data analysis. This commonly involves gathering and using accurate customer information, analysing this information in order to discover trends and critical factors and using techniques such as Pareto analysis, quality function deployment, failure mode and effect analysis, scatter diagrams, Ishikawa diagrams, SPC and so on to solve problems and make more effective decisions. There is no way around the barrier of effective data collection and analysis: without accurate information we are guessing and, as we will see, we are not very good at guessing. There is a clear and urgent need for many managers and decision makers to improve the level of their general numeracy skills. I certainly do not mean by this statement that there should be more 'bean-counters', far from it. Rather we need to develop a greater 'feel' for numbers and probabilities in order that we are able to make better judgements, for it is quality of judgement that commonly differentiates the effective manager from the less effective. In the exercises that follow I have attempted to make the content interesting but also to bring out the underlying lessons to be learned in each case. We will begin by considering a question of probability. Read the description of 'John' given below and then rank-order the statements which follow in terms of the probability that they are true.

John is 33 years old, physically fit and very bright. At university he majored in business administration and marketing, was outgoing, very popular and represented his college in rugby, cricket and athletics.
    Considering the (completely accurate) description given above, rank the following statements in order of probability:

(a) John is a college lecturer.
(b) John is a member of his village rugby club.
(c) John is a bank clerk.
(d) John is a manager in a large multinational company.
(e) John is an insurance salesman.
(f) John is a bank clerk and is active in coaching youth sports.
(g) John is a psychiatric social worker.
(h) John manages his own business importing sportswear.

The majority of people who attempt this exercise rank the probability of John being a bank clerk, option c, pretty low, this of course can be expected given the general description above. The interesting fact, however, is that people commonly place option f, that John is a bank clerk who also coaches youth sports, *above* option c. In other words they feel that it is more probable that John is a bank clerk who coaches children than that he is simply a bank clerk. However, a moment's reflection will show that this cannot possibly be the case.

As we do not know for certain whether any of these statements are true, each must have a probability of less than 1 (in probability theory anything that is absolutely certain is given a probability of 1 and anything that is absolutely impossible is given a probability of 0). Therefore if the probability that John is a bank clerk is taken to be 0.2 (fairly unlikely but not impossible) and the probability that he coaches children is taken to be 0.7 (quite likely but far from certain), then the probability that he does both of these things has to be less than the probability that he does only one of them (two uncertainties are always greater than one). If we use the arbitrary figures given above, the probability that John is a bank clerk is assumed to be 0.2 and the probability that he coaches children is assumed to be 0.7. Therefore, using the rule that the probability that two chance events will happen is equal to the product of multiplying each probability together, we find that the probability that John is a bank clerk who also coaches children would be 0.2 x 0.7 which is only 0.14, considerably less likely than either probability alone. Therefore it must be more probable, whatever the actual figures are, that John is a bank clerk than it is that he is a bank clerk who also coaches youth sports.

Consider another example: 23 individuals are selected at random and placed together in a room, what is the probability that two of them will share the same birthdate? You may have been sufficiently alerted by the previous example to be cautious in your response and you would be correct. The majority of people consider that the probability would be very low when in actual fact it is an even bet: there is a 50 per cent chance that in a group of 23 individuals two will share a birthdate. Most people base their immediate judgement on the fact that as there are 365 possible birthdates it would require a group size of about half that number, i.e. 183, to give a 50 per cent probability of two people sharing the same one. However, as we will see below, this is an error also. Consider a different question, if you were to walk into a room containing 22 other people, what would be the probability that someone there would share your birthdate? The answer, perhaps surprisingly, given the information above, is that it is less than one in ten. This is because of the fact that in the first situation described above the stipulation is that any two people in a group of 23 share a birthdate in common. In the second we are asking that two people have a particular birthdate (i.e. yours) in common. In fact you would require a group size of 253 in order to have a 50 per cent chance of finding that someone in the group shared your birthday, which is precisely the number of combined birthdates possible in a room containing 23 people (there are 23 x 22/2 possible combinations).

Or consider this final example: What would you estimate as being the probability that you will have same-sex descendants for the next 100 generations? In other words what are the chances, if you are a woman, that you will have at least one daughter, who will have at least one daughter, who will have at least one daughter and so on for the next 100 generations? Pretty slim? Well just reflect on the fact that 100 generations ago there existed a woman, your female ancestor, who was destined to have one hundred generations of female descendants, which has culminated in you. And of course the same applies for male ancestors if you are a man. Has this information altered your assessment of the probability that you too may have 100 generations of successive female or male descendants?

I use these examples to highlight the fact that we are generally fairly poor at estimating probabilities and using statistical concepts in order to make decisions. They also show that we are easily influenced by irrelevant information. In the first example for instance the majority of people think it is more likely that John is a bank clerk who coaches youth sports because, given the previous description, it is not unlikely that he would do one of these things, i.e. coach youth sports. However, this has no influence whatever on the probability that he is also a bank clerk, but because the two are paired together they are considered as a single issue. One important lesson that can be learned from this is that people are more likely to believe an improbable statement if it is paired with a probable one.

The second example indicates that people generally have a poor 'feel' for numbers and probabilities; this is a serious handicap to effective management. As we will see in a later section a great deal of management decisions are concerned with probabilities rather than certainties, it therefore bodes ill that people in general (and in my experience managers are no exception) are often weak in this area.

In the final example above, the fact that you had a same-sex ancestor 100 generations ago is completely irrelevant to the probability that you yourself will have 100 generations of same-sex descendants in the future. The fact that *every* living human being had a same-sex ancestor 100 generations ago does not imply that this is a common event but rather that a very great number of individuals alive today share a common same-sex ancestor. The central problem in this case is that we confuse the occurrence of a past event with the probable occurrence of a future event.

An event cannot meaningfully be allocated a probability after it has occurred although it is often tempting to do so. For example, everyone recognizes that it is phenomenally unlikely that four card players will be dealt the full complement of each suit in a fair deal. If it were to happen in a card game today great astonishment would no doubt ensue about the infinitesimal likelihood of its occurrence. However, a full complement of each suit is no less likely than any other hand that can be dealt. Every deal produces a hand of cards that was phenomenally unlikely before the deal was made, but no one says 'Wow, that's incredible—everybody got a mixed hand!' I am aware that the above example can be considered somewhat exotic and perhaps a little divorced from the practicalities of everyday management so I will rectify this immediately.

The case of Robyn and Jack

Consider the following situation: Two sales personnel, Robyn and Jack are in line for promotion to the board of a large company. They are the most successful sales personnel in the organization's history and their records are virtually identical. Being highly competitive individuals they decide to settle the problem of who gets the job by entering into a two-person sales race over a period of 100 days. Because they understand that either of them could get a once-in-a-million chance sale during this period they agree that overall sales volume would not be a reliable indicator of who is the best salesperson. They therefore decide to run the contest on a day-to-day basis and agree that whoever has been ahead in sales on the greatest number of individual days during the period will be promoted to the board. Their progress is detailed below in terms of who is ahead from day to day. An 'R' signifies that Robyn won on a particular day and a 'J' signifies that Jack was the day's winner. The whole 100 days is broken down into 10-day periods as shown below.

Period	*Individual ahead at the end of each day*									
1	J	J	J	R	R	J	R	J	R	J
2	R	R	J	J	R	J	R	R	R	R
3	R	J	R	J	J	J	R	R	R	R
4	J	R	J	R	R	R	R	R	R	R
5	J	R	R	R	J	R	J	R	J	R
6	J	R	J	J	R	R	R	J	R	J
7	J	J	J	R	R	J	J	J	J	R
8	J	R	R	R	R	R	J	J	R	R
9	R	R	R	J	R	R	R	J	R	R
10	R	J	R	R	R	J	R	J	J	J

Let us analyse the results in terms of who is in the lead at the end of each period.

Period	*Leader*
1	Jack (6-4) a lead of 2
2	Robyn (11-9) a lead of 2
3	Robyn (17-13) a lead of 4
4	Robyn (25-15) a lead of 10
5	Robyn (31-19) a lead of 12
6	Robyn (36-24) a lead of 12
7	Robyn (39-31) a lead of 8
8	Robyn (46-34) a lead of 12
9	Robyn (54-36) a lead of 18
10	Robyn (59-41) a lead of 18

These results indicate that Robyn is the clear winner; after an initial faltering start Robyn captured and maintained the lead and, apart from a hiccup in period 7, extended this lead to a convincing 18 days at the end of the 100-day contest.

At this point the reader may object that in fact we cannot be absolutely sure that the contest was truly equal because Robyn may have had some form of advantage in terms of territory, inside information, etc. Let us imagine therefore that we have completely equalized all of the external factors involved in this contest (this is obviously not possible in practice) and that the result remains as above. Would you now take this result as constituting unequivocal evidence that, as far as this period was concerned, the considerable differences in performance must be attributable to differences between Robyn and Jack? Every person I have ever asked this question of says 'yes', or says that they cannot think of any other reason why there should be such a difference. Commonly, when asked to explain what may have happened to produce these results, managers come up with some variation on the following: Jack's early lead prompted Robyn to put in extra effort to pull back and then to increase the lead. Jack made a great effort in period 7 but then Robyn made an even greater effort in period 8 which caused Jack to lose motivation and Robyn coasted home in the final two periods.

All of this is, of course, extremely plausible given the figures, but it is completely wrong. The truth is that *the outcome of this contest was decided by chance factors alone.* How do I know this? Because I simply flipped a coin to determine who was ahead on each particular day, heads it was Robyn, tails it was Jack. Intuitively we feel that results such as this are extremely unlikely to be due to chance factors alone. Clear patterns seem to emerge and we can make sense of these patterns in terms of individual differences. But, as we have seen, chance was the sole arbiter in this case. Again the problem is linked to an inadequate understanding of chance and probability. Because we know that a fair coin has an equal chance of coming up heads or tails we imagine that the absolute numbers of both will remain fairly equal, perhaps even alternating about the average value over a period of flips. This, however, is commonly not the case. Once a chance lead has been fairly well established (as Robyn's was by period 4) it is as likely to increase as decrease and it is probable that a very large number of flips will be required to reverse it. You may argue that this cannot be the case because it is an established fact that as the number of flips increases, the ratio of heads to tails approaches a value of 1. This is true, but a ratio is not a measure of absolute difference.

A ratio is a quotient calculated by dividing the total number of heads by the total number of tails (or vice versa) and as the number of flips increases this ratio will have a tendency to get closer to 1. For example, if we continued to flip the coin in the Robyn and Jack scenario we may find that after 1000 flips Robyn has a lead of 16 over Jack. The ratio of heads to tails is therefore 508/492 which is equal to 1.033. Imagine that over the next 1000 flips Robyn's luck stays with him and he increases his overall lead to 24. The ratio of heads to tails is now 1012/988 which is 1.024. Now this value is closer to 1 than the previous ratio of 1.033 and therefore, although the absolute difference between the numbers of heads and tails has increased, the ratio of heads to tails has decreased.

The astute reader will see that had Robyn's lead increased by an amount greater than 32 then the ratio of heads to tails would also have increased. This, of course, would violate the tendency for the ratio of heads to tails to approach 1 as the number of flips increases. The fact that Robyn's overall lead did not increase by this amount can be accounted for by a statistical concept known as regression to the mean, which is explained in the following section.

Mean statistics

'The luck of having talent is not enough; one must also have a talent for luck.'

Berlioz

Imagine the following situation: Two eminent management theorists argue about whether or not it is more productive to reward exceptionally good performance or to punish exceptionally bad performance. They decide that the issue cannot be resolved theoretically and arrange that the following experiment is carried out.

Airforce officers involved in the training of fighter pilots are instructed either to praise their trainees when they fly exceptionally well or to reprimand them when they fly particularly poorly. Records are kept of the effects of each type of feedback and a clear and systematic pattern quickly emerges. Pilots who are praised for exceptional performance nearly always *deteriorate* following this praise whereas pilots who are reprimanded for poor performance almost always *improve* afterwards. This pattern emerges consistently and the theorists conclude, backed with quantified evidence, that an important lesson has been learned. They therefore recommend that in future instructors should focus on reprimanding particularly poor performances and that they should ignore exceptionally good performances.

The situation described above is not hypothetical; it actually occurred, although the precise circumstances were slightly different from those cited. Amos Tversky and Daniel Kahneman, two psychologists who have undertaken extensive studies in the areas under consideration, reported that officers in the Israeli Airforce noticed the very phenomenon described above and suggested to their superior officers that in future they should castigate pilots for poor performances but not praise them for flying well. Their reasoning, although understandable, was completely erroneous.

Two common misconceptions were at work here. The first error the flight instructors made was to confuse correlation with cause. The mere fact that event A is consistently followed by event B does not necessarily mean that event A is the cause of event B; it may be or it may not. For example, day is always followed by night, but day does not cause night: both are the result of the Earth's rotation relative to the sun. That there is a correlative relationship between them is clear but it is not causal.

To offer another example, research in the USA indicates that children's academic achievement is positively correlated (this is the situation in which an increase in one variable is followed by an increase in the other) with the number and newness of electrical equipment in the child's home. The more new electrical equipment there is, the better the child does at school. However, before you consider purchasing an extra freezer in the hope of boosting your child's exam results, let us look at the situation a little closer. Two events may indeed vary in relation to each other but both variations may be the consequence of a third factor. In the case of the electrical equipment/academic achievement relationship, both are related to income. The more income a family has, the greater is the probability that the household will contain above average amounts of newer electrical equipment and higher income households also tend to have above average interest in the academic achievements of their children. Although each factor in this specific case (amount of electrical equipment and academic achievement) is positively correlated there is actually no causal relationship present. Both are the consequence of above-average income. Correlation between variables therefore does not necessarily equate with cause.

To return to our pilots, it is not disputed that praise for exceptionally good performance was most frequently followed by deterioration while criticism of particularly poor performance was most frequently followed by improvement: these are facts. They are facts but they are completely predictable without recourse to either praise or punishment as explanations. In reality the Air Force instructors could have done absolutely nothing following exceptionally good or poor performance and they would have seen largely the same consequences. Fluctuations of this sort are statistical rather than causal.

Think again about the case of Robyn and Jack described above. In the first 1000 flips of the coin Robyn amassed a lead of 16 and in the following 1000 flips he continued to have good luck and increased this lead to 24. However, as we saw in the calculation above, the ratio of heads to tails actually decreased during this period. This was due to the fact that Robyn's lead from the first 1000 flips (16) was not repeated through the second 1000 (it fell to 8). This is predictable because over a really long period both players' results will tend to approach their mean value. Therefore if either has an exceptionally high or low proportion of wins in a particular period the probability is that they will do worse in the following period. This is known as regression to the mean and it predicts that *exceptional chance shifts away from mean performance values are likely to be followed by compensatory shifts in the opposite direction.*

We can apply this principle to the case of our pilots. Flying an aircraft is an activity that involves an immense number of complex interactions between influential factors, many of which are beyond the control of the pilot. Chance fluctuations in these factors will, on average, balance each other out and a predictable level of performance can be expected. For example, slightly increased air turbulence on one particular day may be compensated for by the fact that the aircraft's manoeuvrability is marginally improved by lower levels of humidity and so on. However, it is inevitable that on some occasions fluctuations will be predominantly 'good' or predominantly 'bad', such as the day when air turbulence is slightly above average and the aircraft's manoeuvrability is slightly below average or, conversely, the day when air turbulence is below average and the aircraft is handling like a dream. Given that all combinations of factors which affect flying performance are possible, it is inevitable that chance performances of an exceptional nature, whether good or bad, will occur on occasions. It is also highly unlikely that this combination will be repeated twice or three times in a row, hence the deterioration in performance following a high and the improvement that follows a low.

This phenomenon is not restricted to aircraft pilots. It applies equally to the footballer who has an exceptional period of goal scoring, is subsequently transferred for huge sums of money and then proceeds to play like a donkey, and to the newly appointed manager who achieves stupendous results one year only to fold miserably the next. Exceptional performances, those which depart significantly from known mean values, should be treated with circumspection. We may be dealing with genius or monumental incompetence (as we sometimes are) or purely with the vagaries of chance (which we more often are).

The key variable, of course, lies in the number of factors influencing performance that is beyond an individual's or an organization's ability to influence. The more of these there are, the more cautious we should be about attributing the cause of exceptional performance to the inherent qualities of the individual or organization concerned, and the more we should expect a compensatory swing in the opposite direction in the future.

The reader will no doubt appreciate that statistical phenomena such as these raise very important and extremely complex questions about processes such as performance appraisal, remuneration setting and promotion. It is clear that chance fluctuations in performance between individuals may be misconstrued as indicating differences in ability and that correlation may sometimes be confused with cause. Although we have absolutely no way of eliminating uncertainty in any of our dealings with the world (it is a highly probabilistic place) an awareness of the vagaries of chance and the tendency for complex systems to behave probabilistically will give us a more sophisticated understanding of the critical processes we must manage.

Puzzles, problems and facts

Puzzle: Contrived to exercise ingenuity and patience.
Problem: Doubtful or difficult question.
Fact: Thing certainly known to have occurred or be true.

The Oxford English Dictionary

A substantial proportion of management books make reference to problem-solving and problem-solving techniques. It is also common for advice on problem-solving to be distilled into a structured plan which contains a number of sequential steps, often arranged so as to form an easily remembered acronym. Examples abound: the KISS approach to the presentation of information: Keep It Short and Simple. The WASP method of structured interviewing: Welcome Acquire information Supply information Parting. The FACERAP technique for fault analysis and rectification: Fault, Appearance, Cause, Effect, Remedy, Action, Prevention and, a very recent addition by a prominent author in the field of TQM. The DRIVE model of structured problem-solving: Define, Review, Investigate, Verify, Execute.

Problem-solving models of this sort are variations on a standard approach that recommends four sequential steps, these steps are;

1. A clear *definition* of what the problem is.
2. A systematic *analysis* of the root causes of the problem.
3. The development of a clear *plan* of action to solve the problem.
4. The *execution* of the plan, with suitable monitoring.

Systematic problem-solving techniques are extremely powerful in generating solutions to many of the operational difficulties that organizations face. There are, however, a number of limitations associated with their use. First, they apply most effectively to a particular type of situation, one that is highly structured and open to data collection and analysis. A number of common examples are given below.

- Optimizing the layout of offices or workshops
- Reducing operation cycle times
- Reducing product development times
- Reducing waste
- Reducing defect ratios
- Increasing materials flow rates
- Sequencing operations for maximum efficiency
- Improving delivery times
- Reducing accidents.

It is clear that the above examples share four important attributes, they are:

1. A desired situation is perceived to exist.
2. The desired situation can be quantified and agreed (e.g. to reduce cycle times by 10 per cent, to improve productivity by 5 per cent, to reduce defect rates to one part per million, to deliver orders within 48 hours of receipt).
3. There is sufficient information available to determine a method of achieving the desired situation.
4. All the critical factors influencing the achievement of the desired situation are capable of being understood, manipulated and stabilized.

These then are the sorts of instances in which a desired situation can be clearly described and there is enough information available to achieve that desired situation. In other words a solution exists if we can find it. The archetypical form of this type of situation is the puzzle. In some instances, such as mathematical puzzles, crossword puzzles, jigsaw puzzles, IQ tests and 'whodunnits' a unique solution, the answer, exists and when it is found it can be shown to be the solution.

Not all puzzles have a unique solution however. For example, we can imagine that a motor car manufacturer wishes to improve the fuel efficiency of a particular model of car by 5 per cent. There are a number of possible ways in which this could be achieved: by reducing the overall weight of the vehicle; by improving the efficiency of the engine; by improving the efficiency of the transmission system; by modifying the aerodynamics; by developing a more effective ignition system, and so on. Different manufacturers may adopt different strategies to achieve the same desired outcome, perhaps combining some of the possible avenues described above, or by using others. It is important to recognize, however, that solutions to puzzles such as these can often be determined theoretically or through the use of experimentation.

Returning to the example above, engineers may calculate that it is theoretically possible to obtain the desired fuel efficiency with minor modifications to the existing body design and the incorporation of an improved ignition system. These modifications can be made to a prototype and the effectiveness of the solution can then be assessed. If the desired improvement is achieved specific design changes can then be incorporated in production models. The important point to note here is that if these changes are rigorously implemented the desired improvement will be achieved on all future occasions. The specified design changes therefore constitute a *guaranteed formula for success*. Timetabling in a school or college is another example of this sort of puzzle. Once a satisfactory timetable has been devised, and provided everyone adheres to it, there will never be two classes in one room at the same time.

Puzzles of this type abound in organizations. They are commonly associated with quality assurance. BS 5750 is essentially concerned with the development of a set of procedures for the solution of specific puzzles such as the production of goods and services to consistent standards. The Kaizen philosophy of continuous improvement is also primarily about the solution of puzzles. Standard Operating Procedures (SOPs), precisely defined methods for producing and assembling components or operating processes, are widely used in manufacturing industries, particularly in Japanese organizations. SOPs are identified through the exhaustive application of puzzle-solving techniques and are continuously reviewed on the premiss that no procedure is ever perfect and therefore incremental improvements can always be made.

Solving puzzles—ingenuity and patience

It is clear from the success of techniques such as Kaizen that an ability to solve puzzles presents us with considerable opportunities for improving the efficiency of organizational processes and procedures. Puzzle-solving ability is consequently a highly desirable skill; it will be useful therefore to examine some of the factors involved.

Puzzles can vary greatly in terms of complexity and difficulty and determining solutions depends on a number of critical abilities. These are: the ability to systematically gather and analyse information, the ability to think effectively and the ability to persevere in the face of difficulty. These abilities can be enhanced with practice and through an understanding of the common barriers that prevent us from being more effective puzzle-solvers. Some practical experience of puzzle-solving will be useful here. Consider the following puzzle:

There are five boys: David, Ian, John, Mark and Robert. We know that the following information is true:

- John is taller than Robert
- There are two boys taller than Ian
- David is shorter than Robert
- Mark is taller than John

Arrange the boys' names in order of height.

This is a straightforward puzzle with a unique answer, the information required to solve it is given in the four statements and only one solution is possible: Mark, John, Ian, Robert and David. The solution to this puzzle only requires that we use information effectively and think systematically.

Now consider a more difficult example. Ian's copy of the phenomenally influential book, *Total Quality—How To Do It In Three Minutes*, has been stolen from his office. Mark, John, Robert and David are the only possible culprits and only one of them could have stolen the book. Each has given the following statement to the police.

- John said that Mark had stolen it.
- Mark said that David had stolen it.
- Robert said he had not stolen it.
- David said that Mark had lied.

An eye witness to the theft tells us that *only one of the above statements is true*; she then promptly disappears. Who is the real culprit?

This is a more difficult puzzle. We only know that one of the statements is true (but we are not told exactly which one) yet this information is sufficient to deduce without any doubt who the culprit is. The solution to the puzzle is given below but I would recommend that the reader spend some time working on it. I am assuming of course that the answer is not immediately obvious! Do not jump to an intuitive solution, however; remember that your answer must be shown to be beyond doubt.

Solution The culprit must be Robert: there is no other possibility. The reasons are as follows. We know that only one of the statements is true; it therefore follows that three must be lies. We can also see that David's statement is a direct contradiction of Mark's, therefore one of them must be telling the truth (because they contradict each other they cannot both be lying). The fact that we now know this means that the remaining two statements must be lies (as we know that only one statement is true and that it must be either David's or Mark's). John must have been lying when he said that Mark had stolen the book and Robert must have been lying when he denied stealing it; therefore Robert must have stolen the book.

The actual truth and falsity of each statement is as follows;

- John said that Mark had stolen it. (false)
- Mark said that David had stolen it. (false)
- Robert said that he had not stolen it. (false)
- David said that Mark had lied. (true)

I have used this puzzle, or variations of it, with very many managers and it usually generates difficulties. People frequently jump to conclusions that are idiosyncratic or unprovable. It is not uncommon for individuals to opt for Robert (coincidentally the correct answer) by virtue of the fact that he is the only individual to have denied committing the crime! I accept that the logic required to solve this puzzle is somewhat convoluted, but it is soluble, and there is only one possible correct answer.

However, a much more important lesson emerges from exercises such as this. It is the daunting realization that people frequently employ extremely unsystematic, bizarre or half-hearted approaches to puzzle-solving. With reference to the exercise above, one person asked if there was any information available regarding the star-signs of each of the characters involved! Such irrationalities aside, one of the most worrying observations is that individuals frequently abandon the mental effort required to think about a logical solution in a relatively short period of time. If an initial answer is found to be incorrect or if the puzzle poses a significant challenge then the clang of mental shutters is almost audible. Some of this is due to the contrived nature of the exercise and people often cite this as the main reason for giving up thinking about an answer. However, I am not at all convinced that this is in fact the principal factor involved.

The vast majority of people begin to tackle the puzzle with a reasonable amount of interest and often with very high levels of enthusiasm. It is when they fail to discover an immediate solution or when they realize that the puzzle is more complex than it at first appears that they begin to lose heart. This may be the result of earlier learning experiences, particularly during compulsory school-ing. This hypothesis seems to be borne out by the observation that people generally give up thinking sooner if they are asked to solve the puzzle individually rather than as part of a group. It may be that this is influenced by the culture that exists within the majority of our schools. Most teachers require children to work alone and discourage them from seeking help from other children when they experience difficulties. I believe that many children consequently develop a coping technique when faced with a seemingly intractable difficulty that may be described as 'apparent problem-solving'. They go through the outward motions of attempting a solution when in fact they have switched off mentally and are either daydreaming or thinking about something that really interests them. This is a form of 'learned helplessness' which I believe many people carry into adulthood.

The solution of complex puzzles requires tenacity and ingenuity. I believe that the vast majority of people are more ingenious than they suppose. Too many have been led to believe that they are not. One of the key challenges of successfully implementing TQM is that we create organizations in which barriers such as these are well and truly laid to rest.

Problems

In the preceding section the formulation of a school or college timetable was offered as a classic example of a puzzle. On the one hand we have the students with their subject choices and requirements and on the other we have the school or college with its buildings, rooms and learning facilities. The challenge, as with a jigsaw puzzle, is to fit the pieces together in a satisfactory way. Of course our timetabler has the advantage that if the pieces do not actually fit he or she can cut them to suit (by adjusting the student side of the equation of course). Ultimately a timetable will emerge which, if adhered to, will work. So far so good. Now, assuming that our students are accurately ensconced in their classrooms, what exactly should we teach them and how should it be taught?

It is immediately obvious that this is not the same type of difficulty as was previously discussed. No precise solution, agreed by all, can be deduced from the information given. Whereas puzzles lend themselves to dispassionate analysis, deduction and solution through the application of systematic techniques, questions of the type described above do not. These are in fact genuine problems. Consider some further examples:

- Who is the customer of the prison service?
- What is the most effective management style?
- How should children be brought up?

These are the sort of questions that defy logical analysis and prescription of the type appropriate to the solution of puzzles. The answer an individual is inclined to give will be strongly influenced by personal and emotional factors, beliefs about crime and punishment, the nature of management, the qualities to be admired in a mature adult and so on. There is no 'correct' answer to be found; people have particular views and each will have its own strengths and weaknesses. Consider some further examples that are closer to the issues discussed in this book:

- How should our organization be structured?
- How should organizational change be managed?
- What criteria should we use to recruit staff?
- What training and development services should we provide?
- How should people be rewarded in our organization?
- What level of information technology should we employ?
- How should we formulate our vision for the next 10 years?
- How should we obtain critical information from our customers?
- How can we best meet the sometimes contradictory requirements of different sets of customers?
- Should we implement a TQM programme within our organization?

It is clear that these questions are neither hypothetical nor facetious; they are vital to the survival of organizations. Decisions must be taken about important issues such as these and the effectiveness of these decisions will dramatically influence future security. The difficulty is that *there can be no sure-fire procedure that will produce a guaranteed solution* to these problems. In fact it is a common and extremely dangerous fallacy to believe that such methods of solution do in fact exist or can be found (usually in the most recent tome to achieve 'Guru' status).

For example, any reputable consultant working in the field of TQM recognizes that preconceived packages, 14-point plans and whizz-bang implementation programmes do not really work. Ultimately each organization must 'grow' its own specific variety of the quality plant. Techniques and systems that work beautifully in one organization may fail dismally in another. That is the nature of the beast. Packages cannot be guaranteed to work because the successful implementation of TQM is a problem and not a puzzle.

Every organization is a unique blend of historical, social, technical and cultural factors and each therefore requires a unique response. The difficulty is that many managers do not fully appreciate this fact. Time and again, in my experience, managers expect to be given a precisely detailed plan for the implementation of TQM within their organization when no such plan is in fact possible.

A common manifestation of this desire for precision in the face of uncertainty and the consequent search for guaranteed answers to complex problems can be seen in the case-study approach to management development so beloved of American business schools. One of the principal attractions of case studies is the implied suggestion that generalizable lessons can be learned from the past successes or failures of organizations (or indeed from the successes of managers such as Sir John Harvey-Jones and Lee Iacocca). If such lessons were not considered to be generalizable there would be little point in studying particular cases. I believe that this is a false hope. Studies of individual managers and organizations can improve our knowledge base in particular areas but they cannot provide us with anything approaching generalizable laws of operation. This is as true in terms of managing organizations as it is in teaching, counselling or playwriting. There are no 'specific secrets of success' to be found lurking within the detailed biographies of successful individuals. Successful teachers, managers, decision-makers and playwrights are successful relative to a *particular set of circumstances that is effectively unrepeatable.* In fact the whole process of searching for laws in situations such as these is, I believe, based on a misapplication of classical scientific method.

Generalizable laws can only be determined when critical variables are held constant between specific situations. This is the basis of the controlled experiment upon which the whole mass of scientific knowledge is predicated. Individuals and organizations, however, are not controlled experiments: they are unique and particular entities that are essentially unrepeatable, and it is extremely dangerous to extrapolate from the particular to the general. What works, or does not work, at a particular place with particular people at a particular time may not apply elsewhere. Bringing up your child in exactly the same way that Mozart was brought up will not necessarily make him or her a great composer!

In a previous book[16] I outlined the potential dangers of the generalized competency model of management effectiveness and this analysis is appropriate here. The principal benefits that can be obtained from a study of successful individuals and organizations include the identification of core values, themes and central principles. These values and principles may then be incorporated into practical procedures that are intended to improve an organization's chances of dealing with critical problems effectively, but the fact remains that success can only be envisaged in terms of probability. Once this point is appreciated managers are less likely to fall into the trap of believing that success is inevitable once 'the plan'; has been detailed. It is also likely that managers will recognize the need for continuous vigilance and accept the fact that operational modifications to any initial plan will almost certainly be required as events unfold in the real world.

The central characteristics of problems

We have seen that problems differ from puzzles in both structure and tractability. This is doubly unfortunate. Problems, as the limited sample above attests, pose the most difficult management challenges and they are commonly the most important influences on the long-term security of organizations. Given their importance it will be useful to understand as much about them as we can and also to examine possible methods of dealing with them. First the main characteristics. Problems differ from puzzles in a number of important ways, by and large:

- Every problem is unique, involving a particular configuration of critical factors. It is highly likely therefore that problems will be only partially amenable to generic 'problem-solving' techniques.
- Problems are commonly non-linear. This means that they are rarely composed of mechanistic cause and effect links but involve complex and often circular interrelationships. For

example, an organization's culture can be considered as being the predominant attitude of mind that currently exists within it. But this attitude of mind will also be a reflection of the established culture of the organization. Organizational culture can therefore be considered as both a cause and an effect of predominant attitudes of mind.

- Problems frequently contain 'soft' information. That is information relevant to the problem may be incomplete, probabilistic rather than certain or qualitative rather than quantitative.
- Problems commonly involve influencing factors that are beyond the complete control of the problem-solver.
- Problems frequently involve unknowable future situations.
- Problems involve perceptions and emotions.

A real-life illustration of the principal differences between puzzles and problems can be seen in the different challenges involved in running an efficient rail and bus service. Running an efficient rail service is predominantly a puzzle. The specific requirements for success (i.e. delivering the timetable) can be determined in advance (reliable engines and signalling equipment, adequate staff, clear tracks, etc.) and a plan of action to achieve this success can be specified. If all goes according to this plan then the railway service will work today, tomorrow and *ad infinitum*. Apart from natural disasters, the principal factors affecting the delivery of the service are (theoretically at least) within the potential control of the railway's management.

Running an effective bus service is a completely different matter. Many of the principal factors influencing success in this situation, such as the level of traffic congestion, possible accidents involving other vehicles, road repairs, traffic light reliability, the consideration of other drivers, burst water mains, etc. are beyond the control of the operating company. And each day brings a different configuration of possible difficulties. Consequently, unlike the situation with the railway, there cannot be a fixed operating plan that will guarantee success when implemented.

It is clear therefore that when faced with problems it is useful to be in possession of an ability that is commonly termed 'good judgement'. This point is critical to many contemporary difficulties in management and organizational development. Because of the rapid and unpredictable nature of change in the modern world managers are increasingly faced with problems rather than puzzles. Whether to embark on some form of quality initiative is itself a problem and one that requires judgement. Judgement, of course, is influenced by knowledge, experience and information. Case studies can add to our knowledge of the interplay of specific factors in specific situations and, given the caveat above, such knowledge is useful.

Experience, of course, must be lived and there is no way around this. However, the mere fact that an individual has a great deal of experience does not guarantee that he or she has learned anything from it. Experience alone does not guarantee the development of good judgement. As with many other critical human abilities, it is more an art than a science. However, the better the quality of information we possess (and consequently the less uncertainty we face) the better equipped we are to make effective judgements. Gathering all available accurate and relevant information is therefore a key requirement in problem-solving. The more accurate and relevant information we possess the more our problems will come to resemble puzzles and the more likely it will be that we can formulate a flexible plan of action to deal with them. Ultimately, however, uncertainty will remain. In a later section I will outline a number of methods for managing these uncertainties.

Facts

The Oxford Dictionary describes a fact as being a 'thing certainly known to have occurred or be true'. The former element in this statement is less open to debate than the latter. For example, no one seriously doubts that the Queen was crowned in 1952 or that President John Kennedy was assassinated in 1963: both are established historical facts. Establishing certainty of truth, however, is a very different matter. Any proposed statement of truth, apart that is from tautologies or claims related to systems of belief, is open to objective analysis and question in a way that established historical facts are not. The established 'truths' of science are no exception to this. Newton's laws of physics, for example, were considered universal truths for a period of some 250 years until Einstein formulated the Special Theory of Relativity. Likewise, the 'truths' established by Einstein, such as the absolute nature of the speed of light, may not be true 250 years hence. The truth component of a fact can therefore be considered as being an assertion that has not yet been disproved.

I hope the reader will forgive this minor foray into the realms of epistemology as there is a practical point! In the preceding sections I outlined the central differences between puzzles and problems and proposed that both concepts are relevant to an understanding of the challenges involved in successfully implementing TQM initiatives. I also indicated that puzzles and problems, although varying in tractability, are 'actionable'. That is, both types of difficulty are, in theory at least, capable of being resolved. Facts, however, are not capable of resolution; they are part of the realities of life. Trying to avoid an unpalatable fact is a fruitless activity because, as the eminent theoretical physicist Richard Feynman once remarked, 'nature always bats last'.

A significant number of hard facts must be faced in relation to TQM and I am personally convinced that a failure to do so lies at the heart of the majority of difficulties experienced with TQ initiatives. Despite a wealth of research and practical experience which clearly shows that the transition from traditional to TQ cultures involves profound change, many senior managers seem unwilling, or unable, to grasp the practical implications involved. Moving to a TQ culture requires a radical shift in previously held assumptions about the nature of organizations and the ways in which they should be structured and managed. To assert the proposition that TQM is not a quick fix has become something of a platitude in current management writing yet a genuine appreciation of the level of organizational change required continues to elude many senior managers.

Below are 10 of the most important facts (i.e. assertions that I have yet to see disproved) that must be faced if TQM initiatives are to succeed within organizations.

Ten facts about TQM

1. Senior management must fully understand the central philosophy and key concepts of TQM.
2. Senior management must be fully aware of the tremendous challenges involved in becoming a TQM organization.
3. Senior management must be totally committed to this aim.
4. Senior management must act in accordance with the principles of TQM (i.e. walk the talk).

5. Senior management must understand that, in the vast majority of instances, major changes will need to be made in terms of organizational structure, culture and working practices.
6. In any TQM programme there is likely to be an initial honeymoon period before the critical challenges begin to emerge.
7. Certain people within the organization, often powerful, will offer strong resistance to the changes that are necessary for TQM to succeed.
8. At some point it will be very much easier to abandon the TQM programme than to keep it going.
9. Everyone will have doubts about the viability of the programme at some point, even the 'quality freaks!'
10. Senior management must give continuous support to the programme and, through their actions, show that they are determined that the programme will succeed.

The term 'senior management' in the list above should be taken to mean 'managers with power'; the terms are not always synonymous. It is a fact that a critical mass of powerful support must develop behind a TQM programme if it is to have any significant impact on the organization. A common failing of many TQM initiatives is to confuse senior management consent with senior management commitment. As I have mentioned in previous sections of this book, the quality trilogy of customers, value and continuous improvement is recited almost universally yet quality initiatives fail to make any significant long-term impact in the vast majority of organizations.

I believe that a major reason for this failure is that the facts listed above are not understood or tackled effectively. In the case of TQM, lip-service by senior management is not enough. The 'we wish you well and we won't stand in your way' attitude is simply inadequate in this context. Senior managers cannot consider themselves as merely the benign observers of a process that will see TQM succeed or fail. If they do not give it their total active support, it will fail. *Denying that these facts exist is a sure recipe for disaster.*

It is a central proposition of this book that TQ initiatives will only succeed if we are able to effectively manage the human dimension of quality. The preceding sections have examined some of the challenges we face in terms of the ways in which we think about certain types of difficulty and the common limitations that exist in the methods we employ when searching for solutions. Many TQ initiatives fail because managers confuse problems with puzzles and deny the existence of unpalatable facts. There are, however, no means of avoiding them. We must improve our ability to solve puzzles, become more skilled at exercising judgement in the face of uncertainty and face up to the fact that TQ will involve dramatic changes within organizations, particularly at management levels. It will now be useful to move away from our discussion of individual challenges and consider those associated with the effective management of groups.

9

Collective irrationality

Psychological research consistently shows that groups perform less effectively in decision-making tasks than individuals. Professor Jerry Harvey calls this tendency the 'Abiline Paradox' which, he says, indicates that *people in groups agree on decisions which, as individuals, they know are stupid.*

There are a number of contributory reasons for this phenomenon. First, group membership satisfies a number of important psychological needs. These include the desire for belonging, identity and purpose. Human beings are social animals and group identity is an extremely powerful way of providing meaning in our lives. There is a strong tendency, again well-documented through psychological research, for individuals to conform to any general consensus expressed within the group to which they belong or aspire to belong. The following sections will detail some of the management challenges which these and other group-oriented tendencies present.

The power of conformity

In a famous series of experiments carried out by the American psychologist Solomon Asch in the 1950s, volunteers were recruited to take part in an experiment ostensibly designed to measure visual acuity. The experiment consisted of showing a group of people a series of cards on which had been printed a line of particular length. They were then shown another card which had three lines of differing length printed on it and were asked to identify the particular line that was the same length as the line on the first card. The form of cards used is shown in Figure 9.1.

It is clear from this example that the correct answer in this instance would be to select line C on the second card as being the

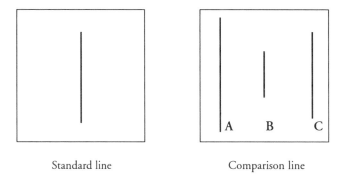

Standard line   Comparison line

Figure 9.1 An example of the type of cards used in the Asch experiments

same length as the standard line. All the test cards (there were 18 in each trial) were constructed in a similar way, i.e. the correct answer was clearly evident. Indeed in 'real' trials Asch found that the error rate was less than 0.5 per cent.

However, in the particular experiments he conducted, Asch contrived to have groups of nine individuals present at each trial of which eight were actually 'stooges', that is, they knew what the true purpose of the experiment was: to test the effects of group pressure on individual decision making. Each trial would typically begin with the 'real' subject (i.e. the one individual who did not know the true purpose of the experiment) being seated in a position that was last but one in the answering order. The cards were then shown individually and, beginning at the end of the group (usually arranged in a semicircle), farthest away from the subject, each person would call out the particular line which he or she ostensibly judged to be the same length as the standard. On the first two cards each of the stooges selects the option that is obviously correct, as, of course, does the real subject. But on the third occasion each of the stooges selects a line (the same line) that is obviously not the correct response, and they do this in 11 other instances also. The interesting question is: what effect does this have on the real subject?

Asch found that 3 out of 4 subjects conformed to group pressure on at least one occasion and agreed that the wrong selection was correct. Almost one-third of the subjects gave 8 or more incorrect answers and 1 in 20 conformed to group pressure in every single instance. When one considers that the nature of the task was not complex or ambiguous—the correct answer was obvious in every case—such high levels of conformity to group pressure, and the suspension of judgement it implies, does not auger well for our somewhat cherished belief in the efficacy of group decision making.

When subjects were debriefed and told the real purpose of the experiment the majority confessed that they had privately believed that the wrong answer was indeed wrong but, for various reasons such as not wishing to appear different or to be made to look like a fool, they had gone along with the wrong answer none the less. Some subjects seemed to have adjusted their perceptions in line with the group consensus and had actually believed that the wrong answers were in fact correct. Further experiments showed that those subjects who felt that wrong answers were being given experienced considerable levels of stress when they disagreed with the stooges (as measured by the amount of plasma-free fatty acids present in the body) but their stress levels fell sharply if they conformed. Asch also found that it was group consensus which influenced subjects most and that a group of three individuals who unanimously agreed on the wrong answer was more influential in pressurizing the subject to conform than a group of eight in which seven people agreed on a wrong answer and one person disagreed.

In a follow-up experiment Asch reversed the stooge–subject ratio and tested groups of 16 individuals in which there was only 1 stooge calling out incorrect answers. Asch found that the reaction of the other 15 was typically dramatic and that the stooge was subjected to sarcasm and ridiculing laughter when incorrect answers were given. This seems to confirm the belief held by subjects in the first set of experiments that being the odd one out is usually best avoided!

The shift to risk

The perceptive reader will rightly note that a tendency to group conformity is not of itself necessarily bad. If, for example, group pressure is in favour of a course of action that is correct, rational or morally desirable then the outcome will be positive. Two further difficulties confront us, however. Experiments have repeatedly shown that groups have the tendency to agree on courses of action that involve lower odds of success than would be acceptable to individual members acting separately. In other words, groups tend to take bigger risks than individuals. Group membership also tends to amplify any commonly held views or tendencies. This phenomenon can be clearly observed in the destructive actions of many groups of football supporters who act collectively in a manner that is frequently greater than the sum of each member's individual tendencies to violence. Combined with this fact is the tendency, particularly likely in situations where there is a charismatic or determined leader, for the group leader to become more extreme in his or her views in direct relation to the level of agreement that is expressed by the group members. In other words a group that provides unquestioning support is likely to encourage extremism in its leader. These individual elements of group dynamics, in combination, constitute a particularly vicious spiral that can be represented in Figure 9.2.

Obviously if this tendency towards ever-increasing extremism and risk-taking is allowed to go unchecked, decisions are likely to become increasingly dangerous and the spiral will continue until the material meets the fan. This may be at a point where the organization incurs a minor loss, is faced with a very serious problem (e.g. IBM) or it may mean total collapse or the abrupt

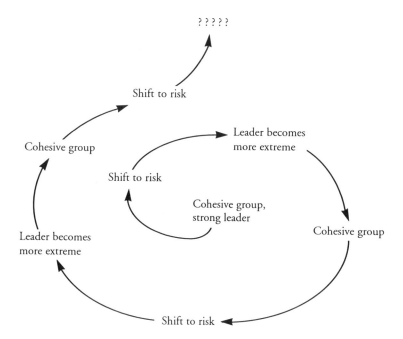

Figure 9.2 The spiral of risk

removal of the leader (witness the demise of Margaret Thatcher). Examples of the spiral are legend and are well documented throughout history, particularly in relation to the actions of the military.[17]

In more recent times, acts of collective stupidity have included:

- The abortive 'Bay of Pigs' fiasco in which President John Kennedy ordered a completely idiotic invasion of Cuba that resulted in the death or jailing of all the invading Cuban exiles within a period of 48 hours and a subsequent payment of 53 million dollars in ransom monies for the return of the survivors.
- The introduction and subsequent withdrawal of the Poll Tax in Britain which cost the country millions of pounds.
- The C5 electric car championed by Sir Clive Sinclair which finished off his company.
- The Hoover 'free flights' fiasco which threatens to cost the already troubled company millions of pounds and has perhaps tarnished its image permanently.
- IBM's decision to maintain its focus on mainframe computers when the market was converting to integrated workstation systems using minicomputers and, eventually, PCs.

In retrospect, each of these decisions can be seen to have been somewhat irrational, indeed after the Bay of Pigs incident President Kennedy remarked: 'How could I have been so stupid?'. Why, then, were these decisions taken in the first place? Although I do not have access to the appropriate details in each of the cases described above it is likely that the critical factors were similar to those which pertained in the case of the Bay of Pigs incident which, fortunately, is fairly well documented.

The 'Bay of Pigs' fiasco: silencing the doubters

We have already noted that groups of people are likely to take greater risks than would each of their members acting alone and that group cohesion encourages the development of increasingly extreme views in group leaders. Also, we have seen that group pressure is a formidable force for conformity. It seems that each of these factors played a major role in the 'Bay of Pigs' debacle. However, Asch's research, which highlighted the considerable power of consensus, also showed that 1 in 4 subjects did not conform to group pressure on any of the 16 trials involved in his experiments. Therefore, assuming that the group of people advising Kennedy was not composed of complete sycophants, Asch's findings indicate that it is not impossible that someone would at least have offered some form of resistance to the decisions being taken. In fact this did happen and it was dealt with in an interesting way.

In the period of time leading up to the abortive invasion attempt Kennedy was surrounded by a group of advisers that was highly enthusiastic about the aims of the operation (i.e. to depose Fidel Castro) but was less than enthusiastic about bringing critical thought processes to bear on the means by which this desired aim was to be achieved. This is a common enough situation; enthusiasm tends to breed wishful thinking and dull the appetite for engaging in objective analysis. However, the records show that one of the advisers, Arthur Schlesinger, voiced his misgivings on the idea fairly early on. He was subsequently taken aside by Robert Kennedy who urged him to support the President because '... he has made his mind up and needs everyone to help him all they can'. In other words Schlesinger's qualms about the logic of the activity was reconstrued as being an act of disloyalty to the President.

What Robert Kennedy really wished to avoid was questioning the basic plan itself which had gathered sufficient momentum to take on something of a life of its own: this is a very great danger with plans. The President was extremely enthusiastic, the CIA had constructed a detailed plan of action (based on six assumptions that were completely wrong) and all were keen to believe that the action would succeed. To throw an element of doubt into this happy situation, to go over old ground, to question fundamentals was simply not acceptable at that stage. The point of no return had been reached. There was, to echo an ominous current political phrase, 'no turning back'.

This situation is not uncommon in groups of all types, be they work teams, families or the boards of multinational corporations. Certain assumptions, behaviours and attitudes become taboos, simply not open to analysis and question. And although everyone is aware that they exist, no one dares bring them up. Harvard's Professor Chris Argyris describes this as a situation that commonly arises within a group whereby certain topics are effectively rendered 'undiscussible'.

The undiscussibles

Undiscussibles are a function of power networks. After all, things become undiscussible precisely because it is dangerous to bring them into the open. My own experiences in consultancy and training strongly indicate that undiscussibles constitute one of the most (if not the most) significant cultural barriers to the successful implementation of quality improvement programmes. One of the important reasons why TQM initiatives frequently grind to a halt after the initial honeymoon period is over is that organizational undiscussibles move closer and closer to the surface. As this occurs junior members of staff often lose their nerve or those in power clamp down on the whole programme.

So what is it about the nature of undiscussibles that make them such a threat? There are a number of generic qualities. In order to understand them, however, it is necessary to accept a current fact of working life (which is usually undiscussible) that has far-reaching consequences for organizational effectiveness. It is a regrettable fact that in the vast majority of organizations people do not tell the truth a good deal of the time. This is often the case when subordinates are communicating with their bosses (and vice versa) and it is particularly the case between managers from different departments. A great deal of ego-massaging, unrealistic self-congratulation, problem denial, reality-bending and downright lie-telling goes on everywhere. That this will happen is completely predictable gives the way most organizations are structured. As Stuart Sutherland rightly observes:

> ... a rational organization will adopt the best means available of pursuing its ends. In practice this rarely happens because its members are often activated by greed or sloth and may put their own ends such as self-advancement or avoidance of risk before those of the organization to which they belong. As a result the organization as a whole acts irrationally. The design of an organization should surely be such as to prevent as far as possible selfish behaviour on the part of its members but many organizations seem to be irrationally structured in ways that reward selfish behaviour rather than punish it.
>
> (S. Sutherland, *Irrationality*, pp. 78–79)

Contained within this extract are a number of points that would normally be undiscussible in the vast majority of organizations. For example, it suggests that some managers may be greedy, lazy, interested in their own self-advancement and have a strong predilection to avoid situations in which they may be shown in a bad light. If this is truly the case we would expect that organizations which are run by such managers would be hierarchical, bureaucratic, secretive, power-oriented, inefficient, callous, characterized by politiking, having a tendency towards blame delegation, be highly resistant to real change and having a clear distinction between the haves and the have-nots. In such an organization, managers (particularly those in the higher echelons) would characteristically allocate themselves such perks as excessively high salaries, lucrative compensation packages should they be dismissed on grounds of incompetence, have a cavalier attitude to the well-being of the workforce, be ensconced in plush and spacious offices, have prestigious company cars or even company aeroplanes, privileged car parking arrangements, separate dining facilities, generous expense accounts and so on.

It is fair to say that the above description is far from hypothetical. Organizations that fit the description completely are now much rarer than they were 20 years ago but they have not disappeared altogether—yet. One of the real challenges in establishing effective quality initiatives is to present the truth to senior managers that practices such as those described above represent the antithesis of the philosophy of TQM. Of course it is difficult to do so because such things are usually undiscussible, therefore they must be alluded to instead. Two practical examples may be illustrative.

I was asked to run a quality development workshop for the chief executive and directors of a particular organization that was funded out of the taxpayer's pocket. The organization possessed extremely good in-house conference facilities yet the workshop was held at a select and expensive commercial conference venue. During the workshop a decision was made to organize quality awareness training for the rest of the organization's staff. It was decided that these training events were to be held in-house.

On another occasion I was contracted to run a TQM awareness workshop for a medium-sized, highly successful distribution company. The workshop for the chairman, managing director and executive board was held in the company's small boardroom over a Friday afternoon/evening and all day Saturday. As a consequence of this workshop, awareness training was organized for the whole workforce (about 120 people) in groups of around 15. The managing director arranged for this training to be carried out in a comfortable hotel nearby and it was conducted during normal working hours.

It is important to recognize that neither of these decisions was taken at a conscious level. This is particularly true in the first instance. At no point during the first workshop did any member of the senior management team discuss the possible message that would be conveyed to the organization's staff as a result of the decisions taken concerning training venues: i.e. plush for us, standard for them. Whether any individual member of the team had reservations or not I do not know, but none were aired. I approached the problem by attempting to draw attention to the symbolism of management actions in a general sense. Everyone nodded in agreement that 'symbolic leadership' and 'walking the talk' were good things but no one seemed to make the connection between the recital of these management liturgies and the decisions that had previously been taken. In the second instance the decision concerning venues was also taken automatically and without conscious deliberation, but the implicit message conveyed to staff was completely different.

Discussing the undiscussibles

If there is one single principle that exemplifies the TQ approach to management it is the overriding focus on clarity and accuracy of information. Information is critical to effective management; without relevant and accurate information effective management is rendered impossible. What occurs in the absence of such information may be described as pseudo-management. I believe that the majority of organizations are pseudo-managed. This is because those responsible for making critical decisions are not in possession of information that directly bears on the operational consequences of those decisions. And the higher ranking a manager is, the less likely it is that he or she will be aware of the fact that serious discrepancies often exist between what is said to be the case and what actually is the case.

At the very beginning of this book I suggested that the majority of managers are aware of only a fraction of the 'unofficial' information that exists within their particular domain of responsibility. Therefore, as we ascend the management hierarchy, this percentage of 'hidden information' increases dramatically. Because hidden information of this sort is not conveyed to the level above, it is highly likely that strategic decisions made at the top of an organization that comprises a significant number of levels will have been based, at least in part, on information and assumptions that are incorrect, distorted or incomplete.

Experience strongly indicates that many organizations comprise official and unofficial elements. The 'official organization' is composed of the ostensive aims and objectives, declared working practices, formal lines of authority and communication, statutory and legal obligations and publicly stated *modus operandi* of the establishment concerned. The 'unofficial organization' in contrast comprises all the internecine power struggles, unauthorized working practices, informal authority systems, rumour networks, shortcuts, unarticulated beliefs and hidden agendas that exist under the surface. In the majority of instances the unofficial organization is the place where all the important action happens. We must ask ourselves why this situation arises and why it is so common.

Them and us

> Work is of two kinds: first, altering the position of matter at or near the earth's surface relatively to other such matter; second, telling other people to do so. The first kind is unpleasant and ill paid; the second is pleasant and highly paid.
>
> *Bertrand Russell*

A substantial proportion of people are, at best, indifferent to the organizations they work for and frequently contemptuous of those who manage them. Too often their feelings are completely understandable. Many managers simply do not have a clue about the essential skills involved in managing people. This is a sad indictment of the working practices current in many organizations and of the philosophy and effectiveness of management development programmes. While I accept that management is often a difficult job and that managers must occasionally take decisions that are bound to be unpopular in some quarters, the general level of dissatisfaction that seems to exist across all sectors of the economy is positively alarming. Let me give a real life example of the extent to which such dissatisfaction can run.

I interviewed a number of front-line employees of a well-known manufacturer of domestic goods that had recently made a spectacular and highly damaging marketing blunder. This had been seized upon by the national press, television and radio. It was an organizational nightmare. However, the reaction of many of the staff I talked to was one of acute amusement at the public embarrassment caused to the company's management and delight in the fact that a number of senior heads had rolled as a consequence of it. This is a very serious state of affairs indeed. The extent of the problem can be further appreciated by the fact that the group I talked to included people with families and mortgages who were faced with the very real possibility of losing their jobs in an area that offered extremely limited opportunities of obtaining another position and certainly none in which they would be able to achieve the level of remuneration they currently enjoyed. Yet it cheered many of them enormously to read the extremely damaging reports of mismanagement which appeared in the national and local press. It was clear that a horrendous division existed between management and workers and it was painfully evident that the people I talked to felt no loyalty whatsoever to their company. Those who found little to feel cheered by were simply contemptuous of the management in general. Why had they come to feel this way? I doubt that they were recruited into the organization with these attitudes, therefore they must have developed as a direct consequence of their experiences within it.

Although this is an extreme case I believe it is symptomatic of a general malaise. Too many people despise their bosses and consequently the organizations in which they are employed. But, of course, such facts are usually undiscussible. Why do such serious divisions arise within organizations? And why do they occur with the monotonous regularity that can so clearly be seen when individuals speak honestly about their feelings towards their organizations and their managers? Serious problems exist, and they are widespread.

The central challenge of management is to structure and operate organizations in ways that maximize the potential of existing resources—physical, financial and human—for the benefit of the organization's customers. And the most important of these resources, by far, is the human one. In making this claim I am very aware that in recent years sermons on the theme of 'our people are our greatest asset' have often been over zealous and sometimes extremely tedious. However, the fact that it is people who make the difference has already become obvious in many sectors and it will increasingly become so in others. The reasons for this are varied but one major contributory factor is the widespread availability of new technology. The much improved flexibility and adaptability of new technology, combined with a parallel reduction in costs, means that competitive advantage cannot be achieved and sustained through technological superiority alone. In many areas, such as banking, insurance, and retailing, the technology is essentially universal. Competitive advantage therefore can only be achieved through the continuing development of innovative products and services, the reduction of waste, improved productivity and the delivery of service quality.

All of these things come from people and not machines. The only thing that essentially differentiates one bank, one insurance provider or one supermarket chain from another is the people who work in them. If one organization corners its particular market by providing a superior banking environment, a more flexible insurance package or a greater range of desirable products then it will be because the people who work for that particular organization make better decisions and provide a better service than the people who work for the others. It is as simple, and as difficult, as that. People are the key to competitive advantage, long-term security, quality and productivity. When organizations are structured and managed in ways that encourage the full development and contribution of their people, the potential for quality and continuous improvement is tremendous. As the example above is pessimistic, let us briefly examine the positive side of the human relations coin.

Front-line workers in a US gear-production plant noticed that the dyes on one or two power presses lasted longer than they did on others. Curious, they tried to work out what the possible cause could be. After investigation and deliberation they concluded that the central reason was that the operator of the particular machines concerned usually switched the presses on before collecting the raw materials required to operate the shift. They guessed that this 15–20 minute pre-heating of the dye in the press made it last much longer, and they were right.

In retrospect this discovery seems obvious, but no one had noticed it before: *and it is highly likely that without the conscious efforts of these front-line staff, no one ever would.* Improvement opportunities such as this, which have a quantifiable impact on the bottom line so beloved of financially oriented 'real world' managers, exist in abundance within all organizations. Many improvement opportunities are, I am convinced, already known to exist by people who have no inclination to communicate them to the organizations in which they are employed. These unrealized improvement opportunities represent real competitive losses to the organization. Of course, if every organization has a similar quota of disinterested or disillusioned employees then the whole system equalizes and, although everyone is missing significant opportunities for improvement, no one is actually disadvantaged in the market-place.

This situation, which was fairly universal until recent years and still exists in many sectors, is similar to the practice of handicapping which is used in horse-racing. As long as individual organizations are more or less equally handicapped in this way the overall impression is that nothing much is amiss in any of them. Problems only emerge when one or more competing organizations begin to rid themselves of their self-administered shackles. This is precisely what happened in relation to the demise of the British motorcycle and electronics industries and it will continue to happen as the pioneering organizations in all sectors break down the internal barriers that are effectively throttling their development. Let us consider the reasons why these barriers arise.

Tribal warfare

A healthy organization should, in many ways, resemble a healthy nation. Unfortunately the reality is usually quite different. Many organizations effectively comprise uneasy alliances between collections of hostile tribes. The general *modus operandi* in such organizations is something akin to an armed truce, with regular skirmishes occurring on the fringes of occupied territories and the occasional pitched battle in centre-field (usually during budget allocation periods). Personal experience has led me to the conclusion that this internecine warfare is often the major reason why many people actually bother to turn up for work. Scoring points off 'the enemy', by thwarting the organization's control systems or, in the case of management, by maximizing the acquisition of finite resources, can become an overriding passion. It is difficult to underestimate the power, and idiocy, of such intrigues and squabbles.

Again a real-life example will be relevant. I once worked in a college of further/higher education (organizations where such activities border on the surreal) in which a small storeroom became available as a result of reorganizing the purchasing function. Anyone who currently works, or has worked, within the further/higher education sector will immediately appreciate the significance of this event. The acquisition of rooms appears to constitute much of senior management's principal concerns in educational establishments.

Once the forthcoming availability of this room was confirmed, via the rumour network, the chiefs of the two leading tribes, engineering and business studies, began what was in essence a detailed military campaign. At first each department head feigned outward indifference while lobbying intensely behind the scenes. However, at the next relevant meeting of senior management the heads of both departments set out formal bids for the acquisition of this room. The style and delivery of these proposals, and the amount of detailed work that had obviously gone into their preparation, would have led a naive observer to conclude that the issue was a matter of life or death for each of the departments concerned. Half a day was wasted on repetitive and specious arguments that frequently referred to events and squabbles that had occurred at various instances in the dim and distant past. It finally concluded in acrimonious stalemate.

The Principal ultimately resolved the issue by privately arranging for the general studies department, an insignificant player in the vast majority of educational establishments, to cobble together a bid and subsequently allocated the room to them. Even then the head of engineering contrived, over a period of some months, to persuade the general studies head to let him have some access to this room. I very much doubt that either department actually needed the room for operational reasons since both could easily have created more space simply by rearranging a few storage areas in their existing domains. It was simply a power game. However juvenile such things are, petty group rivalries of this sort constitute a serious obstacle to organizational effectiveness.

How and why does group rivalry emerge? In order to understand the dynamics involved we must begin by recognizing that group rivalry is based on perceived group differences. After all, if there are no perceivable differences between collections of individuals there can be no group rivalries. Group rivalry therefore begins with the process of in-group identification and out-group differentiation: the realization or desire to communicate that there is a clear division between 'us' and 'them'. In-group identification is frequently communicated through the possession of certain privileges, status symbols, dress and the use of group-specific jargon. The wearing of uniforms is a classic means of communicating group membership, whether it be of the Household Cavalry, Hell's Angels or the local firm of solicitors. IBM acquired the nickname 'Big Blue' as a result of the fact that its sales and management 'uniform' comprised an obligatory dark blue suit and white shirt.

Group identification and the establishment of group loyalties is virtually inevitable; it is simply human nature. We have already seen that groups are important and that group membership satisfies a number of important social and psychological needs. The key management challenge, of course, is to ensure that group identification and group loyalties are consistent with the aims and well-being of the organization as a whole. Interdepartmental rivalries and symbolic expressions of status differentials are extremely damaging to organizations; they encourage feelings of superiority and an inflated sense of self-importance in those who find the need for them, and they create resentment in others.

One of the toughest challenges facing all quality initiatives is finding ways of breaking down the most destructive 'them and us' barrier of all, the one that has historically existed between managers and managed. It is extremely depressing to realize that as we approach the beginning of a new millennium our organizations are largely managed in ways that are more reminiscent of the beginning of the industrial revolution. This historical divisions between 'gaffer' and 'labour' are still to be found all around us. Consider, for example, the symbolically powerful issue of working dress. One has only to enter a branch of any of the larger food retailers to see evidence of the fact that ludicrous class divisions concerning appropriate work attire continue to exist. The unfortunate staff of these organizations are commonly required to wear a working uniform that has clearly been designed by someone who was immensely impressed by the film *2001—A Space Odyssey*. Members of the store's management team, in contrast, usually deck themselves out in the sort of garb that communicates the fact that they in turn have been extremely moved by *Dallas*. While such things are, at an adult level, rather trivial and silly, they actually have serious ramifications for organizational effectiveness. They create and sustain demeaning divisions and they foster resentment and dislike.

I can understand that many organizations such as large retailers, banks, building societies and public services need their staff to be clearly identifiable, as customers require it, but I cannot see any reason for excluding management from this requirement. I, as a customer, do not differentiate between a bank teller and a bank manager or a check-out operator and a supermarket manager. They are both employees of the organization concerned and if it is beneficial for one to wear a specific uniform of identification, why not the other? If this were to be an organizational requirement we would probably witness a substantial reduction in the pomposity and arrogance that frequently accompanies the wearing of a suit. I would also wager that the design of these uniforms would be rapidly entrusted to an individual who actually resides on this planet.

The successful implementation of TQM is as much concerned with the removal of unnecessary and petty institutionalized divisions as it is with the control and continuous improvement of key processes. TQM is about the cost-effective alignment of all the organization's resources in the service of the customer and a belief in the principle of never-ending improvement. This is quite a lot to ask of people. We cannot legislate for it and it cannot be policed. *People must willingly agree to do it*: there is no other way. We will not attain the levels of commitment required to achieve this, however, if people do not believe that they are treated equitably and with respect. Demeaning practices and institutionalized symbols of superiority must be considered very carefully; they create resentment and militate against total commitment. Organizations must ask themselves whether the price of keeping such symbols is actually worth paying.

The introduction of a quality initiative is frequently accompanied by a great deal of rhetoric on the topic of cultural change within the organization. Talk, however, is cheap, and as with most aspects of human life people will wait to see what others, particularly senior managers, actually do as opposed to what they say they will do. Rhetoric is no substitute for action. If managers really wish to ensure that everyone plays a 'team game' then they, above all others, must demonstrate a real willingness to do so. TQM requires every individual in the organization to play his or her particular part to the full. This will not happen if it is institutionally implied that some of the players are second-class citizens. Ultimately, the development of quality is inexorably linked to the development of equality.

SUMMARY AND KEY POINTS

- People are the key to quality and we must understand the ways in which psychological characteristics, individual and social, influence TQ initiatives.
- People frequently act in ways that are directly opposed to their freely-chosen long-term aims. TQ initiatives require that we manage instinctual drives effectively and act collaboratively in pursuit of long-term gains for all.
- Short-term thinking encourages management behaviours that are primarily reactive and may lead to unwarranted risk-taking. It also encourages the potentially damaging attitude that the acquisition and retention of revenue is the organization's governing concern. Long-term thinking encourages discussion and reflection and a tendency to evaluate all short-term opportunities in relation to the achievement of long-term aims. Long-term thinking encourages the notion of *investment* as well as expenditure and revenue enhancement.
- An important constituent of all TQM initiatives is the collection and use of accurate data and the application of statistical concepts and techniques. Managers must develop their general 'feel' for numbers and gain a deeper appreciation of the nature of probability as it applies to individual and organizational effectiveness.
- Organizations are faced with very different forms of challenge in implementing TQM and managers need to be aware of the profound nature of these differences. These challenges can usefully be categorized as puzzles, problems and facts. The solution of puzzles requires effective and thorough data collection and the application of systematic techniques and logical thought processes. Puzzles can be solved theoretically and experimentally and solutions proved. Once a puzzle has been solved in one context the general form of solution used can be transferred to similar contexts. The vast majority of literature

that deals with generic 'problem-solving techniques' is actually concerned with puzzle-solving.

Problems involve specific situations, incomplete or inaccurate data, probabilities, unknowable future situations and unique configurations of key variables. As such, problems do not lend themselves to the application of generic resolution techniques. A great deal can be learned from specific instances of problem resolution. However, what can be learned is best expressed in terms of general values, concepts and principles rather than specific, repeatable procedures. Problems therefore require judgement. Problems constitute the biggest threats and the greatest opportunities that organizations face.

Facts are neither puzzles nor problems but they may be confused for either. Facts are realities. A great deal of time can be wasted on futile attempts at 'solving' facts. Conversely facts may be deemed too unpalatable for consideration and therefore be denied. However, attempting to ignore an important fact in the hope that it will somehow go away, is a sure route to disaster. A number of important facts must be faced in relation to the implementation of TQM within organizations.

- Groups of people tend to take greater collective risks than would each individual acting alone. Poorly managed groups also encourage conformity, tend to suppress sensitive information and inhibit critical thinking. Uncritical group cohesion tends to amplify the convictions of group leaders and encourage them to become more extreme in their views.

- Many organizations are characterized by internal divisions, destructive competition and high levels of distrust between managers and managed. Many of these divisions can be traced to historically institutionalized symbols of inequality. Organizations must act to break down institutionalized divisions and provide an environment in which group loyalties and natural competitive tendencies can be harnessed for the benefit of the organization as a whole.

Concluding remarks

I hope that the reader is not overly daunted by the material covered in this section of the book and the challenges that are consequently revealed. As the psychologist Paul Watzlawick has commented, 'The situation is hopeless but not serious!' It was my explicit intention, however, that this section should adequately describe the nature of the human challenge we face in attempting to implement TQ initiatives within organizations. In many ways the principles and operating procedures of TQM represent a 180 degree turn in traditional concepts of the nature of work, management and the structure of organizations. Unfortunately too many people underestimate the profound nature of this change.

I sometimes wonder, and I must regrettably admit that these periods of doubt have all occurred while in the presence of senior managers, whether TQM will become an early reality in anything other than a limited number of instances. I fully understand the trepidation and covert resistance involved. The changes that will inevitably occur in organizational structures and reward systems coupled with the growth of organizational democracy that is implicit in the philosophy of TQM does not paint a very rosy future for those who covet power or relish status symbols, extravagant emoluments and exalted positions.

Unfortunately such things constitute much of the current trappings of management success. Our concept of effective management, and therefore of effective managers, requires drastic re-evaluation. Some may find the outcome of this re-evaluation disconcerting to say the least. Progress, however, is inevitable, markets will ensure that this is so. I am absolutely convinced that organizations that succeed in developing and harnessing the freely given talents of all their people will inevitably (and much faster than most imagine) supersede those who blindly cling to dysfunctional methods of management and organization. My only concern is for those who will, unwittingly and without their consent, perish along with the latter.

Part III

Evolve and survive

'The tragedy and the magnificence of *Homo sapiens* together rise
from the same smokey truth, that we alone among the animal
species refuse to acknowledge natural law.'

Robert Ardrey

In the previous section I outlined some of the important
psychological challenges, individual and social, that must be faced
if we are to implement the philosophy of TQM within organizations.
In the final sections of the book I will suggest ways in which the
development of TQM can be advanced. I will make use of a number
of models and metaphors for understanding the dynamics of
organizations. I fully realize, however, that the use of models and
metaphors can be a precarious business and I have outlined some of
the more important limitations of modelling techniques below.

10

The evolutionary organization

Writers on organizational theory are fond of using metaphors to expound their views and to discuss the possibilities for organizational development and change. One of the difficulties of using metaphors, however, is that applications can become rather fanciful and divorced from the practicalities of day-to-day operations. After all, metaphors are analogous representations of organizations and are therefore applicable only up to a point. The art, of course, is to know when that point has been reached. However, this caveat not withstanding, it is obviously necessary for us to understand (as best we can) the dynamics of organizations, particularly in relation to the management of change, and the realistic employment of suitable metaphors can be extremely enlightening. The variety available for understanding organizations is considerable and ranges from the mechanical through the political and psychic to the biological.[18] As this book is concerned with the human dimension of quality it is fitting that I should apply the human perspective to an analysis of the structure and function of organizations themselves, while keeping within the bounds of common sense. In the sections that follow I will use human evolution as a metaphor for understanding organizations.

What are the possible benefits of thinking of organizations as being in some senses similar to human beings? I believe that the judicious application of this metaphor can yield important insights about critical organizational processes and help us make sense of the many difficulties we face in implementing TQM. As Tom Peters has rightly commented, organizations, in a fundamental sense, are people. The previous section has shown that people are rapidly becoming the single most important factor in organizational effectiveness and thus competitive advantage. This idea, of course, is pretty standard fare these days, but what about the idea that we can consider the total organization as being similar to a person? A number of interesting and potentially illuminating questions arise when this perspective is taken. For instance, can organizations be usefully considered as having 'personalities'? Do they, in some sense, have 'brains'? Do they have a 'nervous system'? Can they become physically or mentally 'ill'?

Literally, of course, they have none of these attributes or propensities, buy symbolically they do. Every organization I have ever worked in has had a *modus operandi* that could usefully be described as its particular 'personality'. Likewise, the traditional model of organizations has considered management functions, such as strategic decision-making and planning, data analysis and policy-making as representing the cerebral or 'higher brain' elements of its operations (some discussion on the weaknesses of this parallel will be presented in a later section).

The idea that organizations possess 'nervous systems' is relatively unproblematic. The principal function of the nervous system in animals and man is the transfer of information. This metaphor readily applies to organizational communications; indeed the sophisticated IT systems that exist in many organizations are very similar to the nervous systems of living organisms.

As to the 'physical' and 'psychological' condition of organizations, these can be thought of as the organization's material (i.e. capital, manpower, equipment) and non-material (i.e. ideas, creativity, attitudes, moods) resources, respectively. In this way it is acceptable to think of organizations in terms of physical or psychological well-being.

Traditionally, the great majority of management effort and concern has focused on the physical rather than the psychological resources of organizations. This, of course, is understandable; physical resources are readily quantified, controlled and monitored and their impact on organizational effectiveness is clear to see. In many ways they represent the 'hard' elements of organizational and management theories. The psychological elements are, in contrast, much more difficult to quantify and analyse. Such areas represent the 'soft' part of organizational study, the 'touchy-feely' element that turns so many managers off. The problem of course is that it is precisely this soft element that is in fact growing in importance, particularly in terms of TQM. TQM is principally concerned with the dynamics of commitment and capability, which are largely a function of perception, attitudes and feelings of self-worth; they are about 'hearts and minds'. These, of course, are ultimately questions of psychological well-being and they are extremely relevant to an understanding of the challenges we face in implementing TQ initiatives.

At the most fundamental level we must ask ourselves why the implementation of TQM should be desirable in the first place? The answer, or at least a good portion of the answer, must have to do with notions of long-term survival. In order to achieve this aim it is necessary to understand the relevant internal and external forces that are at play. Again we can learn much from a consideration of the evolution of living things, a topic we will explore below.

Using models of organizations

Models and metaphors (from now on I will refer to both as models) are useful to the extent that they enable us to perceive situations in constructively different ways. In other words they are useful when they help us to be more creative problem-solvers. One of the most important potential benefits of using models is that they can help us see possibilities that were not previously available to us. Also, the use of suitable models may enable us to make more effective sense of the situations we face. Models must, however, be chosen with care. If they are to be of practical use there must be sufficient similarity between the situation and the model for realistic comparisons to be made but there must also be sufficient differences present for us to gain useful insights from the transference of concepts and ideas. I list below some of the major similarities, and their relative 'strengths', that exist between organizations and human beings, followed by some of the important differences.

'Strong' similarities between human beings and organizations

- Both are subject to general laws of physics and biology such as the second law of thermodynamics and evolution through natural selection.
- Both are 'open systems', that is, human beings and organizations must interact with the external environment in order to survive.
- Both are 'dynamic systems' that is both are in a constant state of flux about a point of equilibrium.
- Both are composed of functional units with specific capabilities

which must operate effectively and in unison with other functional units.

- Both are susceptible to externally or internally generated pressures.

'Medium-strength' similarities between human beings and organizations

- Both can be considered to progress through developmental stages such as 'childhood', 'adolescence' 'maturity'.
- Both can be considered as having distinctive 'personalities'.
- Both can be considered as possessing a particular level of physical health.
- Both can be considered as possessing a particular level of psychological health.
- Both can be considered as having public and private thoughts, feelings and motives.
- Both can be considered as being capable of learning.
- Both can be considered as being capable of self-generated change.

Major differences between human beings and organizations

- Organizations, unlike human beings, are theoretically capable of existing indefinitely (organizations can be considered as being equivalent to 'species' in evolutionary theory).
- Organizations, unlike human beings, have cognitive capabilities distributed throughout their 'bodies'.
- Organizations, unlike human beings, are theoretically capable of unlimited change.

Understanding survival

I hope that the brief analysis of similarities and differences outlined above provides justification for drawing parallels between human beings and organizations. Both involve complex internal and external interactions and both utilize higher mental functions. Also, as the discussion that follows will illustrate, organizations can be considered as being subject to fundamental pressures characteristic of evolution by natural selection.

One of the principal benefits that can be obtained from a sensible comparison between human beings and organizations stems from the fact that human beings are a 'successful' species in the sense that we have managed to adapt (so far!) to the changes in the external environment which have occurred since the emergence of our primordial ancestors some 2.5 million years ago. Although chance will have played its part in our survival, and although we are far from perfect, we are still here and there are important lessons to be learned from our evolutionary journey. In the sections that follow I will outline the major processes involved in the evolution of living organisms which contain powerful lessons for the development of organizations.

The survival of any living organism (and for the purposes of this discussion an organization can usefully be thought of as a living thing) depends upon two principal factors:

- the ability to maintain internal consistency
- the potential to adapt to a changing environment.

The interplay between these two factors constitutes a delicate balancing act. By internal consistency I mean that the organism must, as a bare minimum, maintain the effectiveness of its vital internal processes over time. For example, if a living thing is to survive it must be able to take in material from its environment (food, air, water, etc.) and convert this material into the energy, molecules, proteins and so on that maintain its vital functions, replace worn cells and repair damage. If the internal processes that convert food into energy and proteins fail, then the organism will die. It is also clear that the processes that utilize converted foodstuffs must remain efficient over time. Cell reproduction is a classic example. The processes through which defunct cells are renewed must be organized so that replacement cells are biologically and functionally appropriate for the organism concerned. If these replacement processes are altered in some way they may produce cells that do not function effectively or, even worse, cells that are lethal to the organism; cancer cells are a prime example. Internal consistency therefore is the process of keeping the organism's key functions stable over time (this is the major concern of many of the central techniques of TQM, particularly statistical process control). Of course this would be fine if the external environment also remained constant but unfortunately it does not. Maintaining constancy is therefore a potentially dangerous strategy for any living organism (or, more correctly, any species) that exists in a changing environment.

Balancing stability and change

In order to combat the potential dangers involved in maintaining constancy in an uncertain environment living things occasionally show random mutations in critical processes. These random mutations create an individual organism that is a variation on the 'standard' model of organism concerned. The amount of 'deviation from the norm' that such mutations produce is commonly very small (for reasons given below) and, of course, there is absolutely no guarantee that any such variation will confer any advantage on the particular individual in which it occurs. Indeed as organisms become more and more complex it is highly likely that any significant changes to the basic design will actually result in disadvantage rather than advantage.

Imagine, for example, that someone makes a random change to the design specifications for the circuitry of a complex computer or the mechanism of a precision mechanical chronometer. It is extremely unlikely that such a random change will improve the functional qualities of either *if the external environment remains constant.* However, if random changes to the design specifications are coincidentally accompanied by certain changes in the external environment, these random alterations may then prove to have positive or negative consequences. For example, if we arbitrarily decide to seal hermetically every single joint in our mechanical chronometer this will have no consequences whatsoever for its reliability or accuracy under normal operating conditions. But if these conditions change substantially, say that the environment becomes extremely humid or dusty, then the hermetic sealing will convey an 'advantage' to the particular chronometer that possesses it in that it will operate longer and maintain greater accuracy.

This is precisely the mechanism through which evolution operates. Small changes to the basic 'blueprint' (the genetic instructions to build a living organism) occur via random mutations and these random mutations result in an individual organism that is slightly different from his or her brothers and sisters. Natural selection then operates in one of three ways. If the difference confers no particular advantage or disadvantage on the individual it is 'ignored' by the environment. If the change confers some form of advantage to the individual it is 'selected in' by the environment. If the change confers some form of disadvantage to the individual it is 'selected out' by the environment. The important point to note here is that changes to the basic blueprint (genetic mutations in the case of living things) occur *before* the environment acts upon them in one of the three ways described above. In other words any advantage (or disadvantage) conferred by genetic mutations is purely a chance occurrence.

This is an important point and it is commonly misunderstood. People frequently talk of animals and insects 'adapting' to particular insecticides or poisons as if internal protection mechanisms had been created within them as a response to the poison. This, however, is frequently not the case. If a species becomes immune to a particular poison it is because the poison has eradicated all those members who did not have some level of natural protection from it in the first place. The introduction of the poison simply confers an advantage on those members of the species who already have some level of natural immunity to it. The main point to note is that until the advent of a poisonous environment (the introduction of Warfarin is a good example here) the genes that conferred protection on particular individuals were probably not at all important in influencing their chances of survival. Until the advent of the poisonous environment it is likely that they were superfluous. However, during the period before the advent of the poison this 'protection' is achieved at a price, the price being the energy required to synthesize the molecules which provide the subsequent protection. The successful evolution of a species can therefore be considered as being based, in part, on the principle of *investment* against uncertainty. The actual nature of this investment can be described as *diversity about a theme*. Nature continually experiments by generating slight variations on a basic design. A proportion of these may prove beneficial in some way to the individual concerned, likewise a proportion will probably confer some type of disadvantage; the vast majority of these minor variations will be neutral. However, continuous variation, that is *continuous change*, is the key to long-term survival in a volatile environment.

11

Management implications

What does all this have to do with the management of organizations?
A great deal. Organizations, like living things, exist in competitive
and volatile environments. In the case of private sector organizations
the competitive environment is the market-place and the bottom line
is profitability. In the case of public sector organizations the
competitive environment can be considered to be the public
spending purse and the bottom line is accountability. In each case
profitability and accountability depend on the relationship between
the resources expended to maintain internal consistency and those
available for action in the particular environment concerned. All
living organisms need a certain amount of energy simply to maintain
vital internal processes. Only energy that is surplus to these internal
requirements can therefore be used to act in the environment.
Obviously it is possible for a situation to arise in which energy intake
is merely adequate to maintain internal consistency, in other words
there is no surplus energy available to act in the environment. In
such a situation a living organism would literally require 'spoon-
feeding' in order to survive. Situations such as this rarely occur in the
natural world, it is not an environment particularly noted for its
altruistic properties. Living organisms that approach such a state will
be highly susceptible to extinction by virtue of the fact that they
either become catatonically ineffective at obtaining the essential
resources that may be freely available (because they become
immobilized by their internal energy requirements) or because
they fail in the competition for limited resources. Although the first
situation (catatonic ineffectiveness) is not a common occurrence in
the natural world there is some evidence that an interesting example
may actually be happening at the present time.

Evolutionary pressures, in general, tend to favour increasing size
in mammals and reptiles. This, of course, is a highly precarious

business for the species concerned (witness the fate of the dinosaurs). Currently, this selection pressure is threatening the future of the African lion. Male lions gain access to females as a result of competition with other males. As far as this competition goes, size is an advantage. But increasing size is damaging to long-term survival. If you are a male lion then the bigger you are the better are your chances of acquiring mates, with the consequent opportunity to promulgate your genes. But the bigger you are the more food you need simply to maintain body functions and the less efficient you become at hunting. Currently, male lions play a very minor role in the acquisition of food, merely helping to flush out game which the female lions then hunt down. There may come a point, if selection for ever-increasing size of males continues, where the amount of food required simply to maintain basic energy levels in male lions is such that females are hunting almost continually and there is little or no time, or indeed energy, left available for the extra-curricular activities required to produce an adequate supply of new lions!

The balance between size and activity is therefore problematic and the limiting factors described above in relation to living things apply equally forcefully to organizations. All organizations must devote a proportion of their resources to the maintenance of internal structures and functions—it is the organizational equivalent of the metabolic overheads required of living things—but these resources are consumed at the expense of action in the environment. Clearly some optimizing mechanism is required to operate if a sensible balance between maintenance and action is to be achieved. Left to themselves, internal organizational processes show a remarkable tendency to follow Parkinson's Law as work (internal work that is) expands so as to fill the time available for its completion. In reality Parkinson was only partly correct in the determination of this law. Practical experience strongly suggests that internal work usually expands beyond the time available for its completion, thus necessitating the recruitment of extra staff and/or the purchase of yet more sophisticated IT systems.

The evolutionary lesson to be learned is that a sensible balance must be maintained between resources devoted to the maintenance of internal functions and those that are focused on the environment in which the organization operates. Personal experience indicates that decisions concerning proposed allocations of resources can be tackled effectively through the use of a few basic questions. The most valuable of these questions is: *How, precisely, will the expenditure under consideration benefit our external customers?* This is commonly quite a show-stopper but it certainly sharpens people up; it also exposes woolly thinking and brings hidden agendas into the open.

The central point, however, is that questions such as this help focus attention on the external environment and prevent the development of an overly myopic focus on the internal. Organizations, if left to their own devices, usually develop a strong internal focus. My own research on this topic indicates that the majority of an organization's employees (at all levels) rarely think in terms of customers or the external environment. This is virtually inevitable given the way most organizations are structured and operated. Research into the agendas and content of many organizational communications indicates that meetings are principally concerned with internal issues, memos are about internal issues, gossip is about internal issues, the rumour network is about internal issues and so on. This amounts to an incredible waste of mental energy. Again we can benefit from a comparison between organizations and living things.

Consider the nature of the complex information mechanisms (such as vision and hearing) that have evolved in living things and then ask yourself a simple question. Are these information mechanisms directed at the internal or the external environment? The answer, of course, is clear. Living things have not survived by systematically focusing on their navels: they have survived because they have evolved increasingly effective mechanisms for obtaining critical information about the world around them. Living things survive because their information-gathering and processing mechanisms are externally focused: information from the environment is accorded paramount importance.

Excessive quantities of internally focused information make the passage of other information more difficult; they create 'noise' in the information processing systems that blocks or distorts messages from the external environment. Of course some level of internal communication is absolutely necessary to survival. Pain, for example, signals that something is amiss within the internal environment. Thirst and hunger signal the need for action. In less complex life-forms internal communications are unproblematic, they are purely functional. In complex life-forms, such as man, internal communications may become dysfunctional; phobias, irrational fears, psychosomatic disorders and some forms of mental illness are classic examples. Again there are strong parallels with organizations. Internal organizational communications become dysfunctional if they generate levels of 'noise' that inhibit the inward communication of vital information from the external environment or prevent important information from the internal environment being registered. This point will be discussed in detail in a later section.

The majority of internally focused information in organizations is concerned with functionality. Such information is typically about 'work in progress' and involves questions of responsibility and prioritization, usually the 'what, where and how' of day-to-day operations. What department do I work for? Where do I work within it? What are the principal requirements of my job? How can I organize these requirements? How can I achieve my work objectives?

Externally focused information, in contrast, is concerned with questions of purpose rather than function. What is the overall purpose of my organization? Why is my section or department important in achieving this purpose? Why is my job important in achieving my section or department's purpose? What is the purpose of organizing in the way I do? Why am I aiming to achieve my particular work objectives? The move away from questions about 'what, where and how' to those which ask 'what for and why' represents a critical shift in emphasis from the inner to the outer. The answer to the first type of question will largely be concerned with established ways of doing things while the second type is more concerned with the purpose and value of various activities.

When organizations ask questions about the purpose and value of specific activities (this is usually a very rare occurrence) they must concern themselves with the proportion of answers that are founded on internal criteria only. In the overwhelming majority of instances the most important criteria upon which organizational activities should be evaluated originate outside of the organization's boundaries, i.e. in the external environment.

Organizations must establish procedures and systems which ensure that important information from the external environment affects the internal environment. It is only through such mechanisms that organizations, or living things, are able to adapt effectively to changing circumstances and the more sensitive these information-gathering mechanisms are the earlier the organization will be able to respond.

The point made above is also, of course, relevant to the various 'internal environments' that exist within the organization's boundaries. These internal environments, commonly known as departments, must be evaluated, at least in part, by those who operate outside of them and are affected by the activities of the particular departments concerned.

Letting go of the horse

In the village in which I live the story is told of a somewhat philosophical farmer who apparently lived in the area during the period of the Napoleonic wars. I am certain that this story, or variations of it, is told in innumerable other towns and villages where, of course, our hero assumes the appropriate nationality involved! In our village, however, there is no doubt whatever that the farmer was Welsh. The story, it is actually more of a parable, is interesting.

Our farmer, a leading light in the community and something of a sage, operates very successfully largely as a result of two particular pieces of good fortune. First, his only son is an extremely talented and industrious worker and, second, he is the proud owner of a remarkable stallion who has no equal in terms of strength and durability. These advantages, along with his own not inconsiderable efforts, enable him to enjoy a prosperous and comfortable lifestyle. One fine day, however, the horse, for no apparent reason, bolts off and disappears into the local mountains. The farmer and his son search for days but with no success. When, however, neighbours express their genuine sympathy at this loss they are extremely surprised by the farmer's response, which is: 'Perhaps, perhaps not'.

Weeks pass and one morning the farmer wakes to find that not only has the stallion returned but he has brought with him two fine wild mares, one of them obviously in foal. A celebration is arranged and now neighbours congratulate him on his good fortune. Again they are perplexed by his response: 'Perhaps, perhaps not'. A few days later his son begins the process of domesticating the wild horses and is thrown from one of the mares, breaking both his legs. Again the consolation from neighbours, and again the perplexing: 'Perhaps, perhaps not'.

In the week following this accident, press-gangs storm the area kidnapping fit young men for forced service in the King's navy, and almost certain death. Every farmer's son, but one, is taken, for of course the gang has no use for a young man with two broken legs.

Apocryphal though it is the story has a relevant message, events can have very different short- and long-term effects. The future, as we have already noted, is unpredictable. It is not utterly chaotic but it is highly probabilistic. We simply do not know what the longer-term effects of particular actions will be.

What organizational lessons can be learned from the discussion so far? We saw in the previous section that biological evolution operates from two fundamental principles: control and variation. That is, the long-term survival of a species depends upon a balance between the stability of fundamental reproductive processes (such as the ability to produce the genetic information required to build a viable human being) and the ability to generate limited variation between individuals within the species, i.e. balance between keeping some things exactly as they are and changing others. Of course the whole point of this genetic variation (I use the word point not to imply purpose but simply to describe consequences, evolution is of course 'blind') is to protect the species from inevitable extinction if a highly contagious disease arose from which no member of the species was naturally immune (at least to some degree). Genetic diversity provides a running chance that some at least may be immune. AIDS is a practical example here. Early predictions of global doom ignored the reality of genetic diversity. Recent studies of high-risk individuals in Kenya has indicated that a proportion have a natural immunity to infection by the AIDS virus.

The organizational implications of all this are clear. We must balance stability with diversity, continuity with change, and recognize the fact that continuous investment is an absolute necessity for long-term survival. We must also recognize the fact that we cannot guarantee that any particular investment will yield benefits in the long term. That is the nature of the game we are in. Long-term survival is a problem and not a puzzle because the future external environment cannot be described with precision.

Having made this point, however, we can take action to ensure that the majority of the investments we make are at least reasonable bets. Organizational evolution has one great advantage over biological evolution: it is not blind. We must ensure that we make use of all the relevant information available to us. In the absence of relevant information, however, investment in variation must simply be a case of 'suck it and see' (which is precisely the way it works in the natural world). Nature essentially plays a 'numbers game', producing random variations on a theme. These experiments are, however, blind guesses and the vast majority of them are consequently of no value to the organism concerned. We, as conscious beings, can at least attempt to model the future, identify trends and aim to act accordingly. But we must not forget that the immense complexity that exists in the world and the non-linear nature of many interactions means that the future will always produce events that we could not have predicted from an analysis of the present. Our attempts at preparing for this uncertain future must therefore include *investments that cannot be evaluated in the short term.*

Basic research and development falls into this category and this book will argue that the notion of fundamental R&D can fruitfully be extended to include the whole organization. Organizations, as we have seen, differ from human beings in that they have cognitive potential distributed throughout their functional elements. There are brains everywhere! I believe that investment in these brains constitutes the best long-term strategy for any organization. Flexibility is the only practical antidote to uncertainty and flexibility is primarily about creativity. We must develop the immense cognitive potential for creativity that exists in all organizations and recognize that we cannot always quantify the precise benefits of every single investment we make. Ultimately an act of faith will be required. Progress and development will not always be linear; life is just not like that. There will be high and low points and a lot of plateaux but continuous investment against uncertainty is a necessity for long-term survival. This strategy, of course, involves an element of risk, sometimes considerable, but from time to time we must find the courage to let go of the horse.

Managing convergent and divergent variation

Much of the literature of TQM, including the first part of this book, is concerned with the philosophy and control of process variation.

As we have already noted the origins of the modern quality movement can be traced to the fundamental principles of statistical quality control pioneered by Shewart in the USA and later developed and espoused by Deming in Japan. Our use of an evolutionary perspective, however, has indicated that the control of variation of critical processes is only one element in a viable long-term survival strategy. Essentially we must manage two different forms of variation, *convergent* and *divergent*.

The vast majority of TQM techniques are aimed at the management of covergent variation only. We saw in Part 1 of this book that the control of variation in the key elements of products and services (as perceived by the customer) is a central requirement of operational success. That requirement is not at all compromised by the ideas that follow. The control of key processes remains one of the fundamental principles of quality management.

Convergent variation

The management of convergent variation (MCV) is concerned with *maximizing the efficiency of existing processes*. The ultimate goal of MCV is the total elimination of variation and the reduction of cycle times until they become identical with process times. This is the theoretically ideal outcome of MCV; the zero-tolerance achievement of a desired target on every single occasion and with the elimination of all forms of waste. This of course represents a perfect process and, as we have seen, it can never be achieved in the natural world because it is impossible to control every single source of variation that exists. However, techniques such as SPC, Pareto Analysis and particularly Kaizen are focused primarily on the challenge of converging on this unattainable goal through the process of never-ending refinements and improvements: the 'journey that never ends'.

The pressures that an over-zealous adherence to such a philosophy can exert on those responsible for Kaizen may be immense. Two recent publications which focus on the negative consequences of a quasi-religious devotion to the principles of Kaizen can be found in *The Nissan Enigma* by Phillip Garrahan and Paul Stewart,[5] a disturbing account of working practices at the Nissan plant in Sunderland, and *Working For The Japanese* by Joseph and Suzy Fucini (see Further reading), an account of similar working practices in the Mazda plant at Flat Rock, Michigan, USA. If the contents of these two publications are accurate, and I know of no reason to assume that this is not the case, then it is clear that neither organization has instituted the quality philosophy that is advocated in this book. Both organizations, it appears, have concentrated myopically on the management of convergent variation only. This may actually be a characteristic of the Japanese approach to quality management, a tendency to become obsessive about controls (even though these controls are designed to be instilled within individuals rather than emanating from an external controlling force) and the elimination of perceived 'waste' such as unproductive time (that is time spent on activities that are not classified as 'adding value').

I believe that in the long term such a philosophy is counter-productive. It is inherently coercive and it will ultimately stifle true creativity. The drive to make improvement suggestions simply because suggestions are expected, or to win a 'numbers game', places extraordinary pressures on individuals. Some accounts claim that pressures to conform to expectations of the 'ideal worker' in Japanese firms have resulted in an average suicide rate of three workers per hour. And those who do not take their own lives must negotiate the perils of 'karoshi', the Japanese term coined in response to the phenomenon of 'death from overwork'. Apart from the dire consequences of idealistic conformance pressures they also cause intense resentment and destructive competition between individuals and teams. Again the work of Garrahan and Stewart is revealing here. We must find a sensible balance between obsessive conformity and chaotic freedom, between the management of convergent and divergent variation, if we are to maximize each organization's potential to deal effectively with an increasingly volatile and uncertain future.

Divergent variation

In terms of TQM, the management of convergent variation has a goal, unattainable though it is, of creating perfect processes. When MCV makes progress, i.e. when functional process improvements are achieved, the process involved is brought closer to a theoretical ideal. The two principal benefits of such process improvements are that they are quantifiable and they have a clear impact on the organization's operational effectiveness. The positive outcomes of process improvements include the reduction of cycle/process ratios, reductions in waste, cost reductions through the elimination of process stages, reductions in faulty components produced, reductions in operating costs, reductions in the cost of internal inspections, no-cost reductions in operating tolerances and so on. It is clear from this list of benefits, which is far from exhaustive, that the application of MCV procedures holds great tangible promise. This is one of the main reasons why MCV has been the central driving force behind the introduction of TQM. It should also be clear, however, that such activities are concerned with refinements to existing processes, equivalent to improvements in the constancy dimension of evolutionary survival described above. Such improvements are certainly of benefit to the organization concerned but they are only one side of the survival coin.

Divergent variation represents the other side. In contrast to MCV activities, the management of divergent variation (MDV) has no specified future goal (if it did then we would, by definition, be aiming to converge upon it). Rather, MDV activities are essentially opportunistic: they are concerned with *activities that may or may not prove advantageous to the organization* (or living organism) concerned. MDV is concerned with the management of risk and the development of flexibility within the boundaries of existing viable operations.

Genetic mutations present a classic example of divergent variation processes in operation. While genetic mutations are completely random the overwhelming majority are contained within a boundary that does not compromise the viability of the organism concerned. Nature does not play around with the fundamental design aspects of living things (human beings do not suddenly acquire gills or the ability to eat wood) rather the process is one of tentative experimentation. The main point to note is that this experimentation is not goal-oriented and its outcomes are unpredictable. However, the process of divergent variation through genetic mutation has proved phenomenally successful in the natural world. It has produced the millions upon millions of species of life we now find on this planet, from microbes to blue whales. Also, of course, it has produced virtually complete dead-ends (such as the dinosaurs) and billions upon billions of variations that have led absolutely nowhere.

Organizations, of course, do not have practically unlimited

resources and organizations are not disinterested in who actually survives in the long run (which is the case with evolution in the natural world). Organizations do not simply want *someone* to survive, they want to maximize the chances that *they* will survive. Organizations cannot therefore afford to countenance the level of risk that exists in the natural world. For example, evolution's most successful and complex product so far (us) has created the first situation since the whole circus began where one species has the capability to halt the process altogether (at least on this planet) or give it a fairly substantial knock.

Some organizational implications

It is increasingly evident that the management of organizations is becoming a process through which an effective balance may be achieved between activities that are designed to maintain stability and those that are designed to promote change. I believe that in the vast majority of organizations historical factors have resulted in the development of management approaches that are overly concerned with stability and the deployment of control mechanisms. Many organizations are over-managed to the point of rigidity. This has led to business failure in the private sector, gross inefficiency in the public sector, widespread alienation and apathy among those who are overcontrolled and it has placed severe limitations on the development of organizational potential. It is time to alter all that and make fundamental changes to our conceptions of the ways in which organizations should be structured and managed. This will not be easy, old ideas die hard, especially when they have worked very successfully for a very long period of time. The problem, however, is that the external environment is now changing at a rate unprecedented in human history. The pace of change in interrelated areas such as technology and business has accelerated beyond recognition. This point was brought home to me in an extremely powerful way quite recently.

While waiting on a deserted country railway station I noticed an old rusted cast-iron vending machine that had once delivered chocolate bars (Fry's 'Five Boys'). The interesting and relevant point about this machine was the fact that the price of these chocolate bars (six old pence) was, along with the product name, cast into the front face. The company involved was obviously not expecting much in the way of price fluctuations for the foreseeable future!

Those days are well and truly behind us and it is time to rid ourselves of outmoded concepts of management that are just as rigidly cast into the psyche and structures of existing organizations as this price was cast into the vending machine. We cannot change the pace of development and progress: it will happen, however we choose to conceptualize or ignore it. The future is coming rapidly; it is time for us to act in order that we have some opportunity of making it a future we desire.

SUMMARY AND KEY POINTS

- Organizations can be considered as having similarities with living organisms, and with human beings in particular. Judicious use of the metaphor of 'organizations as living things' can offer us insights into the central factors influencing organizational survival.
- Traditionally, the majority of management effort has been focused on monitoring the 'physical' elements of organizations such as finance, manpower and equipment. The 'psychological' element of organizational life, such as staff attitudes, organizational culture and personal commitment has received little serious attention.
- A major difference between organizations and living things is that organizations have cognitive capabilities distributed throughout their 'bodies'. However, traditional approaches to structuring and managing organizations have tended to utilize the living things model, that is assuming that cognitive abilities reside with one element only, as in the case of the brain. This 'thinking function' has traditionally been attributed to management only.
- Existing species have survived because of an ability to maintain internal consistency while possessing the potential to adapt to changing environments. Survival is achieved through a dynamic balance between pressures for stability and change.
- Many organizations are predominantly focused on maintaining stability and do not invest resources in activities that may prove vital in the event of a changed environment.
- Organizations must ensure that the resources required to maintain internal consistency are balanced with those available

for action in the environment. An excessive use of resources for internal requirements impairs the organization's ability to act in the external environment (for a practical example of this phenomena see *Big Blues, The Unmaking of IBM* by Paul Carrol (Further reading), a detailed and insightful account of the unmaking of IBM).

- Living things have evolved complex information-gathering mechanisms that are focused on the external environment. Many organizational information-gathering mechanisms are focused inward. This creates 'noise' in information channels and may prevent organizations from detecting early indicators of important changes within their environments.

- Biological evolution progresses through a process that balances consistency and variation. Small mutations in the genetic material of each individual member of a species helps to ensure that a catastrophic loss will not be experienced if a disease arises to which no individual is resistant. Such a disaster could occur if individuals were genetically identical.

- Genetic variation is of no value to an individual unless it confers some environmental advantage. Genetic mutations may confer an advantage in the existing environment or a potential advantage that will only be realized in a changed environment.

- In the vast majority of instances genetic variations do not confer significant advantages in existing environments. Therefore they can be considered as being *investments* against the possibility of significant environmental change occurring in the future. As such their value to the species can only be assessed in the long term. This suggests that organizations must make similar investments if they are to survive in an environment that is considerably more volatile than that in which living organisms exist.

- Organizations must aim to manage convergent and divergent variation. The management of convergent variation (MCV) is focused on error and waste reduction and *the improvement of existing processes*. MCV is one of the principal concerns of TQM and the majority of TQ techniques are designed to facilitate its aims.

- Divergent variation is concerned with investment and the development of flexibility in organizations; it is equivalent to the investment through genetic variation that is observed in living things. The management of divergent variation (MDV) should focus primarily on investment in the cognitive capabilities that exist throughout organizations. As MDV is fundamentally a long-term strategy MDV initiatives may be difficult to evaluate in the short term. In many ways an organization's commitment to MDV can be considered as an act of faith on the part of senior management. However, the evolutionary model counsels that MDV is a fundamental aspect of survival in the case of living things. This book argues that the similarities between the pressures acting in natural environments and organizational environments indicate that MDV should be a critical element in every organization's strategy for long-term survival.

- MDV activities can take a number of forms in organizations and some practical suggestions for action are listed below.

Cross-training activities
Job shadowing
Educational bursaries
Study visits to other organizations
Basic education opportunities in the workplace
Training in statistical concepts for all
Management skills programmes for front-line staff
Opportunities for non-vocational education in the workplace
Establishment of a workplace library system
Language tuition
Effective development of communication skills for all
Computer literacy opportunities for all
Access to organizational resources for the pursuit of individually chosen 'pet projects'
Establishment and facilitation of 'interest clubs' (vocational and non-vocational) within the organization
Sabbatical leave in recognition of service for all
Financial support for the purchase of books and educational materials

Part IV

Making the future

'We must ask where we are and whither we are tending.'

Abraham Lincoln.

'Let us not go over the old ground, let us rather prepare for what is to come.'

Marcus Tullius Cicero (55 BC).

The first three sections of this book discussed some of the key difficulties we face in successfully implementing TQM initiatives. In this final section I will suggest ways in which the development of TQM may be enhanced in organizations. I trust, however, that the assertion made in Part II of the book, that the successful introduction of TQM is primarily a problem rather than a puzzle, has alerted the reader to the probability that no 14-point plans will be forthcoming. This is true. However, the need for comprehensive description and clear understanding is only a part of the challenge we face. Ultimately, of course, someone must actually *do* something if we are to make progress. What follows therefore is a set of tentative suggestions, which should not be considered as specific plans for action but rather as general principles that require tailoring to meet the particular needs of individual organizations. I have grouped these ideas and suggestions into general 'problem areas' as described in the following chapters.

12

Misunderstanding the nature of TQM

The term Total Quality Management is a bit of an oxymoron. In all probability it would be advantageous if the 'M' were to be removed from TQM. Total Quality *Management* strongly implies that Total Quality is primarily a management issue. In one very important sense it is: only management has the authority to make the considerable changes necessary for TQM implementation to succeed. However, the inclusion of the management dimension suggests that Total Quality is something that needs to be managed, and therefore supervised and controlled, presumably by 'managers'. As such it perpetuates the traditional divisive concept of 'management and managed' that TQ is designed to overcome. The implication is that TQM is something that management does to somebody else. Total Quality cannot be 'managed' in the traditional, i.e. supervise and control, sense of the word because it involves factors such as commitment, purpose, vision and trust that are not amenable to mechanistic prescription. Quality can, and must, be managed. Total Quality, however, must be encouraged to evolve. I appreciate that this is a fine point but I believe it is a vital one.

The evolution of TQM will involve an organization in a journey that progresses through a number of specific stages. The sequence of these stages actually results in the T (for Total) element occurring at the end rather than the beginning of the process. The chronological development of TQM is best understood as being first Quality, second Management and third Total, or to put it into the omnipresent jargon: QMT.

Let us examine this notion a little closer. The principal focus of a TQM organization is to provide goods and/or services that meet or preferably exceed the external (or final) customer's expectations in terms of functional requirements, value and cost. This is the baseline and it represents the operational definition of quality. Of course, it is not impossible for a non-TQM (in the sense that TQM is considered in this book) organization to provide quality goods and/or services. Henry Ford did it for quite some time without endorsing or indeed practising any TQ principles (although he certainly applied a number of quality management principles) as did Harold Geneen at ITT. And, over the past few years, all the organizations that have failed in their attempts at implementing TQM programmes presumably still have enough satisfied customers to remain in business. Quality is therefore a necessary attribute of any organization that manages to trade successfully (i.e. to make an acceptable return on investment) in an open market. Monopolies and captive markets are, of course, a different matter.

Therefore an organization that is currently providing goods and/or services which sustain an acceptable level of business is, by definition, providing an operationally satisfactory level of quality. At least for the moment. Such an organization can, if it so wishes, move into the second phase of QMT development, management. Of course the organization involved will have been 'managed' throughout its history but management in the QMT sense means the scientific management of quality, involving the utilization of hard data, statistical concepts and techniques and a process management philosophy. During the development of this quality management phase the organization commonly seeks to control the key characteristics of its existing processes through the management of convergent variance as described in Part 3 of this book, and to reduce its operational costs. I am sure that the reader will appreciate that this is the traditional model of organizations and of quality: it represents the stage at which many 'TQM' organizations find themselves today. However, it can be argued that they are not fully-fledged TQM organizations but principally Quality Management or QM organizations.

QM organizations commonly display the following characteristics:

1. They focus predominantly on quality controls and quality control mechanisms.
2. 'Management' continues to be seen as a function separate from 'production'.
3. They have a strong 'lean and mean' focus.
4. They are predominantly mechanistic rather than organic in structure and orientation.

Many organizations have confused the mechanics of quality management with the development of a TQ culture. The two are not necessarily synonymous. The tools of quality management such as SPC, Pareto analysis, Kaizen, Business Process Improvement can only realize their full potential within an appropriate organizational culture, but they cannot create such a culture. A genuine TQ culture will not emerge as an automatic consequence of using the tools and techniques of quality management in the same way that it cannot be created by simply sticking mindless quality posters on the walls. Too many organizations have learned this to their cost. One of the principal reasons for the failure of many TQ initiatives is the belief that TQ can be successfully introduced without altering the traditional nature of organizations. It cannot. TQM is radical, much more radical than many early practitioners realized and certainly more radical than most organizations have appreciated.

One of the difficult implications of adopting a truly TQM philosophy (as opposed to the QM variety) is the realization that historical notions of management will become obsolete. I believe that the notion of management, as most organizations currently understand it, is doomed. This notion is embedded in the principle of power and control and the principle of power and control can only be morally justified in terms of implied superiority. Managers know best. We must ask ourselves whether this is in fact the case. Do managers really know best? Is the presence of managers as decision-makers, supervisors and controllers justified on the grounds that non-managers are congenitally incapable of effective decision-making and self-generated discipline? I very much doubt it.

My own experience of working in a number of different industries and sectors, private and public, has taught me very clearly that managers are not fundamentally different from anyone else, irrespective of their particular elevation in the hierarchy. In my experience there is no elite class other than that which is perpetuated by the system. Also, within the traditional concept of management there exists a vested interest in maintaining dependency in 'the managed'. In the past, and unfortunately also much of the present, this dependency has been maintained through such organizational devices as rigid job descriptions, banal rules and regulations, minimal opportunities to influence the organization, withholding relevant information, a lack of opportunities to constructively criticize management effectiveness other than through adversarial trades unions, a lack of educational opportunities (I use the word 'educational' in order to make the distinction between the development of convergent skills, commonly achieved through training, and the divergent or 'broadening' skills that emerge from effective educational experiences), a lack of consultation on important decisions affecting working life and so on. Is it little wonder, when we reflect on these institutionalized mechanisms of subjugation and control, that many organizations are finding it impossible to compete in today's rapidly changing, quality-oriented world?

The traditional management view, as applied to the introduction of TQ initiatives, will be highly likely to consider them as being mechanistic projects requiring controlled implementation. The consequences of this view may be observed in failed TQ initiatives across a wide range of industries. No matter what we think we can do, TQM will simply not slot in with 'business as usual'. The most an organization with this management perspective can hope to achieve is to become more efficient at QM. Very often of course failed TQ initiatives do not even achieve this, they actually make matters worse! Also, as we have already seen, QM alone will not help us deal effectively with non-linear change in the external environment.

One of the most important barriers we must tackle is the widely held misconception that the introduction of TQM is predominantly a problem of structure, sequence and logistics. This view is exemplified in the 'X Steps To Quality' approach. This mechanistic view fosters the belief that TQM implementation is essentially a question of effective project management, similar in many aspects to the installation of an improved IT system. This, however, is not the case. TQM is not simply about the realignment of resources and the identification of key processes. TQM is also about beliefs and attitudes, communication, trust and the development of a truly democratic workplace.

We have already seen that the implementation of TQM involves the resolution of both puzzles and problems. Step-by-step implementation programmes only address the puzzle element, and, because they do not address the problem dimension, appear seductively attractive and extremely powerful (the Holy Grail again). It is important to remember that the principal tools of Quality Management, such as process mapping, failure mode and effect analysis, quality function deployment, root problem-solving, SPC, Pareto analysis, Ishikawa diagrams and so on have their origins in manufacturing, and particularly in engineering. It is in the context of engineering manufacture, from research and development (R&D) through to production, that QM has achieved its most spectacular successes.

The inherent nature of manufacturing processes and the levels of calibration and control that are achievable naturally lend themselves to QM principles and provide a fertile ground for the application of QM techniques. It is precisely because of the successes achieved in organizations operating in the manufacturing sector (principally the Japanese) that TQM has become a universal management issue. A problem arises, however, when engineering-biased techniques are applied in non-engineering contexts. One of the biggest weaknesses of structured programmes for the implementation of TQM therefore is that they are conceptually mechanistic, they address structure and sequence, the 'what's and when's', but ignore the 'how's and who's'.

Let us consider a hypothetical example that is based on a representative sample of such implementation programmes. Structured implementation programmes commonly recommend a very similar sequence of steps, as follows:

1. Gain senior management commitment to change and the adoption of a TQM approach to business operations.
2. Create a shared vision or 'mission statement' that communicates clearly the purpose and aims of the organization (mission statements usually incorporate the words customer, quality, excellence, value and service).
3. Specify targets that will provide reliable indications of whether or not the organization is achieving the aims set out in the mission statement (such targets are commonly expressed in terms of customer satisfaction indices, market share, productivity increases, improved cycle times and so on).
4. Specify the critical success factors that will influence the achievement of the organization's targets.
5. Identify the key processes that impact on these critical success factors and bring them into statistical control.
6. Continuously improve key processes through the establishment of process improvement teams.

7. Deal effectively with any difficulties that may arise as a consequence of undertaking steps 1 to 6.

I would not disagree with any of the above steps or indeed the programme itself, I doubt if anyone would. This is always a bad sign! Everything seems so logical and straightforward that one wonders why there is so much difficulty in actually doing TQM! The problem, of course, is that such programmes are overly simplistic. I am reminded of a friend who once planned to market a booklet that guaranteed the purchaser unequivocal business success if he or she religiously followed the advice set out within it. My friend had penned this gem in a matter of minutes and it said:

'To succeed in business you must simply accomplish the following two things:

Step 1 Identify or create a market need.

Step 2 Provide goods and/or services that meet this market need in such a way as to minimize your costs and maximize your return on investment while delighting your customers.'

This appears easy and it is basically what our TQM implementation programme is telling us to do, albeit in much more detail. But the fundamental problem of how to make it happen is not addressed in either case. For example, step 1 of the TQM implementation programme above, gaining senior management commitment (along with *full* understanding: it is relatively easy to get commitment without full understanding), is the single most important and difficult element involved. If this is achieved then everything else is essentially reduced to a puzzle. The problem in achieving commitment with full understanding, however, is that the route to TQM has implications for senior management that may not be agreeable. Implications such as power sharing, information sharing and profit sharing. TQM espouses a philosophy of collective values, teamwork and cooperation. When senior management considers whether or not to embark on the TQ journey one of the questions they are likely to ask themselves is: 'What's in it for me?' Everybody will ask that question; it is naive to think that they won't. So what precisely is in it for them? If the principles of TQM are realistically adhered to (i.e. if an appropriate proportion of the increased revenues and cost reductions which are achieved through enhanced

QM procedures are reinvested in the organization) then long-term survival emerges as the major benefit. This may not actually be a big deal for many senior managers judging by the ludicrously generous 'golden parachutes' that many of them seem to have secured. If TQM is to stand any chance of being successfully implemented, therefore, senior managers must have a vested interest in securing its outcomes, otherwise why should they do it?

Suggestions for progress

TQM cannot be 'managed' in the usual sense of the word (i.e. controlled and supervised). The techniques of Quality Management such as flowcharting and problem-solving must be used with care in the context of attempting to implement TQM itself. Flowcharting the stages and sequences required for TQM implementation may grossly oversimplify extremely difficult challenges and create a false sense of security. It may also foster the mistaken belief that TQM is something that can be 'installed'.

TQM is principally about culture and a culture cannot be prescribed or 'installed'. An appropriate culture will only emerge from appropriate normative practices and behaviours. Senior management commitment therefore means senior management change in behaviour. This implies that the successful transition to a TQM culture requires senior management actions which are significantly different from past actions.

Many organizations confuse Total Quality Management with Quality Management. Quality Management is essentially concerned with the *effectiveness and efficiency* of the key organizational processes that affect the external customer. Its principal focus therefore is the management of convergent variation with the aim of making continuous improvements to existing organizational processes. Quality Management is an essential element in organizational survival, particularly in the short and medium term. Total Quality Management incorporates the fundamental principles of Quality Management but also includes divergent variation or change as an integral element, co-existing with the drive to improve stability in existing processes. In this way it can be seen that 'full blown' TQM represents a dynamic balance between productive stability and productive change and the principal agent involved in suggesting and implementing productive change will be people.

Managing stability and change

Clearly, the actual balance between continuity and discontinuity, stability and change, must be managed effectively. This is a problem and not a puzzle and it therefore requires judgement rather than prescriptive rules. A great deal can be learned from the 'management' of divergent variation that occurs in the natural world. Divergent variation means experimentation and experimentation requires the occasional judicious relaxation of controls. Each organization must find its own acceptable level of experimentation, commensurate with the developing skills and abilities of its staff and the likely consequences of particular actions. One senior manager I talked to dealt with the difficulty of balancing control and freedom in what I felt was a particularly effective way. He used the metaphor of the organization as a boat and his view on autonomous decision-making was (quote): 'Autonomy inevitably means that people will occasionally make a hole in the boat. I can live with the odd hole above the waterline. But if anyone is thinking of doing anything that could make a hole below the waterline, then I want to know beforehand'. The notion of judicious autonomy is central to the philosophy of TQM, but everyone must be aware of the fact that there is a waterline!

As senior management commitment, with full understanding, is a non-negotiable element in the transition to a TQM culture organizations must ensure that TQM education programmes are effective and honest and that incentive mechanisms are established which encourage appropriate attitudes and behaviours from senior management.

'Lean and mean' is an appropriate strategy for short and medium term survival, but a philosophy based purely on cost and time reduction may also be counter-productive in the longer term. Organizational survival depends on both cost reduction and *investment*. An overly zealous lean and mean philosophy may value quantifiable short-term gains above unquantifiable long-term losses, which may in fact turn out to be greater. We must invest not only in the measurable 'value added' activities within organizations but also take note of the 'hidden' investment that comes from activities such as cross training, 'thinking time', skill broadening, information gathering and continuous experimentation. A realistic proportion of the time and resources released through the effective

management of convergent variation must be invested in processes
which encourage an appropriate level of divergent variation.

13

The organizational filter

A living organism's development is influenced by two factors: its genetic make-up and the environment in which it exists. Ultimately the environment can exercise only a restricting effect on development. All that the environment can achieve is to inhibit the realization of genetic potential; it cannot generate characteristics which the organism does not possess the potential to develop. No amount of environmental encouragement will produce wings on a frog! However, the environment may constrain the full potential of the developing frog if it is lacking in appropriate levels of light, nutrients, etc., or if toxins are present.

This is also true of organizations. Organizations can do no more than constrain the full developmental potential that exists within them. For example, within a particular organization there may be half a dozen individuals who are capable of becoming excellent chief executives. Only one person, however, can actually assume this position (and that person may not be any of the six appropriate individuals mentioned); similarly with the position of chief accountant, senior design engineer, marketing director and so on. This is a very sobering thought. As far as the realization of human potential is concerned organizations operate like light filters of varying intensity. A minority are fairly transparent but the overwhelming majority are towards the opaque end of the spectrum. This situation can be shown diagrammatically in Figure 13.1

By and large the vast majority of individuals join organizations with high hopes and a determination to do well at their jobs. If they are extremely fortunate the organization they join will furnish them with opportunities to contribute to the best of their abilities. In reality they are more likely to find themselves increasingly drawn into a culture of despondency and disillusionment. They may find

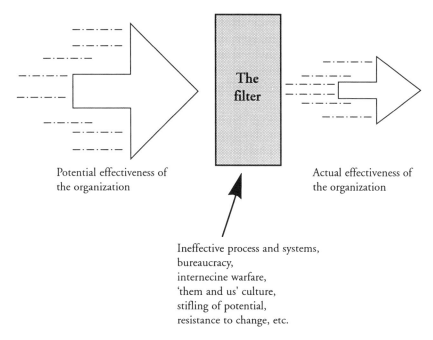

Figure 13.1 The organizational filter

that their immediate supervisor is irrational or has favourites. They discover that there are unofficial working practices in operation; that no one informs them when important decisions are being taken that will affect their future; that their efforts are not recognized while those of others are; that they are unfairly criticized for events that were largely beyond their control; that they are often treated as if they were imbeciles and so on. Devoid of any mechanism for effectively registering their frustration the majority simply switch off. If they are mobile and fortunate enough to possess marketable skills they may move on, but devoid of such an escape route they often move 'underground' instead, keeping a low profile and doing as little as possible. They constitute what a colleague of mine once described as 'the in-house retired'. A proportion move from apathy to cynicism as time passes and become a formidable challenge to management authority.

Anyone who has worked within an organization of any size will recognize that the characterization given above is far from fictional. It has been happening for years, it is happening now and, unless we do something constructive about it, it will continue to happen. The problem is that we cannot afford to let it happen any longer. The intense nature of the modern competitive context is such that organizations simply cannot afford to lose the goodwill of even a small proportion of their workforce. And it is no good blaming them: the overwhelming majority were fine when they joined! So what causes the creeping cancer that emasculates so many organizations? We have already considered some examples; institutionalized divisions, petty rules and so on. However, I believe that the roots of the malaise remain buried in antiquated notions of control and in mistrust.

While I wish to avoid anything approaching a 'sociological' explanation, I must confess that notions of class and class divisions repeatedly emerge as unifying concepts in understanding many of the important challenges facing organizations in this country today. Over the past 7 years or so I have delivered presentations on quality, run training courses on quality techniques and have assisted quality teams with the implementation of their ideas. With one or two very notable exceptions the biggest problems have always been with senior management. The quantities of vapid and captious chatter that constitute the greater proportion of dealings with many senior managers can be positively alarming. Ideas and suggestions are frequently discarded with minimal amounts of rational deliberation and liberal quantities of hubris. There frequently seems to be no real willingness to contemplate change or the possibilities of change, particularly the sorts of change that TQM initiatives require. I believe that this mental inertia stems from an absence of effective critical comment on senior management effectiveness. Too many managers are isolated from the real feelings and opinions of those who work for them and this isolation frequently breeds arrogance. This is a crucially important aspect of the organizational filter that must be tackled in earnest. After all, the most important principle of TQM is that customer information on products and services is the most vital information an organization can obtain. In the 'internal marketplace', however, we typically encounter a completely reversed situation in which the customer is appraised by the supplier. If any form of appraisal system exists at all in organizations it is overwhelmingly of the top-down variety. It is high time that the process operated in both directions.

As I have already stated, organizations can no longer afford the luxury of demotivating a significant proportion of the people who work for them; they must aim to get the very best from all. I have found it useful over the years to consider the problem of the organizational filter from three interrelated perspectives:

- Information
- Trust
- Shared values.

Information

Information, as we have already noted, is the key to quality. This principle applies as forcefully to the internal environment as it does to the external one. Using the model of organizations as being similar to human beings, a situation frequently exists in which the organizational 'brain', i.e. the executive decision-making function, becomes increasingly isolated from its potential sources of information or 'feedback'. This situation can be compared to one in which a human being's nervous system is modified in such a way as to enable functional motor activities to be undertaken while eliminating all sensory feedback to the brain, i.e. with communication going in one direction only, 'brain-to-limbs'. It is clear that in a living organism such one-way communication would be extremely hazardous indeed. Body-to-brain communications such as pain, for example, are a signal that something is wrong. Pain may result from events in the external environment or from some malfunction within the body. Without the ability to register pain, however, a living organism could not know that some form of remedial action was required.

This analogy can be readily applied to organizations. Organizations may appear to be extremely healthy if internally or externally generated pain is not being registered in the organization's brain. It can be argued that the majority of organizations have some level of impairment to their ability to register pain in this way, particularly that which is not chronic. In many instances the level of pain required to trigger some sort of response in the organization's brain is so intense that the underlying causes may prove fatal or near-fatal (witness IBM).

Like all living things, organizations must attend to their general health. This means listening for signs of discomfort from within.

After all, the employees of an organization represent its 'nerve-ends': they are the most important source of information possessed by organizations. That information, welcome and less welcome, must be allowed to register in the organization's brain.

Apart from the need for information to reach the brain, there is also the requirement that information from the brain reaches the body. In living organisms this brain-to-body information is primarily in the form of commands, i.e. 'do this' information. As we noted in a previous section, however, organizations differ from human beings in the fact that they have cognitive capabilities distributed throughout their structure. Organizations therefore differ from living organisms in a fundamental way. Higher animals have separated functions and capabilities for thought and action. Thinking and decision-making are activities which take place in our brains, but our brains are incapable of acting on the environment. Our bodies in contrast are capable of acting on the environment but they are not capable of thought. This model appears to have permeated a good deal of management thought and behaviour.

The classic view of management functions centres on thinking, planning and decision-making (the brain) with the role of everyone else being primarily focused on doing (the body). Of course it is not as simple as that. People, as conscious beings, will not simply attend to what is communicated and act unthinkingly, like robots. They will wonder why it is being communicated, why it was communicated in the way it was, what ulterior motives may have been satisfied through the communication and so on. In other words they will attempt to *make sense* of the communications they receive, and the less facts they know, the more facts they will assume.

The restriction of information plays a very large role in demotivating employees. If we are to build organizational cultures in which everyone gives of their best in the interests of the whole then everyone must feel respected and trusted. I do not mean by this that every single piece of information must be made available to every person in the organization. This is not a sensible way to run a business. I am talking about the petty secrecies that pervade most organizations. Management pay levels are a classic case in point. Why do so many managers wish to keep their remuneration levels secret? Are they ashamed of them for some reason? Similarly with decisions about restructuring, budget allocations, profits, expenses, future plans. In most organizations at present information on topics such as these are restricted to senior management levels only. This is divisive and frequently unnecessary. If an organization is serious about implementing TQM then it must be serious about trusting its employees, and trust begins with honesty. Within sensible business constraints, organizations must give all their employees access to information that is important to the organization's, and therefore their own, futures.

Trust

A colleague recently told me of the experiences of a friend who is training to become an educational psychologist. This training process involves a period of 2 years teaching in a school. After some months she asked her friend, whose placement was in a medium-sized primary school, how things were progressing.

> It is very interesting. Apart from the first week, when a teacher sat with me for a couple of hours every other day, I haven't seen a soul. I have almost 30 6- and 7-year-old children in my class and as far as the school knows I could be teaching them anything. I could be showing them video nasties, inculcating them into some obscure religious cult or just letting them watch cartoons all day. It's obvious from the amount of autonomy they allow me that they think I am a person who can be trusted with the physical and mental well-being of the children in my class, but they will not let me have a key to the stationery cupboard!

The key to the stationery cupboard is apparently kept locked in the deputy headmaster's desk and he must be located when any provisions are required. My colleague's friend estimates that over the months he has been at the school the total amount of time wasted on finding this person, waiting for him to finish whatever he is doing, and going with him to the cupboard, constitutes a considerable financial cost. Multiply this by the 12 or so teachers in the school, and the years in which this rule has pertained, and we are looking at serious waste. But, clearly, the most damaging effect is on the morale of the teachers involved. What message does such pettiness communicate to them? It communicates that they cannot be trusted to act as responsible adults when dealing with the contents of a stationery cupboard! That is quite an insult.

Organizations insult their employees all the time. They insult their intelligence, their powers of creativity, their integrity, their loyalty, their honesty. As I have already stated above, organizations must learn to trust their staff. Again I do not mean by this statement that every employee should therefore have a key to the safe! Trust must be set in relation to knowledge and competence. For example, I trust my young son in very many different ways but I would not trust him to make decisions about my business or to drive my car.

But how does he know I trust him? Because I allow him the freedom to make decisions in areas that are important to him. When I do not feel that what he wishes to do is advisable I explain the reasons why I feel that way. This does not always satisfy him completely but he does not seem to harbour any deep resentment towards me for the occasional restrictions I feel obliged to impose. Most importantly though I believe he knows I trust him because *he is listened to and his opinions are taken into consideration before decisions affecting him are made.*

Trust can be measured by the degree of autonomy an individual is allowed. The values of an organization can be gauged from the areas in which individual autonomy is constrained. In our example of the trainee psychologist described above it is clear that what really matters to the deputy head is that resources are closely controlled. Trust of course operates both ways. If management indicates that it does not trust staff, then staff will not trust management. Trust grows from openness and honesty and a belief that the vast majority of people are willing and capable of creating excellence in what they do.

As trust develops information flows as never before. Real, honest, constructive information. Trust kills the organizational game-playing and points-scoring that presently cripples many organizations, public and private. Trust does not cost the organization a penny and it is not a high-tech investment. Trust begins with the belief that every individual within the organization, from bottom to top, deserves to be treated with common human decency and integrity. Organizations that truly live that belief, create respect at all levels. And in the long run, respect is the only management authority worth having.

Shared values

What are the values of the organization you work for? How are those values communicated? Does your organization have a 'mission statement' incorporating values? Does the reality of day-to-day activities tie in with these professed values? These are pertinent questions. Values, missions and visions currently occupy centre-stage in much management and organizational literature. A great deal of rhetoric has surrounded them and also quite a lot of hot air. Values are important, that point cannot be denied. However, it is the values an organization exhibits through its actions that tell everyone what the game is really all about. Values must be lived if they are to have any credibility whatsoever. And it must be made obvious that they are not merely slogans to be abandoned as soon as climates deteriorate. It is relatively easy to hold high values in good times, sticking with them through the really bad times is the true measure of commitment and this is where the real benefits will be reaped. When people see that senior management is prepared to stick to its values even when that costs money they know they are working for an honest organization. What values should an organization seek to maintain? We can analyse this question by considering the personal values we would wish every employee to work from. This is particularly relevant to our discussion of TQM. TQM, above all else, is a philosophy of commitment and teamwork and it is people-driven: people will make it succeed or fail. If it is to succeed therefore we need to ask ourselves what, precisely, are we expecting people to do? This is a very interesting question; I often ask it on TQM training courses and in management seminars. My own view is that for TQM to work we are asking people, as a minimum, to do the following things:

- To come to work each day unless they are genuinely too ill to do so (no skiving off).
- To have, or be prepared to acquire, the skills and knowledge necessary to carry out their responsibilities effectively.
- To obtain feedback from their internal customers and to strive to improve their skills and knowledge in order to improve the service delivered to their internal customers.
- To communicate freely suggestions and ideas for improving the systems and methods of production/service delivery across the organization.
- To put the overall benefits of the team/organization above personal benefits if there is a conflict of interests.

This is quite a lot to ask of people. The vast majority of these requirements are very difficult, if not impossible, to legislate for or to police. They can only be given voluntarily. We must ask ourselves therefore, why should people do it? This, again, is an interesting and important question. Why should we expect people in organizations to do all of these things, and more? For money? That has never worked and never will. For long-term security? Perhaps. But we cannot assume, and perhaps should not aim to achieve, a permanent workforce. An individual may not intend to stay with one organization for the whole of his or her working life but this does not mean that he or she will necessarily be less than fully committed to it during a period of employment. Task groups and special projects often fall into this category as do organizations that have traditionally employed people for relatively short periods of time. Take the Band-Aid phenomenon. No one involved in that project was looking for a lifetime career but the level of commitment to the ideals of the project was phenomenal. Similarly with organizations such as McDonald's. Very many young people, one of my own children included, have worked for McDonald's without the slightest intention of seeking a career there, yet McDonald's manages to achieve incredible levels of commitment and effort from its young people.

There are no extrinsic means of generating the levels of commitment and effort required to make TQM an operational reality. If it is going to happen then people must want to do it. And they will only want to do it if they trust and respect the organization they work for, which means that they must trust and respect the people who manage that organization. In order to generate that trust and respect the organization must live a set of values that communicate the fact that everyone is important and that everyone can expect to be treated like a responsible adult.

I recently talked to an engineering machinist whose company had been taken over by a large American conglomerate. Quite soon after the take-over the new senior management (American) called the whole workforce (about 800 people) together to talk about the 'new way of doing things'. This apparently consisted of a highly emotional appeal on the general theme of the organization as a united 'family'. The message was highly 'we' oriented and included statements such as: 'we are all working for the same organization', 'we are all in this together', 'we will only prosper if we all work at continuous improvement'. 'We all have an equally important part to play' and so on. The machinist was not impressed. What managers really meant, according to him was, 'We are all in this together but . . . :

- I will be paid a lot more than you will.
- I will be much less likely to lose my job in a downturn.
- I will have more freedom to act than you will.
- I will have a reserved car parking space and you won't.
- I will have an undisclosed expense account.
- I will know important things about the company's future long before you will.
- I will receive more development opportunities than you will.
- I will appraise your performance but you will not be allowed to appraise mine.
- I will work in very much more comfortable surroundings than you will.
- I will be trusted to manage my own time and efforts for the company but you will be measured with a time clock.
- I will be able to find out how much you earn but you will not be able to find out how much I earn.

He is right of course. Gushing management rhetoric about 'families' and common futures does not cut the mustard when institutionalized divisions between managers and managed remain intact; and the problem is not primarily that of remuneration, although obscenely excessive salaries generally lose managers the respect of the workforce. What really matters is that a genuine willingness exists in management to share the day-to-day realities of working for the organization and to be open and honest at a personal level.

Suggestions for progress

Organizations must break down the internal barriers that constitute the organizational filter. Communication is the key to achieving this aim. Communications must be honest and open and they must extend in all directions. This is particularly important in terms of the appraisal of management effectiveness. Organizations should institute *upward* appraisal systems.

Organizations must apply the core principles of TQM to their 'internal marketplace'. For example, the organization should regularly monitor the level of staff satisfaction that exists. One way of achieving this is through the use of staff questionnaires. An example of such a questionnaire is given below.

Sample diagnostic materials

Gauging the feelings of the internal market: Example Staff Questionnaire

Please rate each of the following aspects of the organization and your current job. Your ratings can be anonymous if you wish or you can sign your name in the space provided below. It is entirely your choice. Please remember to indicate the department in which you work. The rating scale is as follows:

Satisfied	*Neither*	*Dissatisfied*
10 9 8 7 6 5 4 3 2 1	0	1 2 3 4 5 6 7 8 9 10

The score you give to each aspect should be in line with the score descriptors given below:

Score	*General descriptor*
0	Neither satisfied nor dissatisfied (neutral)
1, 2, 3	Mildly satisfied/dissatisfied
4, 5, 6	Reasonably satisfied/dissatisfied
7, 8	Very satisfied/dissatisfied
9, 10	Extremely satisfied/dissatisfied

Please circle one number for each of the following aspects

		Satisfied	Neither	Dissatisfied
1.	Working conditions	10 9 8 7 6 5 4 3 2 1	0	1 2 3 4 5 6 7 8 9 10
2.	Training provided	10 9 8 7 6 5 4 3 2 1	0	1 2 3 4 5 6 7 8 9 10
3.	Support from immediate management	10 9 8 7 6 5 4 3 2 1	0	1 2 3 4 5 6 7 8 9 10
4.	Health and safety	10 9 8 7 6 5 4 3 2 1	0	1 2 3 4 5 6 7 8 9 10
5.	Appraisal system	10 9 8 7 6 5 4 3 2 1	0	1 2 3 4 5 6 7 8 9 10
6.	Internal communications	10 9 8 7 6 5 4 3 2 1	0	1 2 3 4 5 6 7 8 9 10
7.	Level of bureaucracy	10 9 8 7 6 5 4 3 2 1	0	1 2 3 4 5 6 7 8 9 10
8.	Resources available	10 9 8 7 6 5 4 3 2 1	0	1 2 3 4 5 6 7 8 9 10

	Satisfied	Neither	Dissatisfied
9. Competence of higher management	10 9 8 7 6 5 4 3 2 1	0	1 2 3 4 5 6 7 8 9 10
10. Equality of opportunity	10 9 8 7 6 5 4 3 2 1	0	1 2 3 4 5 6 7 8 9 10
11. Recruitment process	10 9 8 7 6 5 4 3 2 1	0	1 2 3 4 5 6 7 8 9 10
12. Level of pay	10 9 8 7 6 5 4 3 2 1	0	1 2 3 4 5 6 7 8 9 10
13. Internal systems	10 9 8 7 6 5 4 3 2 1	0	1 2 3 4 5 6 7 8 9 10
14. Having views listened to	10 9 8 7 6 5 4 3 2 1	0	1 2 3 4 5 6 7 8 9 10
15. Support from colleagues	10 9 8 7 6 5 4 3 2 1	0	1 2 3 4 5 6 7 8 9 10
16. Freedom to act	10 9 8 7 6 5 4 3 2 1	0	1 2 3 4 5 6 7 8 9 10
17. Promotion system	10 9 8 7 6 5 4 3 2 1	0	1 2 3 4 5 6 7 8 9 10
18. Competence of direct manager	10 9 8 7 6 5 4 3 2 1	0	1 2 3 4 5 6 7 8 9 10
19. Staff suggestion system	10 9 8 7 6 5 4 3 2 1	0	1 2 3 4 5 6 7 8 9 10
20. Way decisions are made	10 9 8 7 6 5 4 3 2 1	0	1 2 3 4 5 6 7 8 9 10
21. Competence of colleagues	10 9 8 7 6 5 4 3 2 1	0	1 2 3 4 5 6 7 8 9 10
22. Organization's external reputation	10 9 8 7 6 5 4 3 2 1	0	1 2 3 4 5 6 7 8 9 10
23. Recognition of your efforts	10 9 8 7 6 5 4 3 2 1	0	1 2 3 4 5 6 7 8 9 10
24. Approachability of senior management	10 9 8 7 6 5 4 3 2 1	0	1 2 3 4 5 6 7 8 9 10
25. Enjoyability of job	10 9 8 7 6 5 4 3 2 1	0	1 2 3 4 5 6 7 8 9 10
26. Competence of other departments	10 9 8 7 6 5 4 3 2 1	0	1 2 3 4 5 6 7 8 9 10
27. Direction organization moving in	10 9 8 7 6 5 4 3 2 1	0	1 2 3 4 5 6 7 8 9 10
28. Services offered by organization	10 9 8 7 6 5 4 3 2 1	0	1 2 3 4 5 6 7 8 9 10
29. Your advancement prospects	10 9 8 7 6 5 4 3 2 1	0	1 2 3 4 5 6 7 8 9 10
30. Challenge of your job	10 9 8 7 6 5 4 3 2 1	0	1 2 3 4 5 6 7 8 9 10
31. Marketing of organization's services	10 9 8 7 6 5 4 3 2 1	0	1 2 3 4 5 6 7 8 9 10
32. Sense of achievement	10 9 8 7 6 5 4 3 2 1	0	1 2 3 4 5 6 7 8 9 10
33. Trustworthiness of senior management	10 9 8 7 6 5 4 3 2 1	0	1 2 3 4 5 6 7 8 9 10
34. Respect organization shows you	10 9 8 7 6 5 4 3 2 1	0	1 2 3 4 5 6 7 8 9 10
35. Values of the organization	10 9 8 7 6 5 4 3 2 1	0	1 2 3 4 5 6 7 8 9 10
36. General amenities available	10 9 8 7 6 5 4 3 2 1	0	1 2 3 4 5 6 7 8 9 10

	Satisfied	Neither	Dissatisfied

37. Future of the organization	10 9 8 7 6 5 4 3 2 1 0 1 2 3 4 5 6 7 8 9 10
38. General friendliness	10 9 8 7 6 5 4 3 2 1 0 1 2 3 4 5 6 7 8 9 10
39. Payment of expenses	10 9 8 7 6 5 4 3 2 1 0 1 2 3 4 5 6 7 8 9 10
40. Concern for staff	10 9 8 7 6 5 4 3 2 1 0 1 2 3 4 5 6 7 8 9 10

Department ....   Date ....   Name (optional) ....

Scoring procedure

The information obtained from this questionnaire is scored as follows. All 'satisfied' scores (those to the left of the zero score) are given a *positive* value. All 'dissatisfied' scores (those to the right of the zero score) are given a *negative* value.

1. Scores for certain aspects are particularly important and are 'weighted' as follows:

Aspects 14, 23 and 34: these scores are *trebled*
Aspects 3, 5, 16, 17, 24, 29, 30 and 40: these scores are *doubled*

2. Calculate the *total positive score* (the sum of all the scores to the left of zero).
3. Calculate the *total negative score* (the sum of all the scores to the right of zero).
4. Combine these two scores in order to obtain a *single score* (this will be a positive number, a negative number, or zero).
5. Divide this score by 40 to obtain a *final score*.

The final score can be compared with the general descriptor list at the beginning of the questionnaire and related to the individual's general feelings (as a customer) about the organization and his or her current job. Experience strongly indicates that the level of service an individual is prepared to extend to his or her customers (internal and external) will reflect the perceived level of service that he or she receives from the organization itself (if you don't treat your staff well they won't treat your customers well). Someone who scores in the vicinity of zero will be unlikely to do more than the rudimentary requirements of his or her job description. Negative scores in excess of -2.5 generally mean that feelings of disillusionment with the organization have reached a point where the individual concerned is actively seeking alternative employment. It is also disappointing to note that aggregate scores tend to become increasingly negative with length of service—the organization filter at work!

Information obtained through techniques such as staff surveys is extremely important and it must be acted upon. One way of ensuring that this happens is to publicize the scores obtained in individual departments.

Improving departmental focus

Another important contribution to the organizational filter is the tendency for departments to become excessively inward-looking. This situation can be improved through a process of effective analysis of departmental purpose. Again it is useful to start this process moving through the use of structured questionnaires. Some examples of the genre are given below.

Departmental purpose analysis: preliminary questionnaire

1. Who are the major customers and suppliers of your section/ department?

2. How does your section/department currently monitor its performance?

3. What does your section/department do particularly well?

4. Where are the best opportunities for improving the quality of your section/department's services?

5. How does the work you do help the section/department deliver the services you identified in part 1 of the this questionniare?

6. What are the major frustrations you face in trying to do your job effectively?

Departmental purpose analysis (DPA 1)

Please complete the following sentences.
1. The central purpose of my department is to deliver

2. The three most important services we can provide are

3. We can contribute to the success of the organization by

4. We could damage the organization if we do not

5. We can judge how well we are performing by

6. At present our greatest strengths are

7. At present our most serious weaknesses are

Departmental purpose analysis (DPA 2)

1. The people who need our services most are

2. We are important to them because

3. The three most important things they need from us are

4. The most difficult problem we have in delivering a good service to them is

5. The people we most need co-operation from are

6. They are important to us because

7. The three most important things we need from them are

8. The most serious difficulty we have in getting what we need from this is

These questionnaires are principally concerned with the clarification of departmental purpose. This is the first step in the process of developing departmental effectiveness—clarifying who the department's customers and suppliers are and highlighting the major difficulties that are currently being experienced. The next step is to provide the department with some means of assessing its current level of operation. This, of course, is difficult, if not impossible, to achieve from the 'inside'. Ultimately the only opinion that matters is that which is held by the department's internal and external customers. I have found, however, that some form of internally generated performance indicator is a good start. The following questionnaire is designed to give the department some 'feel' for the consistency and stability of its internal processes and procedures. It is based on an analysis of 'day-to-day' activities within the department. Its main purpose is to stimulate discussion about the ways in which the department's processes are currently operating.

Departmental process analysis (DPA 3)

Please give each of the following statements a rating of 1 to 6 where:

1 = This never happens in my department
2 = This only happens rarely in my department
3 = This occasionally happens in my department
4 = This often happens in my department
5 = This happens most of the time in my department
6 = This is the norm in my department

Circle one number on the response sheet for each statement

1. There are some fairly slack periods and other times when I and/or others are rushed off our feet.
2. I have to drop what I am doing to deal with an emergency of some sort.
3. People have shouting matches in earshot of others.
4. It is difficult to get decisions from people.
5. I and/or others are held up through waiting for information or work from other people in the department.

6. Plans are changed at the last moment.
7. There are times when no one seems to be able to answer queries about work.
8. We find that really big mistakes have occurred.
9. Things get lost.
10. People argue about who should have done what.
11. Some people seem to have really cushy jobs.
12. I cannot get the equipment or materials I need to do my work effectively.
13. I get different messages from different people.
14. I work around the department's systems to get things done.
15. I spend time correcting work others have done.
16. Poor performers are not dealt with effectively.
17. We get most of our information through the rumour network.
18. We go from one crisis to another.
19. Problems arise because people do not pass messages on.
20. I have to make decisions without adequate information.
21. There are some things that no one takes responsibility for.
22. I receive unfair criticism.
23. I am asked to do things that I have not been adequately prepared for.
24. I experience frustration in doing my job.
25. The wrong people are promoted.
26. People seem to be working at cross purposes.
27. Management's promises are not kept.
28. There is no clear sense of long-term direction.
29. I have to pick up other people's work.
30. I cover for the mistakes of others.

DPA (3) Scores and analysis

Response sheet
Circle one number in each case

Statement	Score	Statement	Score
1.	1 2 3 4 5 6	16.	1 2 3 4 5 6
2.	1 2 3 4 5 6	17.	1 2 3 4 5 6
3.	1 2 3 4 5 6	18.	1 2 3 4 5 6
4.	1 2 3 4 5 6	19.	1 2 3 4 5 6
5.	1 2 3 4 5 6	20.	1 2 3 4 5 6
6.	1 2 3 4 5 6	21.	1 2 3 4 5 6
7.	1 2 3 4 5 6	22.	1 2 3 4 5 6
8.	1 2 3 4 5 6	23.	1 2 3 4 5 6
9.	1 2 3 4 5 6	24.	1 2 3 4 5 6
10.	1 2 3 4 5 6	25.	1 2 3 4 5 6
11.	1 2 3 4 5 6	26.	1 2 3 4 5 6
12.	1 2 3 4 5 6	27.	1 2 3 4 5 6
13.	1 2 3 4 5 6	28.	1 2 3 4 5 6
14.	1 2 3 4 5 6	29.	1 2 3 4 5 6
15.	1 2 3 4 5 6	30.	1 2 3 4 5 6

Add together each score to give an overall total

Total score = ...

DPA (3) Analysis of scores and general comments

Total score	*Comments*
150–180	Classification: CHAOS. Systems and procedures are totally inadequate. People are frustrated and likely to be very demoralized. The internal reputation of the department is likely to be very poor. Requires major surgery and the introduction of effective systems, communication channels, operating procedures and role clarification. Probably requires senior management intervention.
120–150	Classification: HIGHLY ERRATIC. Systems and procedures are not capable of consistently meeting internal requirements. Major failures likely to occur. People are frequently frustrated. The internal reputation of the department is likely to be poor. Requires urgent attention to major systems and procedures. Probably requires senior management support/assistance to instigate changes needed.
90–120	Classification: UNSTABLE. Systems and procedures need attention and work. Systems and procedures meet internal requirements on average but there are instances of major failure from time to time. People sometimes frustrated. The internal reputation of the department is likely to be average. Changes can be instigated through process review teams and QITs, etc.
60–90	Classification: BASICALLY STABLE. Systems and procedures meet internal requirements on vast majority of instances but would benefit from fine tuning through QITs, etc.
Below 60	Classification: IN STATISTICAL CONTROL. Leave systems and procedures alone, tampering will only create problems. Improvements in outputs can only be achieved through major changes to systems and procedures (but see note below).

IMPORTANT: The fact that *INTERNAL* systems and procedures are in statistical control *DOES NOT NECESSARILY MEAN THAT YOUR CUSTOMERS ARE SATISFIED WITH THE ACTUAL SERVICES YOUR DEPARTMENT PROVIDES.*

14

Making better decisions

We saw in Part II that psychological research indicates that groups tend to perform poorly on decision-making tasks and are prone to take greater risks than would individual members acting alone (the risky shift). Although this is a well-established phenomenon it may be that group dysfunction of this sort is merely a reflection of poor group management. One of the key difficulties, as we have seen, stems from the pressure for group conformance, the tendency for individuals to suppress their discontent with group-favoured ideas in order to remain 'in' or to avoid confrontation with the group leader. A number of techniques can be used to combat this pressure and we will look at some in detail later.

The most important factor influencing group effectiveness, however, is the ability of the group leader. Group leaders must be aware of the fact that individual members may be reluctant to voice their misgivings on issues that seem to be favoured by the majority and consequently important mistakes may be made if suggestions are not honed through effective criticism. Group leaders must therefore positively encourage participants to speak openly and honestly about any important reservations they may have concerning particular decisions. Again it is necessary to strike the right balance between blind acceptance of the perceived consensus and a level of nit-picking that results in complete inertia, the classic 'paralysis through analysis'.

In order to understand the reasons why groups often perform less effectively than individuals we must understand the pressures that group membership exerts and the ways in which these pressures can result in irrational decisions. A major difficulty centres around the highly political nature of many group activities. Meetings and discussions are important organizational events and they often provide individuals with opportunities to impress colleagues and superiors or indeed to settle personal scores. There is also a strong tendency for individuals to jump on whatever bandwagon happens to be passing through the organization at any particular time. These pressures, and others, increase the possibility that irrational decisions may be taken.

How can the group leader deal effectively with them? My own experience leads me to the conclusion that 'open' discussions of views and counterviews can be dysfunctional in groups that have not developed effective process management skills. This may seem to contradict much of what has been said previously but in fact it does not. I have included the inverted commas around the term 'open' because in my experience such discussions are often very contrived indeed. In many cases individuals wait to see what positions powerful or influential individuals will take in relation to a particular topic and they then comment according to this 'lead'. Or, conversely, they may adopt a position which is opposed to that taken by an individual for whom they have some form of grudge and so on.

It is interesting in this context to note the Japanese approach to the presentation of views and ideas at meetings. When Japanese managers meet to make decisions each manager is careful to state his or her (usually his) views with circumspection. It is common for each manager to present a case that outlines the benefits of a particular course of action and to follow this with a consideration of the costs and risks involved and an outline of the merits of other possibilities. Each composition, however, is delivered in such a manner as to clearly indicate what the individual's real preferences are, though these are rarely stated directly. The final decision therefore is likely to be 'bought into' by all concerned as no one has directly stated his or her preferences or objections in anything approaching the forcefulness that typically accompanies suggestions and counter-suggestions in western cultures. Although I am not suggesting that this approach will work everywhere (it requires a certain cultural immersion that most western managers simply have not experienced) there are underlying principles involved which may be utilised to advantage.

Suggestions for progress

One of the most important lessons to be learned from the approach described above is that some degree of anonymity may be advisable in group decision-making. This may seem at face level to involve a contradiction in terms so allow me to take it a stage further. Groups have an enormous potential benefit over individuals in that they bring together a collective knowledge and experience that no individual can possess. The challenge, however, is to harness this collective potential while preserving the uniqueness of each individual's experience and judgement. It is a fine balancing act. A group ceases to be effective when individual contributions reflect the dynamics of the particular group rather than the issues which need to be resolved. In other words groups must focus on external problems rather than internal ones. Of course in an ideal world none of this would be a difficulty. Individuals would leave their private agendas, historical resentments and personal aspirations outside the meeting room and simply get on with being rational, cooperative and objective. If it were only that easy! Groups are a double-edged sword; they offer the enormous potential associated with collective experience and information-sharing yet they frequently counsel irrational courses of action. It is probably impossible to eradicate the irrational tendencies of groups completely: we must aim to manage them within acceptable limits. Two techniques are useful in this aim: they are designed to minimize the effects of negative social and interpersonal factors while encouraging the collective pooling of ideas and opinions. Both techniques help limit the debilitating effects of conformance pressures while calling upon contributions from every member of the group. The first technique, Matched Pairs Analysis, is outlined below.

Matched pairs analysis

This technique, which involves a grid, in Figure 14.1, is used to help groups select priorities from a range of possible actions. The grid was used in a quality development workshop by a group who wished to decide on their priorities in implementing a quality improvement programme within their particular department. The elements included in the grid were obtained through a brainstorming session which aimed to identify the most important issues that would need to be addressed if quality development was to have any real chance of succeeding within the department. This resulted in a list of some 20

		Temps	Poor equipment	Rush orders	Poor communications	Reworks	Staff shortage	Overtime	Suppliers	Materials	Training	Score	Rank
		a	b	c	d	e	f	g	h	i	j	Score	Rank
Temps	a		3	6	⟶								
Poor equipment	b	7											
Rush orders	c	4											
Poor communications	d	↓											
Reworks	e	↓											
Staff shortage	f												
Overtime	g												
Suppliers	h												
Materials	i												
Training	j												

Figure 14.1   Matched pairs analysis

points being made. This was reduced to the 10 most important by combining different elements together where possible and by eliminating others through a show of hands for discussion at a later stage. Each topic was then entered into the grid and the process of matched comparisons started.

The group works along each row and compares the relative importance of each topic to the desired aim of implementing a quality development programme. A total of 10 points must be allocated between the two topics in a manner that reflects the relative importance of each, as seen by the group. In the example above the first comparison is between 'Temps' and 'Poor Equipment'. The group has judged that Poor Equipment is a greater problem than Temps and this difference is reflected in a score of 3 and 7, respectively (the score of 3 is entered in the Temps row and the 7 in the Poor Equipment row). The process then continues with Temps being compared with Rush Orders. In this instance the problem of

Temps is considered marginally more important and a score of 6
and 4, respectively, is given. This process is then continued until all
comparisons are made. Each row is then totalled to give a final score
and the elements rank-ordered. (If two elements end up having the
same total score we can examine the point at which each was
compared directly with the other to see whether a preference was
registered there: if this is the case the preferred element gets highest
ranking, if no preference was registered, a 5–5 score, then the
elements tie in the rank order.)

There are a number of advantages in using this technique. First, it
imposes an element of quantification on the decision-making
process. Second, it breaks the rank-ordering process down into a
relatively large number of sub-decisions (45 in this case). This forces
participants to think about all the issues in some depth and, because
scores are not totalled until the end, avoids the commonly observed
tendency of groups to apply greater levels of rigour to the first three
or so decisions made and to skip through the rest. This can be
observed clearly when groups use the technique with more than six
or so elements. There is a marked tendency for some individuals to
become bored with the scoring procedure after a relatively short
period of time. This reflects one of the major weaknesses of group
decision-making, diminishing rigour, as described above.

Another advantage of the technique is that it promotes a thorough
discussion of all the topics concerned and it allows differences of
opinion to be aired without such differences developing into
entrenched positions. After all, if two people disagree on the
relative priority or points allocation for one particular pair of
elements this represents only a small contribution to the overall
decisions being made. Also, individuals may concede to consensus
pressure on one point, be part of the consensus on another and sway
opinion on a third. There are therefore opportunities for
cooperation, leadership, resistance and advocacy and the end score
will represent an amalgam of the total activities that the group
engaged in. The final scores therefore represent the outcome of a
wide-ranging group process and, particularly where scores are
blocked off as they are made, the final totalling procedure can be
both surprising and enlightening. The main point, however, is that
the final scores result from a process of systematic analysis and
discussion rather than argument and counter-argument about stated
preferences. I have used these grids in a number of different

contexts. They are a powerful tool for building effective teams and developing process management skills. They can also be used to identify differences in perception between groups. For example, I have used the grids with management and staff groups who have worked independently; this process often results in markedly differing scores emerging from each group. The grids can then be used as a basis for discussion which is aimed at clarifying the reasons for differences between the groups and for developing shared perceptions.

Secret ballots

Effective democracies require that individuals cast their votes without promise of favour or fear of retribution. This idea can be usefully applied to group decision-making in general. As we have seen, 'open' discussion in many groups is not open at all. Publicly stated views may represent what an individual feels is the most prudent position to take on a particular issue rather than the one he or she genuinely believes to be the most effective course of action. Also, when an individual with power, experience or influence indicates a particular position, it is difficult for less powerful or less experienced members of the group to remain uninfluenced. The situation is particularly difficult for those who are directly responsible to such an individual; they will need to muster considerable courage indeed if they are to voice any disagreement publicly. Factors such as these constitute the root problem in dysfunctional group processes. People are often simply afraid to speak their minds. And it is naive to believe that statements avowing the right to speak without fear of retribution hold any water. People, as everyone knows, bear grudges. We must therefore look to introduce some level of anonymity into group decision-making processes if we are to avoid compromising the individual's autonomy and rationality. One such means involves the principle of the secret ballot which is intended to avoid some of the negative possibilities involved in public declarations of beliefs. One practical decision-making tool that utilizes this approach is known as the Delphi Technique and it is used when a choice must be made between a number of alternative courses of action. The procedure operates as follows:

1. All relevant information about each possible course of action is documented.
2. A group of experienced individuals (six to eight is ideal) is brought together to examine and discuss the information given on each option and they are told that a choice between the options must be made.
3. Everyone is given an opportunity to ask questions or seek clarification about the alternatives as required but no discussion on relative merits is allowed.
4. When all queries have been answered each participant is instructed to write his or her preference (a single choice) on a piece of paper and to pass this to the group facilitator.
5. The group facilitator then totals the individual choices and, if no clear preference has emerged, informs the group what the least preferred option was. This option is then removed from consideration and the process resumed until a preference is obtained.

If the process culminates in a draw (avoidable by ensuring that the group contains an odd number of participants), it may be necessary to obtain more detailed information about the options or to bring the matter into open discussion for a while before resuming the balloting process. I must stress that in situations where judgement is required (problems rather than puzzles) there is no perfect process available for reaching an effective decision (i.e. one that proves to be workable in the long term). The Delphi technique, however, is designed to dilute the negative influences associated with many group decision-making processes. The fact that each individual makes a private decision means that power issues are less important. Also the fact that the process involves a group of experienced individuals rather than a single 'expert' means that personal idiosyncrasies and biases may be balanced out. Also, in the event of an inconclusive first ballot, the group is only told which option was least preferred; no information is given concerning the option that was 'favourite', for example, or whether two or more options tied. This lessens the chance that individuals will be influenced by the decisions of the majority.

15

The role of the individual in TQM

Organizations are ostensibly composed of individuals who come together in the pursuit of a common aim. Experience of the day-to-day realities of organizational life frequently contradicts this description, however. We have already noted that destructive internecine squabbles and self-directed behaviours are common occurrences in many organizations. If TQM is to become an operational reality it requires that every individual in the organization acts according to a set of fundamental principles that have been discussed in some detail throughout this book.

Ultimately, as we have already noted, TQM can only function on a voluntary basis because it is predicated on the principle that every individual is prepared to commit his or her mental and physical capabilities to the achievement of organizational aims. Again the reality is often very different from the theory. It is a regrettable fact that in many organizations a sizeable proportion of individuals merely ensure that they are physically present for the amount of time legally required of them. During this period of attendance they commonly maintain a standard and quantity of output that is adequate to deter open confrontation with others but constitutes little more than the minimum they believe they can get away with. Such people make up the in-house retired. Personal experience strongly suggests that the great majority are not employed in front-line operations where work pace and effort are predetermined by production schedules. Rather, they are in those organizational niches that afford some degree of autonomy combined with an opportunity to effectively disappear or become engaged in some spurious activity that can be passed off as constituting bona fide work.

One of the most arduous tasks involved in the transition from traditional to TQM cultures is the effective management of human resources. The Total in TQM means just that: the involvement of everyone. There can be no passengers in TQM. I do not mean by this statement, however, that TQM organizations must consequently be staffed with hyperactive workaholics. There is a danger that TQM can be interpreted in this way, indeed it is one important barrier to acceptance. I do not believe that it is a productive interpretation. By involvement in TQM I mean that everyone must share a genuine commitment to the organization and a willingness to respond positively to any reasonable requests that are placed upon them. This is a potentially difficult area. We must not deny the fact that TQM, like any ideology, can be interpreted in a range of different ways. It can be employed as readily to legitimize oppression as to encourage liberation. The Japanese notion of the 'salaryman' stands as a classic example. The general expectation of the salaryman is that he will subjugate his identity to that of the company. Consequently he will be expected to put the needs of the company above his personal needs or the needs of his family. In other words he will be required to display blind obedience.

This is self-defeating on a number of fronts. First, blind obedience, as we have already seen, leads to cognitive atrophy and mindless conformance. Second, it requires personal characteristics that are rapidly disappearing from the market-place. It can be argued that the Japanese economic miracle was predicated upon the existence of a workforce that had experienced ignominious defeat in the Second World War, was the product of a highly conformist culture, had lived through quite severe hardship and needed to build its industrial infrastructure virtually from scratch. The success of the Japanese can be primarily attributed to an outstanding ability to manufacture large quantities of high quality consumer goods at relatively low prices. This demands conformity, hard work and financial prudence, qualities that are, or at least have been, widespread throughout post-war Japan.

Things, however, are changing. The consumer markets of the late 1950s through to the late 1970s were crying out for change. Western manufacturers, stupefied by the growth-driven, demand-led nirvana that followed the end of the Second World War, were easy targets. They have since been literally kicked out of their stupor by the Japanese. Those that are still in business have learned a lot of hard lessons and they are now serious competitors in an intensely customer-focused market-place (witness the progress made in recent years by Rover).

It is also fair to say that the emerging generation of Japanese workers does not necessarily share its predecessor's attitudes to work or accept the subjugation of personal wishes that were previously assumed without question. This generation has grown up in a different world, one in which the only memories are of consistent growth and increasing wealth rather than defeat and hardship. All of these factors, combined with the Japanese tendency for convergence rather than divergence, present Japanese organizations with considerable challenges in the coming years. Still, we should be so unfortunate!

Blind conformance is not a viable strategy for confronting the economic and social challenges we face in the coming years. Commitment and the willing application of intelligence and creativity by everyone in the organization offers the only sustainable means of survival. This demands yet another management balancing act, between control and autonomy, and requires a particular management approach, an issue we will explore shortly.

Evidence strongly suggests that personal responsibility is a cornerstone of TQM. Quality is, in the final analysis, a personal issue. Quality will only happen if everyone is prepared to play their part to the full. This brings us back to the thorny issue of the in-house retired. Practical experience of implementing TQM initiatives repeatedly indicates that this is a critical issue and it is one that management cannot afford to ignore. People simply will not put in the effort required to implement TQM if they see that some individuals are being allowed to opt out. One of the most important signals that management can send about the seriousness of its commitment to TQM is to ensure that no one is exempt from the requirements of the basic philosophy. As far as TQM is concerned, *total means total.*

The rule of thirds

There is commonly a distinct partition of attitudes towards the introduction of TQM within organizations. I have observed this on so many occasions that it has become something of a general operating principle. Practical experience indicates that in the majority of organizations (particularly the medium-sized to large ones) a 'rule of thirds' will probably apply regarding initial attitudes to TQM.

This rule of thirds counsels that in most organizations roughly one-third of the people are, to some extent, already doing TQM. To be more exact, they are applying many of the fundamental principles of TQM as best they can given the constraints within which they have to operate. This group of people commonly welcome the philosophy of TQM with open arms, it legitimizes and clarifies what they have, often unconsciously, been doing, or trying to do, for some time. They are the self-converted. The next third consists of what may be described as the 'wait and see' group. This group will come on board gradually provided that initial training and awareness programmes are effective and that they can be convinced that TQM is not just another fad and that management is serious about its commitment to quality. The final third range in attitude from complete indifference to marked hostility. This group of individuals represents the most serious threat to the success of any TQM initiative and it must be managed effectively. It will comprise individuals from all levels within the organization and they will use a range of techniques in their attempt to thwart any TQ initiative, from studied indifference through muted cynicism to covert and overt resistance.

Management at the highest level must recognize that resistance of this sort is practically inevitable: to ignore it is to precipitate failure. It is inevitable because TQM constitutes bad news for a proportion of individuals within the organization and they will not wish to see it succeed. These individuals must be marginalized by senior management if the greater body of staff are to believe in the sincerity and credibility of any TQ initiative. They should then be given every opportunity to contribute to the programme but when push comes to shove management must have the courage to take difficult decisions. Ultimately it must be a case of 'if you can't change the people, change the people'.

The structure of individual competence

TQM relies heavily on the twin notions of commitment and individual competence. One of the important questions we must ask therefore is: what constitutes individual competence? A common response to this question is usually something along the lines that job competence is the product of an individual's attitudes, skills and knowledge (the 'ASK' model). This analysis, as far as it goes, is fine.

It does, however, neglect a crucial dimension, that of organizational constraint. Models of competence based on 'ASK' principles represent the traditional notion of the individual's role within the organization. Let us consider this notion further.

'Attitude', as it applies to individual competence, can be equated with 'motivation'. Having the right attitude means having the right motivation, i.e. wishing to do one's job well. (One heuristic for determining the reasons for poor performance suggests that asking the question: 'Could the individual do this if his or her life depended on it?' provides important information. The answer 'No' means that you have identified a training need. The answer 'Yes' means that there is a problem with motivation.) 'Skills and Knowledge' can be combined in the notion of 'Capability'. Therefore, using the traditional concept, an individual is commonly described as competent if he or she is suitably motivated and possesses an appropriate level of capability to carry out the tasks required of his or her job. The principal implication of this model of course is that *competence resides within the individual.* I believe that this is a limited and static notion of competence that is founded on the traditional notion of the organization as a machine and the individuals who work in it as cogs in that machine. The principal weakness of the model is that it ignores the fact that variables such as organizational structure, the distribution of power and the dynamics of social relationships (components of the organizational filter) are also extremely important determinants of competence. The model, throughout, tends to focus human resource efforts on the development of individuals *in isolation from the systems and processes in which they are obliged to operate.* It is time we moved away from this outdated, static notion of competence, towards a dynamic model in which organizational constraints and opportunities are also included. Principally, we must extend the notion of competence to include not only the individual in isolation but also the role of organizational power, or control. When we include the power dimension it is clear that an interaction between motivation, capability and control will determine the overall effect that an individual will have on an organization. It is effect that is the key; motivation and capability alone, the traditional keystones of competence, only represent potential for effect. For example, the most capable goal-scorer in the world will only be effective if his team-mates are willing and able to give him the ball. Effect then can be represented by the following formula:

Effect (E) = Motivation (M) × Capability (C) × Control (C)

This can be easily remembered as $E = MC^2$.

$E = MC^2$

It is clear from this formula that effect is a *product* of the three variables concerned. This model offers interesting possibilities for understanding the potential effects that the actions of particular individuals can have on organizations. Consider the role of the chief executive officer: he or she will score very close to a maximum 100 on the control dimension, possessing considerable freedom to act. If we assume that our incumbent is also a highly motivated individual, we are presented with an interesting situation. A highly motivated individual with virtually unlimited authority to act represents a very powerful force for good or bad. The effect that our chief executive will have on the organization therefore will depend on his or her capability: this will be the key variable.

At the opposite end of the organizational ladder things are different. The effect that a front-line worker can exert on the organization will be primarily related to the control variable. He or she may be a highly motivated genius but this will not translate into positive effect for the organization if there is little or no opportunity to influence (or control) organizational activities. It is clear from this analysis that the potential effect that an individual can exert on an organization will depend on the particular configuration that exists between the variables of motivation, capability and control. It is clear, however, that control is the key variable influencing effect. Where the control element is particularly high (i.e. where an individual has the authority to make significant decisions) then effect will be a direct consequence of the individual's levels of motivation and capability.

In terms of organizational effect, motivation can be considered as comprising a spectrum that has high positive potential at one end (a strong inclination to act in the interests of the organization), high negative potential at the other (a strong inclination to act against the organization's interests) and a complete lack of any form of potential (total indifference to the organization's interests) in the centre. This spectrum can be represented diagrammatically in Figure 15.1.

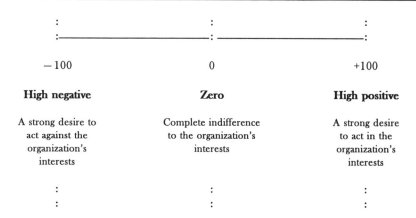

Figure 15.1   The motivational spectrum

Capability can also be conceptualized in this way, ranging from high positive at one end (an accurate/objective understanding of critical variables and the actions required to deal with them) to high negative at the other (an inaccurate/erroneous understanding of critical variables and the actions required to deal with them), with a zero rating at the centre (an awareness that critical variables are not understood). Again this can be represented diagrammatically as shown in Figure 15.2.

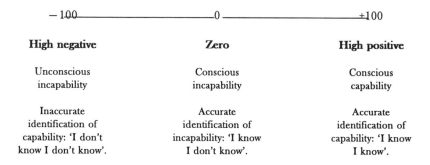

Figure 15.2   The capability spectrum

Finally, the control factor can be considered to vary between a value of +100 (total autonomy) to zero (total constraint): this representation is shown in Figure 15.3.

Figure 15.3 The control spectrum

It is clear from a study of this model that individual competence, as traditionally conceptualized, is a notion that is limited to the maintenance of existing levels of organizational effectiveness. In terms of the principle of continuous improvement, however, competence can only be translated into organizational improvements if competent individuals have the power to change organizational procedures and practices. It is also clear that the three variables: motivation, capability and control, are inextricably linked and have far reaching implications for the organization. Ideally the level of control an individual is allowed to exercise should be commensurate with his or her level of motivation and capability. Any mismatch between these variables is likely to result in problems for the organization and/or the individual concerned. An individual who is both motivated and capable will be frustrated if unreasonable restrictions are placed on his or her ability to make autonomous decisions. Conversely the individual who has authority without capability can wreak havoc on the organization!

This model has important implications for human resource management. It suggests that as individuals improve their levels of capability and motivation they should be given increased levels of autonomy commensurate with their development. As I have written elsewhere, one of the major weaknesses of many HRD efforts is that they are not linked to a commensurate relaxation of organizational constraints. Individuals often return from developmental experiences highly motivated and keen to put newly learned techniques into practice only to find that existing systems and entrenched attitudes do not allow this to happen. The consequences of such experiences are highly predictable, i.e. demotivation and a lack of faith in the credibility of the organization's HRD efforts.

The role of management

It is clear from the discussion above, and from the discussion of related topics in this book, that the introduction of TQM has considerable ramifications for the nature and practice of management within organizations. We have seen that organizational improvements will only emerge if individuals are able to make changes to existing organizational practices. Historically, the authority to institute changes to existing practices has been the sole prerogative of management. Managers have traditionally made decisions and issued directives which others have followed.

Managers, in this model, constitute the brain of the organization and are consequently charged with cerebral functions such as planning, organizing, directing and decision-making. Non-managerial staff, in contrast, can be considered as representing the physical body of the organization and are charged with the task of carrying out management's instructions by 'moving matter about in space' as Bertrand Russell put it. Managers are thus the 'thinkers' and non-managers the 'doers'.

Of course this situation is fine if every organization adopts the same working definition of managers and managed (as was the case for the greater part of this century). Under this model organizational survival becomes primarily a function of management competence: the better the quality of management, the better the organization's chances of success. The model is fatally flawed by the assumption that management alone is capable of providing the cognitive input necessary to operate and sustain the organization. This is a fallacy.

An important factor influencing the success of the Japanese has been the belief that *everyone* in the organization has the potential ability to improve on the way things are done. This, of course, is not a simple act of faith as great care is taken in the selection of employees, substantial amounts of time and effort are invested in training and developing them and potential organizational barriers to involvement are systematically eradicated. Management's role therefore is moving away from a traditional focus on the control of physical and non-physical resources to an emphasis on the liberation of competence, particularly cognitive competence. What management attributes are therefore appropriate to this changing role? It may be useful to consider this question in terms of the common weaknesses in management performance that have emerged as a consequence of the introduction of TQM initiatives.

Common management weaknesses in TQM

Some of these weaknesses are listed below.

- Failure to act as a convincing role model.
- Failure to act decisively in difficult situations.
- Failure to reward TQM behaviours effectively.
- Task avoidance (particularly avoiding dealing with difficult staff and/or long-standing problems).
- Lack of ability to build and motivate a team.
- Lack of ability to develop individual staff.
- Inability to communicate a clear vision of the future.
- Fear of risk-taking.
- Failure to support staff initiatives effectively.
- Inability to 'let go' of authority.
- Inability to maintain the momentum of the programme.

These weaknesses have been highlighted primarily as a consequence of the particular challenges involved in managing in a TQM culture, they are not likely to emerge in traditional 'command and control' environments. It is also clear from an analysis of these weaknesses that the personal qualities of managers will assume a much greater role in TQM organizations than they do in traditional ones. TQM requires a particular style of management and consequently a particular style of manager. I list below some of the key personal qualities needed.

Personal qualities required for managing in a TQM organization

- Honesty
- Openness and approachability
- Integrity
- Enthusiasm

- The ability to lead by example
- The ability to communicate effectively
- The ability to inspire confidence
- The ability to think long term
- The ability to accept change
- The ability to tolerate ambiguity
- The ability to tackle difficult problems and act decisively
- The ability to develop individuals and build teams
- The tenacity to see projects through to completion.

These qualities are emerging as key factors influencing effective management but they are not addressed effectively in many management development programmes. The fact that an individual possesses a DMS, a management degree or an MBA tells us precious little about important personal qualities or their ability to actually do any of the things listed above. This is a serious weakness. As we move away from traditional concepts of organizations towards ones in which the flexibility and cooperation of resourceful individuals constitutes a central aim, the role of management will become increasingly focused on the balance between leadership, facilitation and problem resolution.

Managers will be required to build bridges and demolish barriers rather than direct and monitor the work of others and they will ultimately be responsible for making difficult decisions in ambiguous and complex circumstances. This will require certain personality traits that may be difficult or indeed impossible to nurture in some individuals. This point is usually undiscussible in management development circles because it implies that to some extent effective managers may be 'born rather than made'. My own view is that some individuals will find it very much easier to develop these qualities than others.

Suggestions for improvement

One of the key factors influencing the successful introduction of TQM initiatives is a clear indication from management that it is serious. One of the most important means of underscoring this commitment is for management to endorse, ideally through powerful symbols such as promotion, the attitudes and behaviours of those individuals who have displayed particular commitment and capability to the aims of the programme. It is crucial that management supports these individuals, irrespective of traditional factors such as age, seniority or academic qualifications.

Traditional models of competence have focused on personal qualities such as attitudes, skills and knowledge. These qualities are necessary elements in the notion of competence but they are not sufficient. I suggest that in order to understand the full complexity of the situation, a further dimension, that of organizational control, must be taken into account. It is necessary to appreciate that individual competence merely represents potential for effect. Translating this potential into effect involves considerations of autonomy and responsibility. HRD initiatives must address wider organizational issues than have been the case in the past (for an in-depth analysis of this topic see Total Quality Training, Chapter 9).

The traditional role of management will remain important to the successful implementation of TQM initiatives. The key variable, however, is degree. The degree to which management decides, controls and directs day-to-day activities requires critical examination. It can be argued that traditional notions of organization have assumed that one of the principal functions of management is to ensure that work gets done and that it gets done to acceptable standards. I believe that the institutionalized controls and checks that have followed from this assumption have operated as self-fulfilling prophecies. In all probability a significant number of individuals unconsciously adapt their attitudes and behaviours in line with the perceived lack of trust and esteem that the organization communicates to them. They have largely become what the organization has tacitly assumed they are. I accept that this assertion is a value statement, but I stand by it. Experience and personal research has consistently indicated that the vast majority of people at the 'lower' levels within organizations are immensely more capable, and more importantly, have much greater potential than organizations give them credit for. For example, Tom Peters' assertion that front-line employees are committed, intelligent, creative, vigorous, etc. 'except for the eight hours they are at work' has, in my own experience, been shown to be true time and again.

The implicit balancing variable that underpins the 'staff are incapable' assumption is the counter-assumption that 'management is capable'. It frequently seems evident to me that many organizations are subtly operated on the assumed dynamic between these seemingly contradictory elements, 'competent' management and 'incompetent' staff. I am sure that there are instances in which such an analysis constitutes a realistic appraisal of the way things are. But in these instances we must ask ourselves why the situation has come to exist. Is management recruiting incompetent staff or is it making them incompetent?

One of the most difficult and challenging implications of TQM is that management must reassess its role in organizational life. I believe that the old model of management is doomed; it will be killed by the success of organizations that do not adhere to it. I also believe that, at a fundamental level, the basic operating principles of TQM do not constitute rocket-science. I hope that the general approach taken in this book has convinced the reader that the fundamental challenges we face in attempting to implement TQM are not about leading-edge technology or complex notions of management science, they are principally about people dealing with other people.

In my view a great deal of common sense has been obscured by the increasing intellectualization of management practices. The explosion of post graduate management degrees seems to be a knee-jerk response to a basic insecurity among practising and would-be managers. The difficulty is that this intellectualization appears to blind many senior managers to the fact that basic human interactions constitute an extremely important element in organizational success.

Management expertise in such areas as strategy development, procurement, marketing, finance, law and, increasingly, international considerations are obviously of vital importance to the organization. But they do not constitute the whole picture: they are essentially concerned with planning rather than doing. Ultimately, however, every grand plan must be translated into operational reality. This is where most organizations are weak.

Organizational experiences of attempting to introduce TQM are a classic example. As I indicated at the very beginning of this book the vast majority of TQM initiatives do not fail because of flaws in the implementation plan; they fail because people cannot make the plan work. My fear is that management development programmes increasingly emphasize the intellectual aspects of management to the exclusion of everything else. What is required is balance. Management development programmes must also address the management qualities needed to get things done in the real world.

This increasingly means the ability to harness the total support of every individual in the organization.

Managers, particularly senior managers, frequently seem to forget that their actions, and consequently the attitudes that these actions imply, are closely scrutinized by everyone in the organization. The assumptions that are made about these actions will have a significant impact; for good or ill, on the organization's chances of success in any venture. The time in which management could in effect 'go it alone' (i.e. command and control from the top) is rapidly coming to an end. Success in future will depend on close collaboration between groups of individuals who will become increasingly equal in terms of technical expertise and organizational authority. In this situation qualities such as leadership earned through respect will become the principal determinants of managerial authority.

It is clear that the emerging requirements of effective management and the considerable personal dimension involved inevitably draws us into a consideration of individual psychology. I am aware that this is a controversial topic and one that has received a 'mixed press' from practising managers. It is essential, however, to discuss some of the more important variables involved. First we must consider the notion of personality as it applies to the requirements of managing in a TQM culture and ask ourselves; what key personality characteristics are required in order to be an effective TQ manager? This of course begs the question of what exactly we mean by 'personality'.

Different managers have different styles of operating, different priorities, concerns and principles. Each has his or her own private theories about what makes people tick and what constitutes the principal responsibilities of a manager. What I would like to discuss (briefly) in the remainder of this section therefore are the practical consequences of these internalized belief systems. It is probably reasonable to speculate that individuals carry out their organizational responsibilities in order to satisfy two needs, intrinsic and extrinsic. Intrinsic needs stem from the basic personality characteristics of the individual. For example, the majority of individuals will be drawn to occupational areas that require them to act in ways that are congruent with their fundamental personality traits. The highly extraverted individual is likely to gravitate towards occupations that involve high levels of activity, socialization and change. The highly introverted individual, by contrast, will probably be happier in an occupation that requires dedication, reliability and concentration.

These are broad generalizations but experience (and a good deal of psychological research) counsels that they are not wildly unrealistic. It would therefore be in an organization's interests to ensure, as far as it is possible to do so, that the requirements of a particular occupational niche are matched to the principal personality traits of the individual who is placed into it. The growing employment of psychometric techniques for aiding the process of selecting and promoting personnel bears witness to the fact that such variables are assuming increasing importance.

As to extrinsic needs, these can be described in terms of a desire to gain the esteem of others, the recognition obtained through the realization of organizational goals and the status associated with particular forms of employment or with particular occupations. Of course there are also material needs involved, the need to meet one's financial responsibilities is an obvious example.

Ultimately we must ensure that the satisfaction of the individual's psychological needs are commensurate with the requirements of the jobs they occupy. Many people are attracted to particular occupations for reasons that do not necessarily enhance their possible effectiveness in those occupations. This can be clearly seen in the case of local and national politics. It seems evident to me at least that a considerable proportion of individuals who are attracted to political office of some form or other do so in order to satisfy their own ego needs rather than the professed reason of serving the community.

Similarly, I have known a number of individuals who, in my opinion, would make excellent politicians, but in the vast majority of instances they have absolutely no desire to become so. Managers, likewise (and this is particularly true in respect to TQM) must be selected in terms of the personal characteristics that are known to be advantageous to the emerging demands of the role. In the section above I listed some of the management weaknesses that have become evident as a result of the introduction (and often failure) of many TQM initiatives and I also indicated some of the personal qualities that are emerging as important factors in the success of such programmes.

In the section that follows I will briefly describe a technique for analysing management style and suggest an approach to management development that addresses the major challenges involved in establishing TQM cultures within organizations. Again I will make use of a questionnaire. I have used variations of the questionnaire which follows with a considerable number of managers, trainers and teachers over the past 5 years and a systematic pattern of behaviours has begun to emerge. Before we discuss this in any detail it will be useful for you to complete the questionnaire which follows. The questionnaire requires that you rate a number of statements in terms of whether or not, and to what degree, you agree or disagree with them. Please try to avoid the tendency to 'work out' what the questionnaire is after and answer as honestly as you can. In this way you will obtain an insight into your preferred management style. An explanation of the theory on which this questionnaire is based, and the implications for TQM is given in the sections that follow.

Management styles inventory

Analysis of management style questionnaire

Give each of the statements below a rating of 1-6 where:
1 = very strongly disagree   4 = mildly agree
2 = strongly disagree   5 = strongly agree
3 = mildly disagree   6 = very strongly agree

1. Work teams must be structured so as to have clear lines of individual responsibility and authority.

---

2. The role of management is to ensure that people and processes work in the most efficient manner.
3. Organizations have to take risks if they are to survive long term.
4. Training is really about helping people to learn and grow.

---

5. The key skill of management is the ability to adapt to realities.

---

6. When an individual is at work, personal problems have to be left at the door.
7. Ultimately, all management decisions need to be evaluated in terms of clearly measurable financial costs and benefits.

---

8. It is an important part of a manager's job to get people moving, to put a bit of life into them.

9. Management's caring responsibilities to their staff are as important as their financial and production responsibilities.
10. Effective management is essentially about working around obstacles.
11. Managers must be in control of all the critical factors that influence organizational success.

12. The most important function of an appraisal interview is to accurately inform people about their strengths and their development needs.

13. Really effective managers usually have untidy desks.
14. People would be much better at their jobs if organizations showed genuine care and concern for them.

15. The best way managers can improve is by gaining the comments of their staff.

16. A manager's responsibility is to manage effectiveness and ultimately this means controlling personnel difficulties.
17. A completely thorough research of facts and information is absolutely essential if management is to be effective.
18. The vast majority of meetings are too long, full of waffle and boring.

19. A manager is really a facilitator of learning, a guide, a helper and a friend.

20. Wherever possible, managers should try to adapt work requirements to the needs of individual staff.
21. It is a responsibility of managers to control personal emotions and take difficult decisions in the interest of the organization.

22. A wider use of information technology offers the best potential for improving organizational performance.
23. Managers need a sense of humour as much as anything else.
24. One of the most important qualities managers must have is the ability to support others and help them overcome their difficulties.
25. Managers can only be effective if they operate in very close consultation with their staff.

26. If people are just not up to doing an adequate job then management has a responsibility to replace them.

27. To be truly effective, job descriptions must be thoroughly researched and comprehensively detailed.

28. Managers have to enthuse their staff by leading from the front.

29. Teams will only be effective if the people involved genuinely care about each other.

30. All that any manager can really hope to achieve is to make the best of the staff and resources that are available.

31. In terms of redundancies, managers must have the final say in who goes and who stays.

32. A manager's main responsibility is to organize efficiently.

33. Managers ought to overlook the odd misdemeanour, especially at festive times such as Christmas.

34. It is essential that managers have a genuine concern for the care and well-being of all their staff.

35. In the long run a consensus decision is always better than a directive.

36. If people are being paid adequately to do a job then they have a responsibility to give of their best at all times.

37. The most effective methods of recruiting staff are based on psychometric testing and objective skills analysis.

38. Most people do not work hard because they are bored out of their minds.

39. Real effort will only emerge in a warm, caring and trusting work environment.

40. The key factors affecting organizational success or failure are really beyond the control of management.

41. The most effective way to manage is to lay down clear duties and rules that all can understand.

42. Staff appraisals will only be effective if they focus on established facts and do not involve emotions.

43. Too many managers take themselves and their work responsibilities much too seriously.

44. Appraisal interviews are really counselling interviews.

45. In order to do my job as a line manager I need detailed guidelines and instructions from higher management.
46. In truth, delegation is usually more trouble than it is worth.

47. Improved management performance is most effectively achieved through structured learning experiences.

48. Most appraisal interviews are an embarrassing joke.
49. It is inevitable that personal problems will affect people's work and managers need to understand and accept this.

50. It is important that mangers try hard to meet the needs of all their staff.

51. In the real world it is impossible to have honest appraisals if staff are allowed to see all management reports on them.
52. Thorough planning and preparation are the keys to effective management.
53. To be a good manager you must passionately believe what you say.

54. All managers would benefit from training in counselling skills.

55. All managers probably experience deep feelings of inadequacy from time to time.
56. The vast majority of organizational problems can be directly attributed to weak management.

57. People in organizations will change when they see the logic of changing.

58. Management really has to be the most committed group of people in any organization.
59. Happy working relationships are the most important aspect of any effective organization.
60. In terms of management, the customer is always right.

The questionnaire is based on the theory of Transactional Analysis (TA) developed by the Canadian psychotherapist Eric Berne in the 1950s and 1960s. I have used TA as a framework for analysing the behaviour patterns of effective and less effective managers, trainers and teachers over a period of 5 or 6 years. Before we go through the process of scoring the questionnaire it will be useful to outline TA theory. In common with all psychological theories which aim to explain the complexities of individual personality, TA has the usual complement of strengths, weaknesses, enthusiasts and detractors. However, TA is practical, simple without being simplistic and, most importantly, believable and usable. Although we will not explore the theory in great depth (for such an analysis see Total Quality Training: Chapter 8) an outline of the basic principles will be necessary.

TA is a theory of personality and communication that employs the notion of 'ego states' to help us understand a wide range of human behaviours. An ego state is a set of internal feelings and perceptions that lead us to act in a particular way. Our internal ego state influences the way we interpret the world around us and consequently the way we act in that world. In Berne's basic model of personality he outlines three major psychological factors that influence a person's behaviour:

- the internalized values and opinions we have learned, mostly from our parents;
- the child-like qualities we take with us into adult life;
- our ability to think independently, rationally and logically about ourselves and the world around us.

These basic psychological factors, which Berne considered to comprise an individual's three fundamental ego states, result in a number of personal attributes that he referred to as 'ego functions'.

Thus the 'Parental' aspect of personality (the attitudes, beliefs and behaviours learned mainly from parents) can be considered to have two different functions, a 'Controlling' function and a 'Nurturing' function. After all, real parents spend a considerable amount of time doing one or the other with their children.

The 'Child-like' aspect of personality also has two functions, the 'Free' or 'Natural' function and the 'Adapted' function. The Free function represents the personality characteristics of the very young infant whereas the Adapted function results from the process of socialization that all children go through.

As to the final aspect of personality, the ability to think rationally and logically (which Berne referred to as the 'Adult'), this develops as the young child grows to maturity. The mature personality can therefore be considered as a mixture of values and beliefs learned mainly from parents; the natural abilities, emotions and drives experienced as a young child; the social behaviours and attitudes we were taught and our ability to think logically and rationally. Although everyone theoretically has the full complement of ego functions available for use it is not uncommon for one or two to dominate an individual's personality.

In general terms the Controlling function of the parental ego state (Berne called this the 'Controlling Parent') is concerned with monitoring and controlling the external world. The Nurturing function (the 'Nurturing Parent') is concerned with the care and well-being of others. The Adult function is value-free and is concerned exclusively with information, facts and the resolution of problems based on an analysis of data. The Free function of the child ego state (the 'Free Child') is inner-directed and involves creativity, emotion, and the desire to meet internal needs. The Adapted function (the 'Adapted Child') in contrast is concerned with adapting to the needs and requirements of others and to the external world.

This then is the basic framework, which is inevitably a simplification of the complexities of individual personality but it offers us a means of understanding and interpreting many important behaviours. Let us consider Berne's assertion that personalities are often dominated by one or two ego functions. We could imagine a situation in which an individual's 'Controlling Parent' was the dominant ego function. Such an individual would have a strong psychological need to control the environment and consequently the individuals who make up that environment. They would be likely to have little faith in the competence of others, to be highly critical of any perceived weaknesses and to control activities with an iron hand. They will be attracted to positions of authority and power. As leaders they are likely to be both forceful and dynamic. Does this description invoke memories of a former female Prime Minister?

An individual with a dominant 'Nurturing Parent' ego function would be quite different. Such an individual would have a strong psychological need to help and care for others and would consequently be strongly attracted to roles that offer such opportunities. An individual dominated by the 'Adult' ego function would be likely to be attracted to areas in which the exercise of analysis, information gathering and inference played a major role. The individual who is dominated by the 'Free Child' ego function is frequently an energetic self-starter. Although primarily driven by self-directed needs such individuals often attract followers and thus become unwitting leaders. The individual whose personality is dominated by the 'Adapted Child' ego function is likely to be happiest in a situation in which major decisions are taken by others; they prefer to be followers rather than leaders.

The above descriptions are of course something of an exaggeration (although fairly extreme examples of each personality type are not uncommon) and the vast majority of individuals will display personality tendencies that include aspects of each of the five ego functions described. Some element of dominance, however, is common, this after all is what makes up the striking variations of personality between individuals.

The central point, however, is not to describe a theory of personality but to use it in order to understand the personal qualities required for effective management in TQM cultures. This point will be addressed in the sections that follow.

Five key activities

I have found it useful to consider management actions as being grouped under five category headings. These category headings are:

- Controlling
- Informing
- Enthusing
- Supporting
- Adapting

Virtually every activity that a manager, trainer or teacher carries out can be classified under one of these headings. What is of interest, of course, is whether effective and less effective individuals display markedly different behaviour patterns. For example, do effective managers spend more time supporting than controlling? How much time do ineffective managers spend informing their staff? Are effective managers characterized by the use of adapting actions?

The questionnaire aims to clarify your own preferences in respect to these key actions. The scoring procedure is given below.

Scoring the questionnaire

Add your scores to each individual question in the following way;

Add together your scores for questions 1, 6, 11, 16, 21, 26, 31, 36, 41, 46, 51 and 56. This is score A.

Add together your scores for questions 2, 7, 12, 17, 22, 27, 32, 37, 42, 47, 52 and 57. This is score B.

Add together your scores for questions 3, 8, 13, 18, 23, 28, 33, 38, 43, 48, 53 and 58. This is score C.

Add together your scores for questions 4, 9, 14, 19, 24, 29, 34, 39, 44, 49, 54 and 59. This is score D.

Add together your scores for questions 5, 10, 15, 20, 25, 30, 35, 40, 45, 50, 55 and 60. This is score E.

Each of these final scores (A to E) indicates your particular response to a set of questions aimed at detecting any preference towards one of the five key actions described above. The first set of questions (score A) is designed to assess your preference for *Controlling*, the second (score B) for *Informing*, the third (score C) for *Enthusing*, the fourth (score D) for *Supporting* and the final (score E) for *Adapting*.

The maximum score obtainable is 72 and the minimum is 12. Aggregate data suggest that for any dimension only 2 or 3 per cent of respondents score below 24; roughly 15 per cent score between 24 and 34; 65 per cent of respondents score between 34 and 48 on most dimensions, roughly 15 per cent score between 48 and 62 and only 2 or 3 per cent score above 62 on any particular dimension. It must be remembered that this questionnaire, used in isolation, constitutes a fairly blunt means of identifying managerial preferences. It does, however, represent a starting point in analysing what managers do on a day-to-day basis and questioning whether or not this is what is most effective to do.

My own research in this area indicates that effective managers employ a particular combination of key activities. They are first and foremost effective leaders. They are excellent at communicating their enthusiasm, setting challenging targets and acting as role models for their team. They are also effective at making difficult decisions, they do not practise task avoidance and they do not sit on the fence. In this respect they employ the Control function of the five key actions effectively, that is *when it is necessary to do so*. Their general style, however, is not characterized by use of the Control function. Effective managers do not shirk from making necessary decisions and clarifying standards but they focus the bulk of their attention on implementation activities, on the process of *ensuring that decisions are implemented and carried through to completion*. In general terms effective managers spend the greater proportion of their time utilizing the key activities of *Informing, Enthusing* and *Supporting*. They also adapt to realities when it is appropriate to do so and avoid the waste of time and effort associated with futile attempts at solving facts.

Effective managers therefore are effective decision-makers and effective implementers of decisions. They are excellent communicators and motivators and they are able to support individuals and teams in difficult circumstances. They lead by example and they are prepared to share responsibility and, most importantly, they are effective at recognizing effort as well as achievement.

The question we must ask ourselves of course is, can these abilities be developed? My own view is a qualified *yes*. They can be developed in the right individuals and with the right development techniques. Experience suggests that certain individuals have psychological needs that militate strongly against the development of the personal characteristics required to manage effectively in TQM cultures. We must therefore consider the appointment of TQ managers with considerable care and ensure that due consideration is given to fundamental aspects of an individual's personality as well as his or her experience, technical skills and academic qualifications.

My own view is that there is often a considerable gap between an individual's ability to make the appropriate theoretical responses about a particular activity and his or her ability to be effective in that activity. Management is a classic case in point. Without wishing to deride the efforts of business schools (I occasionally teach at one, so any such derision would be hypocritical), I firmly believe that an essential dimension of management effectiveness is not addressed in a majority of instances. The problem, of course, is that this dimension of management effectiveness cannot essentially be taught, it can only be acquired. It seems to me that the crucial developments which have occurred in recent years—and the advent of TQM is a classic example—have shifted the practice of management away from its presumed affinity with science towards one that more resembles an art. It seems increasingly clear that one of the most important requirements of modern managers is that they possess the ability to exercise sound *judgement* in the face of uncertainty.

However, management development seems to be broadly viewed as a process of acquiring specific knowledge and techniques which are accredited in the examination room or, in the case of NVQs, the workplace. I would not disagree that the acquisition of knowledge and practical techniques constitutes an important element of management effectiveness, but they do not constitute the whole. Some critical aspects of management effectiveness simply cannot be categorized and measured in these ways. I am increasingly drawn to the idea that what the majority of management development programmes lack is an element of *education*. There seems to be an overwhelming focus on the acquisition of technical and pseudo-technical competences at the expense of what may best be described as 'all round development'.

I am well aware that this is boggy ground, but nevertheless the impression persists. Perhaps it is time that management educators recognized that wisdom often develops through seemingly esoteric activities such as the examination of fundamental assumptions about values and by discussing notions of meaning, purpose, truth and morality. Of course 'arty-farty' topics such as these do not often appear in the traditional business school curriculum, but these are not traditional times.

The effective management of time

The mismanagement of time constitutes one of the most important reasons why many TQ initiatives flounder. In the early stages of many programmes TQ activities tend to be seen as disturbances from 'real work'. The question I have heard most often during TQM training courses and at various stages of programme implementation is: 'How do we find the time to do TQM?'

There are a number of points to consider here. First TQ

activities, because they are alien to most organizational experience, tend to assume the role of 'time bandit' in many cases. Most people have a fairly full schedule at work, that is, their day is usually filled with activity of some form or other (whether it is productive activity is of course a different issue and one we will consider in some detail in a moment) and 'fitting TQM in' constitutes an added pressure. This is a real problem and it must be tackled effectively if TQM initiatives are to succeed.

The first difficulty involves the attitude, which is completely understandable early on, that TQM activities are separate from work activities. Work activities are primarily associated with the achievement of short-term results, particularly when these involve the resolution of immediate pressures. Clearing the in-tray, producing the report on time, sorting out the sales problem, arranging an alternative supplier when materials run short, getting the heating fixed and so on. These are *urgent and constructive* actions and they require immediate attention.

Of course the mere fact that an action is urgent does not mean that it is necessarily constructive. For example when the phone rings in a manager's office it requires urgent attention. However, if on answering we find that the caller has been misdirected to us and that we have to spend a period of 5 minutes redirecting the caller to the correct recipient our time has been effectively wasted and the caller is unlikely to be impressed. Activities such as this can be described as being urgent but not constructive. Urgent activities are those over which the individual can exercise little real choice, in other words, they are more or less mandatory. Constructive activities are those that have the potential to impact positively on customer satisfaction (although, in the example given above, our caller is ultimately connected to the correct individual, he or she is unlikely to be impressed by the fact that the mix-up was finally sorted out). Conversely, activities over which the individual can exercise choice are considered not-urgent (i.e. they are not monitored and not doing them will incur no consequences in the short term). Activities that have the potential to impact negatively on customer satisfaction (such as connecting them with the wrong person) can be described as not-constructive.

Common organizational activities

These concepts can be used to create a matrix as shown in Figure 15.4. This matrix can be used in order to understand the effective management of time and help us resolve the difficulties frequently associated with the implementation of TQM initiatives.

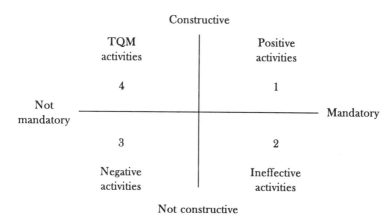

Figure 15.4 A common matrix of organizational activities

It is clear from this matrix that common organizational activities can be grouped under four headings. Those contained in quadrant 1, constructive–urgent, include such things as dealing effectively with customer queries, work-in-progress problems, staffing shortages and so on.

Those falling into the category of quadrant 2, mandatory–not constructive, include things such as chasing information, being required to attend unproductive meetings, having to compensate for the inadequacies of systems or colleagues and having to deal with misdirected queries. (The reader will note that such activities do in fact contribute to getting work done and therefore, ultimately, affect customer satisfaction. But the effort involved would be unnecessary if systems and procedures were improved.)

Quadrant 3, not mandatory–not constructive, comprises the negative activities so often seen within organizations, such as interdepartmental rivalry, the externalization of quality problems, cynicism and defensiveness (of course because such activities are not mandatory we don't have to do them!)

Lastly, the activities that comprise quadrant 4, not mandatory-constructive, can be best described as TQM activities. Because they are not mandatory individuals can *choose* whether or not to do them and they may consequently be avoided or be continuously sacrificed in favour of 'urgent' activities. However, as they appear on the constructive side of the horizontal axis they have the potential to impact positively on customer satisfaction.

Actual times spent in each quadrant of the matrix

Again, as I am not aware of any formal studies in this area, I must refer to my own research in order to estimate the proportion of time that individuals (particularly managers) engage in activities that fall in each of the four quadrants described above. This research indicates results shown in Figure 15.5.

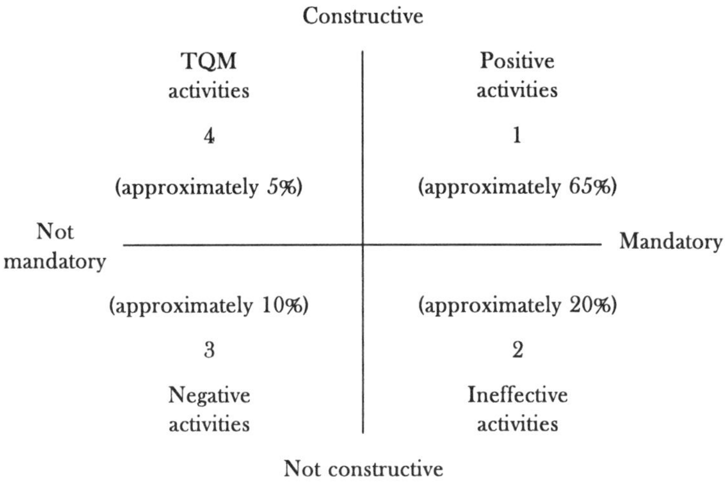

Constructive

TQM activities	Positive activities
4	1
(approximately 5%)	(approximately 65%)

Not mandatory   Mandatory

(approximately 10%)	(approximately 20%)
3	2
Negative activities	Ineffective activities

Not constructive

Figure 15.5 Approximate percentage of management time spent in each particular quadrant

I must stress that these percentages are approximate but I am convinced that they are not wildly inaccurate. Let us consider their implications.

What is immediately clear is that time spent engaged in activities that fall below the horizontal axis is *wasted time*. It is clear therefore that this represents a 'time reservoir' that can be tapped in order to facilitate the move to TQM. This process must start with a reduction in the types of activity found in quadrant 3 (those that are effectively the free choice of individuals). This is usually a considerable challenge as institutionalized attitudes, historical divisions and destructive relationships are difficult to change. However, it must be achieved and senior management must ensure that its commitment to this aim is not compromised.

The activities contained in quadrant 2 are primarily the result of ineffective processes and systems and defunct or unnecessary rules and regulations. Cross-functional process improvement teams, quality circles and staff suggestion schemes, effectively organized and managed, can be extremely productive in creating considerable improvements in these areas. A more detailed listing of the activities commonly associated with each quadrant is shown in Figure 15.6.

It is clear therefore that with commitment, effort, and support the greater proportion of time that is wasted in non-productive activities associated with quadrants 2 and 3 can be transferred to quadrant 4, TQM activities. When this is achieved, the extra time devoted to error prevention, teamwork, process improvement and the elimination of bureaucracy will reduce the necessity for many of quadrant 1 activities, making further time available for forward planning and encouraging the MDV activities outlined at the end of Part III of this book. A truly virtuous circle.

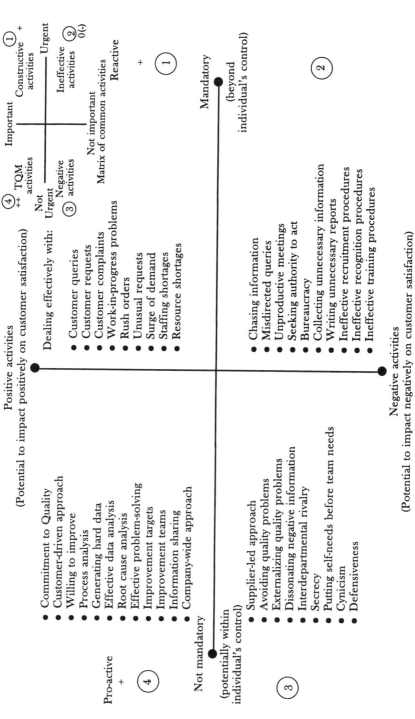

Positive activities
(Potential to impact positively on customer satisfaction)

Pro-active +

Dealing effectively with:

- Customer queries
- Customer requests
- Customer complaints
- Work-in-progress problems
- Rush orders
- Unusual requests
- Surge of demand
- Staffing shortages
- Resource shortages

- Commitment to Quality
- Customer-driven approach
- Willing to improve
- Process analysis
- Generating hard data
- Effective data analysis
- Root cause analysis
- Effective problem-solving
- Improvement targets
- Improvement teams
- Information sharing
- Company-wide approach

Not mandatory
(potentially within
individual's control)

- Supplier-led approach
- Avoiding quality problems
- Externalizing quality problems
- Dissonating negative information
- Interdepartmental rivalry
- Secrecy
- Putting self-needs before team needs
- Cynicism
- Defensiveness

- Chasing information
- Misdirected queries
- Unproductive meetings
- Seeking authority to act
- Bureaucracy
- Collecting unnecessary information
- Writing unnecessary reports
- Ineffective recruitment procedures
- Ineffective recognition procedures
- Ineffective training procedures

Negative activities
(Potential to impact negatively on customer satisfaction)

Important   Constructive + ① Urgent
                                   activities
                                   Ineffective   ②0(-)
                                   activities
                          Not important   Reactive
                          Matrix of common activities
                                                    ① +

Mandatory
(beyond
individual's control)

                                                    ②

++ TQM   ④
   activities
Not   Negative ③
Urgent activities

Figure 15.6 A detailed matrix of organizational activities

16

The challenge of change

'People talk fundamentals and superlatives and then make some changes of detail.'

Oliver Wendell Holmes Jr.

There is change and there is real change! We are all familiar with the former variety, the superficial change that occurs *within* a particular system but leaves the fundamental system itself unaltered. Many 'empowerment' programmes fall into this category. Staff are often seduced by the promise of autonomy and freedom of action only to be bitterly disappointed when they discover that empowerment really means 'empowerment to a point'. *Real* power commonly remains exactly where it has always been.

The transition to TQM requires real change and that is why it is so difficult to achieve. Many organizations attempt to fit TQM into their existing culture and general mode of operation, they commonly see it as a programme aimed at *improving* the way things are done. It is not, it is a programme aimed at *changing* the way things are done.

In the introduction to this book I stated that Peter Drucker had commented that TQM was a good idea but that like a lot of good ideas it had the unfortunate tendency to degenerate into hard work. He is right, TQM will be hard work in the vast majority of organizations. It will be hard because it will require individuals, and managers in particular, to do things that they have traditionally preferred not to do. Such things as:

- Generating accurate data rather than relying on assumptions, personal perceptions and wishful thinking.
- Accepting that our own behaviours may need to change instead of blaming everyone and everything else.

- Committing the effort necessary to design and deliver goods and services that meet customers' requirements (internal and external) rather than our own.
- Sharing real power and information with others rather than pretending to do so.
- Confronting the root causes of endemic problems rather than ignoring them or merely dealing with their symptoms.
- Relinquishing divisive status symbols and behaviours rather than generating specious justifications for keeping them.
- Committing resources to activities that will secure the long term rather than focusing on short-term returns.
- Reacting thoughtfully to adverse or critical information rather than ignoring, rationalizing or denying it.
- Monitoring real-time processes rather than operating from time-lagged data.
- Saying what we honestly believe to be true rather than what we believe to be acceptable, political or prudent.
- Utilizing resources for the benefit of our customers rather than ourselves.
- Leading by doing rather than leading by talking.

TQM therefore requires that real changes are introduced and sustained. This is the central challenge and it is a substantial one. Again we can use the metaphor of human adaptation to understand the nature of the difficulties we face.

The transition from traditional concepts of organizing and managing to those associated with TQM can be likened to the effects that abruptly moving to a higher altitude will have on a human being. An individual who goes from sea level to high altitude fairly rapidly will be likely to experience heart palpitations, breathlessness and a reduced capacity for physical activity. These effects are quickly removed if the individual returns to sea level post-haste.

This happens with many TQM initiatives. A rapid ascent into the TQ stratosphere commonly puts great strains on existing systems and methods of working and creates real problems. The easiest way of dealing with these problems is to get back to base.

However, individuals who resist the urge to descend to safety and remain at high altitude for some time become progressively acclimatized to the new environment and function with increasing effectiveness, although the majority will not be able to do all the things they were capable of at normal altitudes.

Organizations show similar tendencies. Substantial change programmes that are not allowed to falter at the 'panic and panting' stage create stresses in the system (some people will inevitably resist new ways of working and many processes and procedures will be found inadequate for changed requirements). This usually results in operating difficulties and a reduction of efficiency in the short term (things get worse before they get better). This is the stage at which senior management commitment will be most seriously tested.

Finally, of course, there is adaptation through genetic variation and mutation. Some individuals will find that they are surprisingly well equipped to deal with a high-altitude environment (as indeed high-altitude dwellers are) and they will constitute the source of future generations.

And so within organizations, many individuals (remember the rule of thirds) will be eminently suited to the new TQ way of doing things and they will excel. Others will find that they have the will and ability to adapt. It is senior management's prime responsibility to ensure that these individuals receive adequate recognition and reward. In this way new forms of operation will gradually evolve, and a TQM organization will be born.

Welcome to the future!

Bibliography/Recommended further reading

I suggested in the final chapter of this book that much current management education lacks breadth and that many problems stem from the view that effective management involves the acquisition and application of discrete 'competences' (chiefly of a financial nature). My own view is that the illusive and vital element of all effective management is *judgement* and that judgement cannot be taught. Judgement *emerges* from an interaction between knowledge, experience and reflection. Devoid of knowledge we act blindly, devoid of experience, knowledge is merely dogma and devoid of reflection we cannot change. Also, judgement is enhanced through *variation* of knowledge and experience, exploring different disciplines, different ways of seeing and of being can pay unimaginable dividends.

This book draws on many disciplines, including statistics, quality management, sociology, mathematics, biology, psychology, physics and philosophy. In the following list I suggest, with all due humility, a range of publications that I have personally found to be particularly useful in understanding the complex difficulties we face in attempting to harness the immense potential of organizations. I sincerely hope that they may be of use to you. I have grouped them, in no particular order of importance, under the general topic to which they relate.

References

1. B. Thomas, *Total Quality Training*, Maidenhead: McGraw-Hill, 1992, p.52.
2. 'Japan's faltering car industry', *The Economist*, 27 Feb 1993, pp.84–88.
3. 'Japan's faltering car industry', *The Economist*, 27 Feb 1993, pp.84–88.
4. T. Peters, *Liberation Management*, Basingstoke: Macmillan, 1992, p.677.
5. P. Garrahan and P. Stewart, *The Nissan Enigma*, London: Mansell, 1992, p.38.
6. L. Mobley and K. McKeown, *Beyond IBM*, Harmondsworth: Penguin, 1989, p.9.
7. J.F. Love, *McDonald's*, London: Bantam, 1986, pp.178–181.
8. A. Morita, *Made In Japan*, London: Fontana, 1988, pp.58–59.
9. L. Martel, *Mastering Change*, London: Grafton, 1988, pp.23–24.
10. M. Mitchell Waldrop, *Complexity*, London: Viking, 1993, pp.34–46.
11. M. Imai, *Kaizen*, Maidenhead: McGraw-Hill, 1986, p.30.
12. *The Independent*, 13 June 1993, p.27.
13. W. Schmidt and J. Finnigan, *The Race Without A Finish Line*, Jossey-Bass, San Francisco, USA: 1992, pp.336–337.

14. A. Morita, *Made in Japan*, London: Fontana, 1988, p.84.
15. A. Morita, *Made in Japan*, London: Fontana, 1988, p.86.
16. B. Thomas, *Total Quality Training*, Maidenhead: McGraw-Hill, p.73.
17. N.F. Dixon, *The Psychology Of Military Incompetence* and *Our Own Worst Enemy*, London: Futura, 1979 and 1987.
18. G. Morgan, *Images Of Organization*, London: Sage, 1986.

Quality/Quality management

Aguayo, R., *Dr Deming*, London: Simon & Schuster, 1990.
Amsden, D. *et al.*, *SPC Simplified for Services*, London: Chapman & Hall, 1991.
Chang, Y., G. Labovitz and V. Rosansky, *Making Quality Work*, London: Harper Business, 1993.
Drummond, H., *The Quality Movement*, London: Kogan Page, 1992.
Harrington, H.J., *Business Process Improvement*, Maidenhead: McGraw-Hill, 1991.
Imai, Masaaki, *Kaizen*, Maidenhead: McGraw-Hill, 1986.
Ishikawa, K., *What Is Total Quality Control?*, London: Prentice Hall, 1986.
Mitra, A., *Fundamentals of Quality Control*, London: Macmillan, 1993.
Robson, G., *Continuous Process Improvement*, New York: Free Press, 1991.
Schmidt, W. and Finnigan, J., *The Race Without a Finish Line*, San Francisco: Jossey-Bass, 1992.
Whiteley, R., *The Customer Driven Company*, London: Business Books, 1991.

Organizations/management

Morgan, G., *Images of Organization*, London: Sage, 1986.
Senge, P.M., *The Fifth Discipline*, London: Century Business, 1990.
Hannan, M. and T. Freeman, *Organizational Ecology*. Harvard: Harvard Press, 1989.
Parkinson, C.N., *Parkinson's Law*, London: Readers Union, 1957.
Fucini, J. and S. Fucini, *Working For The Japanese*, New York: Free Press, 1990.
Garrahan, P. and P. Stewart, *The Nissan Enigma*, London: Mansell, 1992.
Martel, L., *Mastering Change*, London: Grafton, 1988.
Love, J.F., *McDonald's, Behind the Arches*, London: Bantam, 1986.
Carroll, P., *Big Blues, The Unmaking of IBM*, London: Weidenfeld & Nicolson, 1993.
Ritchie, B. and D. Marshall, *Business Risk Management*, London: Chapman & Hall, 1993.
Pascale, R. and A. Athos, *The Art of Japanese Management*, Harmondsworth: Penguin, 1981.

Psychology/biology/philosophy

Adams, J., *The Care and Feeding of Ideas*, Harmondsworth: Penguin, 1986.

Berne, E., *Games People Play*, Harmondsworth: Penguin, 1961.

Dixon, N.F., *Our Own Worst Enemy*, London: Futura, 1987.

Gazzaniga, M., *The Social Brain*, New York: Basic Books, 1985.

Glasser, W., *Reality Therapy*, Harper & Row, 1975.

Hacker, P.M.S., *Insight and Illusion*, Oxford: Oxford University Press, 1986.

Illich, I., *Deschooling Society*, Harmondsworth: Penguin, 1986.

Jones, S., *The Language of the Genes*, London: HarperCollins, 1993.

Kelly, G., *The Psychology of Personal Constructs*, London: Norton, 1963.

Kopp, S., *If You Meet the Buddah on the Road, Kill Him!*, London: Sheldon Press, 1985.

Kuhn, T.S., *The Structure of Scientific Revolutions*, Chicago: University of Chicago Press, 1970.

Pinker, S., *The Language Imperitive*, Harmondsworth: Penguin, 1994.

Rose, S. *The Making Of Memory*, London: Bantam Books, 1992.

Smail, D., *The Origins of Unhappiness*, London: HarperCollins, 1993.

Sutherland, S., *Irrationality*, London: Constable, 1992.

Watzlawick, P., J. Weakland and R. Fisch, *Change, Principles of Problem Formation and Problem Resolution*, London: Norton, 1974.

Watzlawick, P., *The Language Of Change*, New York: Basic Books, 1978.

Watzlawick, P., *Ultrasolutions*, London: Norton, 1988.

Watzlawick, P. (ed.), *The Invented Reality*, London: Norton, 1984.

Weeks, R. and L. L'Abate, *Paradoxical Psychotherapy*, New York: Brunner/Mazel, 1982.

Wilson, E.O., *On Human Nature*, London: Bantam, 1979.

Wittgenstein, L., *Philosophical Investigations*, Oxford: Blackwell, 1981.

Wittgenstein, L., *On Certainty*, Oxford: Blackwell, 1979.

Wittgenstein, L., *Culture and Value*, Oxford: Blackwell, 1980.

Index